OPEN WIDE THE DOOR

The Story of the University of Minnesota

FOUNDED IN THE FAITH THAT MEN ARE ENNOBLED BY UNDERSTANDING
DEDICATED TO THE ADVANCEMENT OF LEARNING AND THE SEARCH FOR
    TRUTH
DEVOTION TO THE INSTRUCTION OF YOUTH AND THE WELFARE OF THE
    STATE

Dedication, The Cyrus Northrop Memorial Auditorium
University of Minnesota

OPEN WIDE THE DOOR

THE STORY OF
THE UNIVERSITY OF MINNESOTA

JAMES GRAY

G. P. PUTNAM'S SONS · NEW YORK

To Maxine B. Clapp and Alma Scott
whose creative co-operation
made the writing
of this book
a pleasure

SOURCES AND ACKNOWLEDGMENTS

THIS STORY of the University of Minnesota is regarded by its recorder as a collaboration on the part of hundreds of men and women all associated, in more or less conspicuous ways, with the rapid growth of the institution. Though, in its one hundred seventh year, the university is seven years older than the state of Minnesota, its history has been conveniently compressed, by circumstance, into the capacious portmanteau minds of certain enormously creative people. One of these, the first president, William Watts Folwell, had the additional gift of longevity. He survived to be a sprightly ninety-six and generously permitted his distinguished brain to be picked by a curious undergraduate at Minnesota who, of course, had no notion at the time that he would ever become the chronicler of what he was told but who simply enjoyed being given free access to that fine intelligence.

In 1948, that same frequent interviewer of Folwell was invited to write a book to appear three years later as a part of the university's centennial celebration. The large volume was issued by the University of Minnesota Press. The present work was prepared within the year especially for this series of studies of the great American universities. Its text is entirely new and it brings the account down to date with a consideration of the administration of the present head of the university, James Lewis Morrill.

However, the investigation conducted in the preparation of the earlier book uncovered much of the material presented in this one. Sources for both were either the same or similar.

7

The first step was to interview everyone with a long memory, taking these, with the investigator's grim awareness of the realities of life and death, in the order of their probable disappearance from the scene. Included, along with former presidents, their wives or widows, were deans, professors, football coaches, campus "cops." This procedure proved to be highly productive. The academic is notably (only to the ungrateful is he notoriously) communicative. His analytical flow can be counted upon to continue as long as it is not interrupted. Their properly appreciative interviewer never permitted any limitation, except that of the professors' own time, to be imposed upon them.

The second step was to help channel into the university archives the scattered papers of scores of departments on the several campuses. An understandable reluctance to part with documents—to the academic almost anything on paper is holy writ—at first tended to baffle the investigator. But the persuasive gifts of a succession of extraordinarily energetic archivists began, at last, to prevail. When all the sluggish influences had been removed the stream proved to be copious, indeed, containing the papers of presidents, the reports of deans, lecture notes, manuscripts of papers read before convocations and dining clubs, fragments of biography and autobiography, minutes of department meetings (in fair or foul longhand), letters (public and private), summations of committee findings. This last source was perhaps the most useful of all. The University of Minnesota has had from its earliest days a habit of self-appraisal, and the tone of these surveys was unvaryingly revelatory. Estimations of past efforts and speculations about proposals for experiments to be tried in the future vied with one another in the vivacity of their candor.

In certain instances the exigencies of time and temperament had tended to make the stream of documentation run thin. The earlier administrations were the least well represented. An exception was that of Folwell, whose own interests as historian made him an undefeatable conserver of significant records. His private papers, distributed between the archives of the univer-

8

sity and the manuscript collection of the State Historical Society in Saint Paul, contain a wealth of evidence. To this he added in his four-volume history of the state passages dealing with the university which are immensely valuable for their keenness of observation, their wisdom in the interpretation of educational philosophy, their objectivity of judgment and their magnanimity of appraisal.

It was the habit of Northrop to use a wastebasket as his filing case for university reports. This eccentricity of administrative procedure opened alarming gaps before the investigator. But these were filled from four sources of evidence: a fragment of autobiography; a vast collection of family letters donated by the second president's nephew, the late Dr. Joseph Warren Beach; the affectionate account of personality and purposes contained in E. Bird Johnson's *Forty Years of the University*; and the equally beguiled and beguiling biography, *Cyrus Northrop: A Memoir* by the late Professor Oscar Firkins.

An unaccountable lapse of judgment once permitted a self-styled "efficiency expert" to swoop through the records of the pre-Coffman days. With the insensate fury of a female Attila she pillaged and burned. The chief result of her scorched-file policy was to leave the important Vincent administration virtually a wasteland. Fortunately, the third president left vivid evidence of his powerful individuality, his administrative energy and his idealistic outlook everywhere in department records. A man who cannot speak without being both witty and profound is not easily relegated to obscurity. Vincent could be readily put together out of the brilliant fragments of himself that were scattered through all the documents contemporary with his administration. The days of Vincent's youth were revealed delightfully in the opening chapters of an autobiography which the author did not live to complete. It was put at the disposal of this recorder by the former president's widow.

A university piles up to impressive, even overwhelming, heights the souvenirs of its collective temperament. The printed work of its scholars offers, either by intent or by unconscious testimony, evidence of its philosophy. Official publications, student newspapers, humor magazines, literary reviews —short-lived or long-lived—all uncover lively glimpses of day-by-day procedures, dominating personalities, changing mores. The files in the archives of the *President's Reports*, the *Board of Regents Minutes*, the *Senate Minutes*, the *Minnesota Daily*, the *Alumni Weekly* under its many aliases, now the *Gopher Grad*, *Ariel*, *Shi-U-Mah*, the *Minnesota Quarterly*, *Minnesota Chats*, the *Ivory Tower* have been consulted with varying degrees of pleasure and profit, amusement and fortitude.

Because the number of collaborators runs literally into the hundreds, it would be impossible for the author of these pages to list them all in this note of thanks. It would be quite as inappropriate snobbishly to single out a few because of their pre-eminence in university circles. But gratitude is owed to them all both for the scrupulous attention that they gave to questions and for the personal kindness they displayed toward the questioner.

For their special services of many kinds a word of thanks must go also to Dr. Edward B. Stanford and his staff of the University Library; William L. Nunn, director of University Relations; William T. Harris, director of the University News Service; and the vice-presidents of the university, Malcolm M. Willey and William T. Middlebrook.

J. G.

CONTENTS

Sixteen pages of illustrations will be found following page 64.

PROLOGUE

NATURAL HABITAT OF THE
CIVILIZED SPIRIT

THIS IS THE STORY of an experiment in education, American style. The University of Minnesota in its administrative structure encloses, as dramatically as does any institution of the group of land-grant colleges, the theory of universal education which is America's unique contribution to the record of man's effort to collect and to distribute knowledge.

The day-by-day history of the university's progress toward that goal unfolds in illuminating detail the development of the idea that every sovereign citizen of the state is entitled to all that his mind can accept and his abilities advance in the way of wisdom. What he may gain of understanding it is his duty to turn back to the service of the state in ways that will promote still farther the well-being of all men everywhere. The instruction that he receives must be transmuted into a disciplined eagerness to explore the secrets of science, into a quickened awareness of the opportunities offered by the arts for the enrichment of the human spirit, into a facility for functioning intelligently in the life of the community.

The land-grant idea sprang into the mind of a mid-nineteenth century pioneer of thought. He envisaged a place where "such branches of learning as are related to agriculture and the mechanic arts" could be taught as "leading object" but without the neglect of the interests of traditional education.

Like many another new idea this one had a difficult birth and a precarious infancy. Yet in the pattern of such institutions as the University of Minnesota it has survived, grown strong, become dominant in the minds of educators. Indeed it may be claimed that the University of Minnesota is archetypical of the land-grant school. Its whole history is based on the belief that it is possible to develop an enormous university system in which every sort of theoretical and practical interest of education is represented. Agriculture and technology are closely integrated with other schools to form a unit capable of serving every concern of the people of the state.

Its metropolitan location offers another advantage, enabling its leaders to be in constant, easy communication with other leaders in every field of community life.

The administrative unity of the university has helped to keep its parts functioning smoothly under a discipline that insures the ready support of one by another. Yet the philosophy of autonomy for each individual college within its design has allowed each function to develop its own strength with uncramped spontaneity.

In all of its policies and practices the University of Minnesota shows the effects of the revolution in educational theory which reformers of the nineteenth century struggled vigorously to bring about. For that reason a report of its progress may have something of special interest at a moment when, midway of the twentieth century, reformers are once more deeply concerned with fundamental attitudes.

A few contrasts may offer a suggestion of how great the changes of a hundred years have been.

When the University of Minnesota was first created, in the minds of a group of pioneers, statehood had not yet been achieved. the Territory was a wilderness, its lands were unsettled; its resources were undiscovered. . . . Today, the university exercises a powerful voice in the affairs of all the rich Upper Midwest region—in its industry, in its agricultural development, in its pursuit of science, in every phase of its way of life.

14

The first building was actually nothing but a candlelit preparatory school pitifully ill-equipped to teach even the rudiments of reading, writing and arithmetic, let alone the advanced subjects of genuine university work. . . . Today, the university has a huge plant with three main campuses at Minneapolis, St. Paul and Duluth, and eleven other units scattered across the state. Many of its units have facilities for instruction and equipment for research that are equal to any that exist in the world.

In its precarious early days the university found it difficult to persuade hard-pressed pioneers to send a score of their sons and daughters into its classrooms. Even much later, a single student might present himself for enrollment in one of its departments. . . . Today one of the chief problems the university faces is to keep up with its own growth. During the period of the "veterans' bulge" the enrollment reached 29,-000. The university looks forward, with the equanimity of experience, to the probability of having to receive some 43,-000 students by the year 1970.

Once the operation of the university was very much a family affair. Well into the teens of the century, enrollment was drawn almost exclusively from within the borders of the state. . . . Now there is a constant demand for admission from students in every corner of the country. In recent years sixty nations—and more—have been represented among candidates for advanced degrees. Fifteen per cent of the total enrollment of the Graduate School is accounted for by foreign students. Simply to stand on the mall and watch the picturesque parade of exotic costumes, trailed through January snowdrifts, offers assurance enough that the University of Minnesota has a following throughout the world of learning.

Long ago, the university was torn by the jealous wrangles of a tiny group of teachers each of whom feared the disruptive hand of change; each fought for what he considered to be the threatened rights of his little realm with Homeric resolution. . . . Today an enormous faculty conducts its intramural

15

affairs with so great a degree of harmony that a great majority of its members happily claim the cooperative temper as the identifying feature of the academic spirit at Minnesota. "Where else," one of them once asked, "could you find four important physiologists working in different specific fields who can come together over the luncheon table or in the conference room to pool their knowledge and help each other toward solutions of major problems?" Ease in crossing departmental lines to enlist a colleague as collaborator may well be regarded as an important test for the fitness of an institution to do high-grade work in research. And, as its own men believe, it is this attitude that has produced, at Minnesota, an extraordinary amount of significant work in studies of wheat rust, nuclear physics, cancer and diseases of the heart.

There was a time when the university was so impoverished, indeed so deeply in debt, that the less stalwart among its own regents were ready to close the doors and forget their own grandiloquent hopes. . . . Today, the legislature is usually generous in appropriations for support, and there are many private individuals, industrial organizations, federal and national foundations to come forward with resources for research. In some conspicuous instances the donations from other-than-normal channels equal the funds for a department's work that appear in the printed budget.

A curious hostility on the part of town toward gown once plagued the university's efforts to serve. . . . Today, a spiritedly possessive temper envelops the university. Groups of every kind rap on its door asking for help with hundreds of problems. Usually they bring large funds for the support of such undertakings.

If these notations suggest a belief on the part of the tabulator that for the university the millennium has already come, anyone within the academic circle would quickly and emphatically deny the suggestion. In a world where there is so vast an amount of work to do if the values of civilization are to be made secure, the trained investigators know better than any layman could how long the way is and how rough underfoot. At Minnesota they would perhaps be willing to say no more than that a favorable climate exists in which to stimulate an energetic pursuit of knowledge and that its leaders are committed to such a pursuit.

It is well understood at Minnesota, also, that today American education stands accused of significant failures, even of a tragic misdirection of its fundamental effort. A candid observer must acknowledge that, in its self-conscious determination to demonstrate the feasibility of universal education, the land-grant college may well be suspected of having neglected to identify and to train the superior student. And who else can deal with the drastic emergency to which the recent successes of Soviet-trained scientists have called our alarmed attention?

Minnesota has been in the forefront of the struggle of theorists to justify the idea that "education for democracy" means receiving all applicants for instruction and giving them as much as they are able to digest. The catch phrases of "general education" and "terminal education" have been used by certain thinkers to evoke the image of an institution of learning that is "student-centered" rather than "subject-centered" and where "adjustment to the life experience" is the goal rather than a high level of exact training for complex responsibilities.

These phrases have been spoken often at Minnesota. The university once had on its faculty (though only briefly) that same John Dewey who, at the moment, is being made the whipping boy for all the supposed sins of the twentieth-century trend in education. One of Minnesota's most effective presidents, Coffman, was a leading exponent of attitudes which have fallen into disfavor since October, 1957 with the dazzling appearance of *sputnik*. The spirit of self-abasement in which educators now indulge tends to present the concept of mass education as the friend of mediocrity and the enemy of fine achievement. But this apologetic temper will need to run the full course of its understandable chagrin and reach a positive program before any really serviceable reform can be accomplished.

Meanwhile it would perhaps be well to remember that what Coffman and other educators of his kind really believed is that there is no essential antagonism between the idea of training the many in such ways that they may be able to run the ordinary affairs of daily life with greater intelligence and insight and, at the same time, of training the brilliant few to conquer the future.

Minnesota, if it must answer the charge (leveled sometimes with the air of confronting a criminal) of graduating thousands of students each year, might very well answer that it is also the place which stimulated the mind of a dedicated, completely unselfish scientist to establish U 235 as responsible for the slow fission in uranium. It is the place where two doctors worked together in such sympathy with their colleagues and such comfort in their intellectual environment that they were able to win the Nobel prize for their discovery of cortisone.

This account of the university's development will undertake to show that from the time of the first president there has been at Minnesota a tradition of responsibility toward the values of the "genuine university." To attract original intelligences, to give them sympathetic circumstances under which to work and to expect of them in return contributions of significance to the world of knowledge—this has been the program of nearly all the men who have occupied posts of importance and influence within the university's administrative pattern.

Always preoccupied with theoretical problems of education, the university has served often as a way station for teachers and deans en route to presidencies of other institutions. Harry Pratt Judson paused at Minnesota on his way to the presidency of the University of Chicago; James Rowland Angell on his way to Yale; George McLean to Iowa; Frank McVey to Kentucky; Kendric Babcock to Arizona; Alfred F. Woods to the Maryland State College of Agriculture; Ada

Comstock to Radcliffe; Roscoe Thatcher to Massachusetts State College; Alvin Eurich to the University of the State of New York; Frederick Hovde to Purdue; William Carlson to a startling succession of presidencies; and Thomas McConnell to the University of Buffalo. The influence of the Minnesota tradition would seem to have reached far.

And the pageant of its private life has always been lively. In every period men and women, capable of many different kinds of challenge, have strolled provocatively or catapaulted violently through its routine. Frank Billings Kellogg, before he served as Secretary of State and won the Nobel prize for peace, served as lecturer on law in its faculty. Pierce Butler—rubicund, positive and dedicated to the spirit of the law as he saw it reflected in his own unintimidated eyes—served as a regent before going to Washington and the Supreme Court. Sinclair Lewis, flailing about him with his wit—like a Don Quixote riding Rosinante backward as he stormed his windmills of pretense and hyprocrisy—bounced in briefly to teach creative writing. Curiously insecure of himself, despite the fact that he had just received the Nobel prize, he bounced out again without finishing the course. Harold Stassen, using the little world of the campus as a tryout arena for his later exercises in the great world of politics, took his law degree at Minnesota, winning from his dean an unequivocal endorsement as the most brilliant student he had ever had. Minnesota's present governor, Orville Freeman, prepared for an early debut in politics by mastering and disciplining all the discursive loquacities of campus intrigues.

There was never a time when literature was not well represented from the era of Richard Burton, Arthur Upson and Joseph Beach on. Before she went to Smith, Mary Ellen Chase sharpened her wit on the minds of her better students and gave some of her first stories to student publications. She and Marjorie Nicholson (in Miss Nicholson's pre-Columbian days) sharpened wits on each other in a cheerful company of young faculty members. (These people gathered at the boardinghouse of a woman who would be delightedly remembered if only for her name, Mrs. Scripture.) Robert Penn Warren, balancing his dark philosophy with a private companionability of the most abundant good nature, drew into his courses on the novel and on poetry all the graduate students in English and, along with them, as many under-graduates as could crowd in. Max Shulman, like a fully clothed Puck with an elaborately droll invention in every pocket, trained for his career as a best-selling writer of frenzied comedy by writing a column for the *Minnesota Daily*. Eric Sevareid edited the same daily with a fierce devotion to principle and a readiness to take on any adversary up to and including the president of the university. Tom Heggen, dark and withdrawn as his elders saw him, a Byron in homespun, wrote searchingly of solitary young men in anticipation of the complete success in portraiture that he was to have with *Mr. Roberts*.

After the early days of struggle, when the institution had become "our university" to many graduates, a fine representative group among them became its generous benefactors in other ways besides those having to do directly with revenue. James Ford Bell become founder of General Mills and a kind of universal genius of the democratic way of life as conservationist, collector of books and silver, amateur musician (he once composed a song which Galli-Curci added to her repertoire) and philanthropist. He became also a regent of the university and was forever supervising its alcoves of learning as well as its major interests. He and a group of private citizens financed and built a Museum of Natural History as a tribute to their friend, Dr. Thomas Roberts, creator of the masterpiece *Birds of Minnesota*. In an access of the bountiful spirit he gave his famous collection of the Jesuit *Relations* and similar materials to the university and furnished a beautiful room in the library to house it.

Other collectors have been prompted to make similar contributions even though Minnesota was not their alma mater. Because the library is one of the largest and most distinguished in the country (it has, according to an impartial survey made for the *Library Quarterly* in 1942, some forty areas that offer the highest rewards to scholarship), it has seemed to many discerning men to be the proper place to serve as a bookman's treasury. To it have gone, as though by power of natural attraction, the collections of H. V. Jones in the fields of printing and newspaper history, the library of Dr. Irwin Kerlen of Washington, D.C., and the Leslie Ames library of books on India.

The university has become, in fact, what such a center ideally should be: a stronghold of intellectual values to which responsive people in the region take all their good things for safekeeping. The Minneapolis Symphony Orchestra which since the turn of the century has had an uninterrupted career used to vibrate between halls in Minneapolis and St. Paul. Now it has found a permanent home on neutral ground between rival cities. The Cyrus Northrup Memorial Auditorium on the campus offers room for the orchestra's large following and ideal conditions for performance. Eugene Ormandy, in his first major assignment, matured his talent there. Dimitri Metropoulos followed with his fine, hyperthyroid fervors.

Nor is the platform reserved for distinguished outsiders. On other campus stages the students alternate between offering pleasant copies of the conventional theater's exercises and ingenious experiments in the untried. Grateful lovers of drama remember a performance of *Romeo and Juliet* that glowed with youth and was eloquent with an understanding of how verse should be spoken to preserve, all at once, its meaning, its rhythm and its passion. They remember, with the enduring surprise that clings to any bold creative adventure, the urgency of power that students poured into the original theater version of Robert Penn Warren's *All the King's Men*. Not often in the American theater has the tragic sense of vigor, maimed and misdirected, been so effectively communicated.

The student stage at Minnesota has offered a laboratory for the first experiments of men and women who have become valuable professional players. The late Roman Bohnen, born old and able to understand, in his teens, the sorrows and perplexities of old men, offered many anticipations of the mature talent that served the Group theater and Hollywood well for many years. Gale Sondergaard (she was Edith to her contemporaries at Minnesota) played routine comedy with an intensity which suggested that if she could have her rights she would be playing *Strange Interlude,* as she was later to do when Lynn Fontanne was through with the play's central role. Richard Carlson presented in his youth an already clear statement of that authority in the interpretation of sophisticated American types which has recommended him to many studios where films and television entertainments are made. By a curious, but also characteristic irony, Henry Fonda had to do with student drama at Minnesota although, as a student of engineering, he worked only backstage and never acted at all.

None of these interests makes the University of Minnesota unique—not the offering of itself as a laboratory for experiments with theories of education, nor the work done in many fields of research, nor the successful effort to broaden its range to cover all the arts. But taken together these undertakings show it as a place of vitality where pressure toward achievement is regarded as stimulating, not oppressive; where effort is demanded, originality is encouraged and talent of a high order is provided with a favorable atmosphere in which to mature. The treadmill exercises of routine instruction, so widely associated with the concept of mass education, do not characterize its daily life. Indeed, it may be claimed without inappropriate enthusiasm that it has become a kind of natural habitat of the civilized spirit.

To retrace the steps by which this evolution has been accomplished may be useful to those who wish to believe that the American university of the twentieth century is an institution which has been nourished in the past by an indestructible faith in learning, which is well equipped today for the further conquest of understanding and which is dedicated to the idea that the promises it has made to the future are its first and its deepest concern.

CHAPTER ONE

PARAGON OF PATRONS

IN THE YEAR 1851 the first bold, but still uncertain steps were being taken to make a new world on the Northwest frontier. Minnesota had been a territory for just two years. Its reputation in the East for being an all but impenetrable frozen wilderness had not deterred some 6000 white men from making it their home. Of these fewer than a thousand lived in St. Paul; fewer than 600 in the village of St. Anthony. Perched high on the banks of the Mississippi, above the Falls which the explorer-priest Father Hennepin had named for his patron saint, this tiny community struggled between infant hope and infant fear to establish its identity.

Power, abundantly available from the Falls, had attracted settlers. A sawmill was in operation for the benefit of those who wished to build houses and barns on the good agricultural land of the left bank. There the city of Minneapolis was presently to flourish but it had not yet been born. Shops had sprung up along the muddy paths that served as St. Anthony's thoroughfares. A newspaper, the *St. Anthony Express*, had begun publication. Its pages were full of hearty assertions about the town's fine destiny; the muscular language of the competitive spirit made every sentence referring to the rival, St. Paul, swell with aggressive pride.

But all this brave show of energy was obviously the compensatory gesture made by the pioneer who knew what an enormous task he had assumed. Far the greater part of the territory's land still belonged to the Indians. The Sioux and the Winnebagos were in the habit of setting up their tepees in the village square of St. Anthony. There they conducted their tribal life in full view of an audience which had no wish to share in their rituals of "gaming, dancing and drumming." Later in the same year—1851—the Treaty of Traverse des Sioux was to be signed by which the tribes would be induced to give up most of their lands for release to white settlers. The struggle of civilized man to control and to improve his environment was taking only its first small step in this new world.

Yet it was at this moment that the pioneers decided they must have a great university. There was nothing in the least modest about their plans. If the Colony of Massachusetts Bay could, within a few years of its founding, call Harvard into existence, there was no reason why the territorial leaders should not, as one of their first official acts, work a similar miracle. But the men of Minnesota were not content with the idea of duplicating the success of Harvard. Spokesmen for the enterprise talked vaingloriously of creating an institution so richly endowed that it would "put Harvard in the shade."

Alexander Ramsey and Henry Hastings Sibley were the two men who did most, in the early stages, to implement this wild dream. As governor of the territory and its delegate to Washington, Ramsey and Sibley badgered an indifferent Congress persistently for support in the form of an appropriation of land. Their efforts were fruitful at last and on February 26, 1851 the University of Minnesota came, at least hypothetically, into being.

What the community actually got was far from impressive. The outward and visible sign of Minnesota's inward and spiritual dedication to higher learning was a two-story "prep" school where, for $4 a quarter, a retired clergyman taught reading, writing and arithmetic to a score of village children.

Even this faint adumbration of a great concept was to have a short and insecure existence. During the ordeal of the early years every kind of disaster fell on the blameless, but frequently bowed, heads of the board of regents. First, the land on which the prep school stood in the midst of the village was virtually drawn from under it; the regent who had offered it as a gift but never given clear title decided that he wanted it back for commercial purposes. A new site—the university's present one—was chosen. The land was a mile away from the village and, in the opinion of the *St. Anthony Express*, its bucolic charm surpassed that of the Hudson. On it the regents decided to erect a building that would cost $49,000. Ramsey considered this to be mad extravagance and said so. But the regents, obsessed by their dream of grandeur, brushed his objections imperiously away.

A tragic series of circumstances brought them to abrupt awakening. The Rum River which flowed through the university's lands suddenly dried up and it became impossible to float out the logs the profits from which were to have paid the bills.

This act of God was followed by an even more blighting sequence of events resulting from the reckless acts of man. The financial disaster of the year 1857 fell upon the whole country. As the doors of eastern banks slammed shut, the reverberation shattered the economy of the frontier.

Trapped in a maze of responsibilities, the regents could seem to think of no way to run but forward. They went doggedly on with their plans to build the strange structure that came to be known as "Old Main." (From the original central portion of this architectural oddity wings were to be thrown out as they were needed ever wider and wider. But financial troubles very sadly clipped those wings.)

When the regents found that their resources were quite exhausted they persuaded the legislature to authorize the sale of $40,000 worth of bonds, secured by the university's lands. But these new funds served only to let the wavering duel between man and circumstance go pitifully on.

During these trials even the preparatory department had ceased to function. But on May 28, 1858 it was able to reopen in its new home with a new principal. Professor A. H. Barber

27

earned an unenviable fame by trying to take an official stand against the admission of "females" to the school. "Nonsense," said Jane Grey Swissholm, writing in the pages of her strongly feminist paper, the *St. Cloud Visitor*. "If you want the boys of today to be good citizens a few years hence you must educate them with their sisters and their future wives." Professor Barber was promptly overruled.

But, if justice could be made to prevail in a matter of abstract principle, it still could not prevail over circumstance. Minnesota had achieved statehood in 1858. But whatever advantage this gave her in the way of prestige it did not immediately improve her economic status. The settlers simply could not afford to send their children to Professor Barber's school and it closed within six months. Another effort to reopen in 1859 failed completely.

Then came the great interruption of the Civil War. Minnesota, youngest of the states, organized three regiments of volunteers and sent many of its most valuable civic leaders along as officers. The Indians, dissatisfied with the results of the settlement of Traverse des Sioux, chose this awkward moment to conduct uprisings against the settlers at home. In this cruel emergency men like Sibley became responsible for the very lives of their fellow pioneers; they were preoccupied for years with the crisis.

No one had time to give to the florid wish-fulfillment of which Old Main was the bleak reminder. It stood on its impressive height above the river, deserted except by wild turkeys and even wilder squatters who had taken possession of its shelter. When a committee of the board of regents visited the building, they found the doors hanging loose from hinges, the floors ruined by the wood-chopping exercises of the squatters, the fixtures torn away by vandals. A noble effort was crumbling, with an air of sullen self-contempt, into ruin.

But in that end was a beginning. At a moment when it faced extinction the university had the nearly miraculous good fortune to enlist the championship of a man who believed in education with something very like religious fervor.

John Sargent Pillsbury himself had had little formal schooling. Yet he became known as "the father of the university" because nothing in all his strenuous life seemed to him so important as the task of keeping that institution alive.

It was during the Civil War that Pillsbury was first drawn into the university's affairs. A typical entrepreneur of the period, he had come to Minnesota to set up a hardware business. Branching out with the spontaneity of his special kind of genius, he became involved in real estate, in banking and, most important of all, in the creation of the milling empire that still bears his name. He survived all the threats of extinction that nature and circumstance had flung in the way of his various enterprises and earned a reputation for scrupulous integrity. It was inevitable that such a man should be drafted by his neighbors to serve them in the state senate and later in the governor's chair.

In 1863 the affairs of a university that really existed only in the minds of a group of stubborn, unyielding men were in a very bad way indeed. Its debts were so heavy, its bonds were so entangled in red tape that one regent reported to the board: "Nothing more can be done." Liquidation, he told them dolefully, would wipe out the university's inheritance.

One of the university's many creditors was John Sargent Pillsbury. As dealer in hardware he held a bill of $5.50 for "locks, nails and iron" against the builders of Old Main. Also some of the university's bonds had passed into his hands in the course of negotiations that had dispersed them far and wide.

In a homely frontier version of the story of Paul on the road to Damascus, Pillsbury was converted from creditor into champion. The episode occurred when, quite unexpectedly, he found himself host in his hardware store on Main Street to the governor of the state. The governor's errand was to ask him to become a regent of the university.

At first Pillsbury declined, saying that he was "unfit" for such an assignment because he himself had no academic degree. Then, all at once, a sense of mission must have seized his mind. Saving and developing the university became in that instant the creative task to which, in the midst of a multitude of other duties, he gave most enthusiastically of his energies. There was not a spot on earth, he once said, where he would rather be remembered than on the campus. And, though his name still gives a great business its official signature, Pillsbury has had his wish. He is remembered with the most vivid kind of gratitude at the university for the laconic eloquence and patient altruism with which he refused to accept defeat when nearly everyone else would have done so. Indeed, he occupies a niche unlike that of any other man in local history. Minnesota honors him as the completely unique zealot: a self-educated man who made it the strongest passion of his life to preserve at the university an opportunity for millions to acquire education.

Forgetting his own share of the university's vast $80,000 debt, Pillsbury set out to satisfy the other creditors. To facilitate negotiations he persuaded the legislature to create a temporary board of regents limited to three members. It was easy enough to persuade the others to resign from an assignment that had had all the uncomfortable features of martyrdom except actual dismemberment. As they put on their hair-cloth shirts Pillsbury, Captain Orlando Merriman and Senator John Nicols were by no means sure that they did not face even that fate at the hands of angry creditors.

But the truth was that some of these people were playing rather ruthlessly at the Shylock game. Pillsbury knew that many of the holders of bonds had paid only a fourth of their face value for them. The exigencies of the panic had enabled them to pick up what they considered to be bargains. It was Pillsbury's task to persuade them to surrender the bonds at the same bargain prices.

Traveling back and forth across the country, the triumvirate of regents sought out creditors—the argumentative, the tearful and the obdurate. They met many obstacles. But each time that they seemed to have reached the end of a blind alley, Pillsbury faced blankness with unimpaired resolution.

30

"I'm not giving up yet," he would say, and start again.

At last in 1867 he was able to report to the legislature that the last claim against the university had been paid. "The slate is clean," he said.

The situation proved in the end to be by no means as unhappy as the dealers in doom had described it. Of the 46,080 acres that Congress had originally given the university, more than 30,000 remained, together with Old Main and the ground on which it stood.

"The faith and fire" within John Sargent Pillsbury had now taken full possession of his imagination. The university, he insisted, must begin to operate again without delay. The triumvirate asked the legislature for $15,000 with which to put Old Main into decent repair.

It was still only a preparatory school that they hoped to start. The citizens of St. Anthony began scouring the neighborhood to find likely boys to fill its seats. As a gesture of loyalty toward home industry, one former regent brought his own son back to Minnesota from the Military Academy at Chester, Pennsylvania, where he had been.

When Principal W. W. Washburn opened the doors on October 7, 1867, he had a dozen pupils and a faculty of two: Gabriel Campbell, to teach Latin and Greek; Ira Moore, to teach mathematics and "the English branches."

There were girls among the students, too. Again—with Campbell and Moore spiritedly dissenting—the question of coeducation that had been settled in favor of rights for women.

The most significant of Pillsbury's services, after that of saving the university from its suffocating burden of debt, was to take the first step toward establishing the basic philosophy by which it lives today. This is the belief that an educational institution exists to serve the community of which it is a part, offering itself as a laboratory for the solution of all its practical as well as its intellectual problems and the development of its social interest quite as much as its humane studies.

Pillsbury's acute ear caught up the first faint hint of this idea as it reached him from the tongue of Justin Morrill.

This prophet of the movement that created the land-grant colleges of today was a congressman from the state of Vermont. In 1857 he had spoken his first public word on the subject when he introduced a bill proposing that the federal government donate large tracts of public lands to the support of institutions that would teach "such branches of learning as are related to agriculture and the mechanic arts." Morrill was a prophet in more ways than one. But central to all his values was that of soil conservation. Farming, he insisted, must be taught "as a learned, liberal and intellectual pursuit" so that waste of the land through ignorance might end.

Like many prophets Morrill had far to go, by a tortuous and sometimes torturous route, before he could achieve his simple, shining goal. His bill for the creation of colleges to teach agriculture was passed by Congress in 1859. It was promptly vetoed as unconstitutional by that genius of ineptitude, President Buchanan. The bill was passed again in 1862 and this time enacted into law. By its provisions each state in the union which was willing to create a college to teach agriculture and mechanic arts was to receive 30,000 acres of land from each of its representatives in Congress. This meant that Minnesota, with two senators and two representatives in the House, was entitled to 120,000 acres of land.

For a time in 1862 it seemed likely that an Agricultural College of Minnesota would be created, with this backing, at the town of Glencoe. An extremely active advocate of its claim was Glencoe's leading citizen, John Harrington Stevens. But five years were consumed in the business of getting clear title to the lands. In the meanwhile war, rebellion and riot had both matured and hardened the character of life on the frontier. John Stevens had become Colonel Stevens, hero of many campaigns against the Indian uprisings. At the end of his service, wearied by controversy at its most violent, he had retired to the new town of Minneapolis and Glencoe saw him no more.

So Pillsbury was able, at a strategic moment, to gather up the Agricultural College and fit it into his own design.

Minnesota, he felt deeply, must not deplete its educational effort by trying to support two weak institutions. Pillsbury—a state senator now—had been right so often that no one undertook to challenge him. The Agricultural College became, by act of the state legislature in 1867, a unit of the university.

With his usual paternalistic zeal, Pillsbury immediately arranged to justify his foster child's pretensions by giving it a farm. This tract of one hundred twenty acres he had lately bought for his own use but now he surrendered it at the price he had paid. Lying close to the academic campus, this land seemed well chosen. The soil, however, proved to be unsatisfactory and a new farm later replaced it. Meanwhile the university had made a profit by selling off, bit by bit, as residential property the acres of the first farm.

This was the situation of the University of Minnesota in 1868. It was not unlike a faltering adolescent who had lived through a full set of the diseases of infancy. A university only in name, it had no clear idea of how it was to attain the grandeur dreamed by its ardent creators. It did not let its right hand, the preparatory school, know what its left hand, the Agricultural College, did, chiefly because neither hand was at all sure of its performance.

But simply to have survived was an achievement. This was a dazzling surprise to the citizenry as a whole. To Pillsbury it was the solid reward of five years' dedicated effort.

And now his school was ready for its first well-planned experiment with the principles of what was being called in the world of nineteenth-century visionaries "the new education."

Pillsbury continued to give disinterested loyalty to the University of Minnesota throughout his life. The record must surely be unique in the history of education in America. Though he was not the son of a university he became the father of one. He will be remembered always on the campus which became the shrine of his faith as the paragon of patrons.

33

CHAPTER TWO

ARCHITECT OF THE FUTURE

WILLIAM WATTS FOLWELL was by any intellectual measure a man of extraordinary stature. Not by the yardstick, however. He stood under average height. But he had a soldier's carriage, a scholar's mind, and the temper of Chaucer's "verray parfit gentil knight."

He assumes prominent place in this record as the first man to carry the title President of the University of Minnesota.

(Actually, the law creating the university authorized the board of regents to chose a "chancellor" of the university who should be also president of the board. But the habit of referring to the president of the university has long since confirmed this as the title by which, in the popular mind, authority over the university's administrative design is held.)

It is not merely for his primacy in the parade of presidents that Folwell is noticeable. He commands respectful attention as one of the leaders among young educators who during the renaissance of American values, following the Civil War, fought indefatigably for new standards and new principles.

Folwell failed as president of the university because his ideas were too bold to please the subservient citizens of the Right, the intransigent citizens of the Left, the obstructionists who planted themselves in his way and the stubborn lovers of tradition who tugged at him from the rear. But his failure was a kind of triumph because it left his personal honor unmarred and his imperishable influence actually increased.

There was no aspect of learning that did not appeal to

Folwell. As his successor, Cyrus Northrop, said of him, he was "interested in everything from Plato to hog cholera." But "interest" is a poor, flaccid word with which to debase Folwell's intense, unwavering pursuit of all the intricacies of Greek, Latin, mathematics, philology (with particular emphasis on Sanskrit and Arabic), engineering, political science, law, the violin, history and library science.

No dabbler in academic disciplines, Folwell would, after his graduation from Hobart, have been welcome at any of five distinguished colleges as teacher of languages or of mathematics. As a colonel of army engineers during the Civil War he had had laboratory training in bridge building. He created pilot courses in political science at the University of Minnesota and all during his presidency doubled in brass as chief administrator and head of the library. He wrote the definitive history of the state of Minnesota, the final volume of which he had just completed when he died at the age of ninety-six.

Though he was not a "popular teacher" in the sense of the bustling academic who flatters the ego of the adolescent by pretending to share the most vulgar of his values, the most rudimentary of his jokes and the tawdriest of his tastes, Folwell genuinely loved and respected youth. In his very old age he preserved both the warmest of sentiments and the staunchest assets of dignity. He became "Uncle Billy" to many generations of undergraduates. Yet he wore his avuncular pride "with a difference," that of a superb personal reserve.

In the late years of the 1860s Folwell had been examining his mind soberly and he knew that he wanted to be a teacher, preferably the head of a large university system. During his years of postgraduate study in Germany, just before the Civil War, he had discovered, as his diary reports, that he could not "endure to have learning piled on me. I want not to be instructed but to be informed," he wrote.

By extension this personal preference was later developed into the principle that "It is absurd to require a student to drudge and agonize over a mere gymnastic. There should be a noble and practical motive for all the lessons and exercises of a school."

This was in sympathy with the ideas of several prominent young educators of the time. Folwell while he worked faithfully but without delight at a job in his father-in-law's mill at Venice, Ohio, had corresponded regularly with these leaders. One of them was Charles Eliot, president of Harvard, who in an essay published in the *Atlantic Monthly* had formulated the program of what he called the "new education."

It should be the aim of all Harvard's friends, Eliot urged, "to second the movement now taking place by which it is gradually changing from a gymnasium or college into a true university. The distinction between a college and a university is that in one all the students are taken through a prescribed curriculum; in the other they have many and various departments of knowledge offered to them. A college is a place to which a young man is *sent* to go through the appointed list of studies; a university one to which he *goes* to get instruction and help in the pursuit of science. A university should give opportunity for universal culture; it should provide faculties in language, science, law, theology, medicine, engineering, architecture and all the arts."

Folwell must have read this essay and murmured: "Hear! Hear!" He picked up two phrases from it, "new education" and "true university," and made them cornerstones in his own philosophy.

Presently he began an active campaign to find an assignment in which he could put his ideas to work. A brother-in-law who was also a brother in intellectual sympathy became his ally. George Leonard Chase, pastor of the Episcopal parish of Gethsemane in Minneapolis, knew that the institution across the river at St. Anthony was badly in need of guidance. Unhappy Principal Washburn was wavering toward resignation; the regents were without experience. An idealistic conspirator, Chase wrote to Folwell: "You know the change in the requirements and the methods of Education that is now

36

taking place. You want only the opportunity. Would you have it here? Ay, merry!"

When Washburn made up his mind, at last, to resign, Chase pushed the campaign for his friend vigorously. On August 23, 1869 Folwell was elected president of the university.

The extraordinary quality of his inaugural, delivered in the assembly hall of Old Main on December 22, was its clairvoyance. Here was a man who had little more than a preparatory school to run projecting his imagination into the future and foreseeing what a university must become. It could be, Folwell declared, no mere "overgrown college." It must be a "federation of professional schools thoroughly imbued with the scientific spirit." Obedient to the demands of the new education, America must create a threefold scheme: "first, the common schools, second, the colleges; third, the university." The elective system must be encouraged in order to find out and stimulate the new talents needed by society. The university should offer itself as a laboratory for the development of new values. "We purchase a telegraph, the phonograph, a new motor, the spectroscope, the lucifer match or chloroform at the price of fifty years of seemingly fruitless laboratory work. The university should be the natural resort and resource for counsel and information."

It was to the service of the community that Folwell stood ready to dedicate his university. "I urge," he said, "that the university is essential to the well-being, rather than to the being of the state."

And he foresaw, too, that if the university were to serve the sovereign people worthily, the people must support the university with generous allowances. It was to their immediate, as well as their long-range advantage to do so. Therefore let them "count the cost and take the million for unit."

Yet no matter how bold his dreams might be, Folwell was able to accept the realities of the situation that he faced in the 1870s. With the reserved benevolence that the young find reassuring in a parent he presided over a curious collection of students. Only half of the three hundred that made up the average enrollment of those years were in what was called "the collegiate department." The "Latin school" still offered preparatory work for some one hundred pupils. There were also the completely unclassifiable products of the pioneer community who were untrained even for the discipline of the secondary school and needed, quite simply, to learn the rudiments of arithmetic and English grammar.

The system coddled no one. All students were required to report for chapel at eight-thirty; they received demerits for failure to appear. Only the morning was devoted to classroom instruction (five short periods); the rest of the day was given over to the work by which a student supported himself. Folwell estimated that a young man or woman needed five dollars a week with which to get through the academic year. This allowed $16.84 for books and $1.88 for "society expenses." To enable students to "live decently" he arranged, in the first year of his administration, to set aside dormitory space in Old Main. For $3 a term the rudimentary comforts of "stove, mattress, bedstead, washstand, table, bookcase and chairs" were provided. Later, when every square foot of Old Main was needed for classroom work, the president still considered it to be his duty to find living quarters for his young men and women. He would walk from door to door with a new matriculant urging the neighbors to take him in. Diaries of that early period reflect the gratitude of farm boys for whom Folwell found lodging over a "wagon shop" or store.

Old Main could hardly be called a triumph for the foresight of those who had impoverished the university to build it. Folwell once described the structure, in a characteristically blunt report to the regents, as being "about as ill-adapted to its purpose as possible." Its one staircase was "narrow, tortuous, ill-lighted." (Fortunately when, many years later, Old Main justified the president's criticisms by burning to the ground, it had the tact to do so in the middle of the night so that no human lives were destroyed with it.) The only heat in the building was supplied by forty-three wood stoves of various dimensions the combined efforts of which did little to offset the austerity of the Minnesota winter weather. The assembly hall in particular presented so stern a setting for chapel exercises that the most ardent of all the prayers ever uttered in it came from one devout but chilled Christian to another as they mounted the stairs. "Pray short, John," the supplicant urged. "It's going to be cold up there."

Equally far short of Folwell's vision of the "true university" were all the educational facilities. The library had no reading room; the laboratories, only the most abecedarian of equipment.

Still Folwell persisted in shooting the arrow of his purpose into the seemingly blank space all about him. In 1870 he announced his "Minnesota Plan" which the regents unanimously, though it must be suspected uncomprehendingly, adopted. This implemented the intention outlined in Folwell's inaugural address for creating the genuine university by carving out securely the three levels of an educational system and of directing the effort of the University of Minnesota toward the full development of the highest of these levels. The elementary department was to be sloughed off as quickly as possible, not because Folwell scorned its responsibilities, but simply because it was like a vestigial organ having no function in the system to the care of which he was committed.

Then the really difficult task was to begin. Here Folwell quite startlingly displayed his ability to anticipate developments that have become general practice since his time. He wished to broaden the curriculum of the collegiate department, "throwing the usual work of the freshman and sophomore years out of the proper university course and merging it into the old preparatory department." To him it seemed to be almost a law of nature that "the close of the sophomore year is a well-marked era in college life. Grammar, drill, blackboard drudgery are over; a new field of humanizing, literary and reflective subjects opens. At this point the optional studies, if they can be afforded, come in to vary the old dull routine." In short, he foresaw the growth of the junior college and of the senior college as both exist today.

But his preoccupation with the top level of effort was so great that he proposed, as soon as the collegiate department had developed strength enough to stand alone, to give it independent existence just as a wise father surrenders a mature son to his own way of life. "The third step in our enterprise," Folwell wrote, "must be after separating superior and inferior instruction to get rid of the latter in order to use our resources for the development of the proper university work."

To his faculty all this sounded, as Folwell himself once said with characteristically indulgent humor, like the "rant of the wild educational mutineer." Among his teachers were two retired clergymen, one of whom Folwell described as "a courteous and genial man with whom it is pleasant to associate"; another cannot be defended against the charge of having lived his life in a chronic rage. Both of these men opposed Folwell and his Minnesota Plan on practical grounds. They saw it as their clear duty to teach the boys and girls who came to them what it was good for them to know, indulging, meanwhile, in no "trifling or speculative" hopes for the future. To think of banishing freshmen and sophomores even before an impressive company of them had been brought together seemed like a "vain and illusory dream." The courteous gentleman said: "We cannot afford to lose our young men. When Professors have built up classes from the foundation it cuts the sinews of our courage to have these classes depleted." The angry opponent accused Folwell of wishing to set himself up as dictator and warned of a crisis like that through which the University of Michigan lately had suffered at the hands of an educational revolutionist (H. P. Tappen). Both thought the Minnesota Plan subversive to a system that had been "born, bred and matured in America."

That this was a hazy, sentimental untruth Folwell was quick to point out. No "American system" existed, but just as surely one was in the making. It called for workable ways

40

of meeting the needs of "young people preparing to be engineers, merchants, architects, chemists, miners, journalists, naturalists, astronomers and agriculturalists." The real waste of time and effort lay in sending them "into voluntary exile" to foreign countries "in search of the culture not to be found on this side of the Atlantic." The educator's duty lay in forwarding "a powerful tendency in the direction of comprehensive state and national control of education." A state university must form an integral part of a state system of education and be its crown.

In this first brush with his conscientious but obstructionist faculty Folwell had a major triumph. On a July day, which left all other participants limp with uncertainty, the stanch soldier, Folwell, summoned witnesses to his defense. Among these were four distinguished presidents of universities— Porter of Yale, White of Cornell, Runkle of Massachusetts Institute of Technology, and Angell of Vermont—all by proxy. Their letters agreed that the Minnesota Plan showed, in Porter's words, "just recognition of the value of literary, scientific and professional culture." The regents drew a collective sigh of relief and voted that "Folwell was master of the situation."

The president who had entered the meeting with a letter of resignation in his pocket ended the day with his hand strengthened. He went out immediately to preach his gospel across the state. In August he told a convention of school superintendents that they should work "to bring about a vital, organic connection between the University and the High Schools." A great gulf still existed between them. Students who had no intention of seeking higher education should not, of course, be neglected in the high schools. But, as Folwell said with a courage and vigor that were remarkable considering the doubtful temper of his audience: ". . . We believe the high schools while carrying it [instruction on the secondary level] with utmost efficiency can at the same time undertake with economy the preparation of students looking forward to the University."

41

Perhaps, in the end, the most enduring of Folwell's contributions to educational theory in his own realm may be found in the fact that Minnesota was the first state to provide "free secondary instruction in public schools for all qualified pupils within its borders."

Four years after Folwell became president the first graduating class was presented to the regents at a great public banquet. There were just two members of that class, but, as Folwell said, Minnesota need not apologize for that modest showing. The lioness of Greek fable, when she was twitted by the wolf for bringing forth only one cub at a time, responded, "Yes one—one, but a lion." And Folwell echoed: "We present you twin lions of whom we have no reason to be ashamed."

Minnesota was by no means an impoverished institution during the 1870s. Ramsey, now in Washington as senator, had persuaded Congress to give two more townships to the university on the ingenious theory that the first grant had been made to the "territorial university" and that the "state university" deserved equal consideration.

The next step was to get agricultural instruction established. Here progress was maddeningly slow. Though entrance requirements were modest (virtually anyone over sixteen could apply) no one appeared. Farming, to the pioneer, was a matter of bending one's back over a hoe, not over a book. Several excellent men, serving in succession as "chief professor of agriculture," made honest efforts to attract students. The regents thought up fancy curricula. Members of all the existing agricultural societies—the State Grange, the Patrons of Husbandry, the State Agricultural Society, the State Horticultural Society—were invited to visit the farm. Amazingly, it proved to be news to them that an agricultural college existed. From time to time two or three students presented themselves to hear lectures on How Crops Grow and Farm Drainage. But circumstance, with an ironic perversity that had become all too familiar, drained away even this trace of interest and, in

1880, the enrollment sheet for the agricultural college again was completely blank.

Responsibility toward the Morrill Act of 1862 weighed heavily on Folwell's sensitive, inflexible conscience. It is not difficult to imagine how he must have winced when a woman member of the faculty tried to whip up enthusiasm with this shrill treble call to the clan:

> So, it's back to the farm boys for luck, luck, luck.
>> Hear the neighing, mooing and the cluck, cluck, cluck.
> Our sheepskins wrapped by Ceres will be our mascots true;
>> Our motto: Scientific farming, cock-a-doodle-do.

It was not until 1881 that there was any occasion for triumphant crowing and even then the success was of a personal rather than an ideological kind. Folwell had found in Edward D. Porter a man of experience, one who was also tirelessly enthusiastic and innovative. He had been at Delaware College for thirty years and, at the age of fifty-five, still wanted hard work to do. He found it certainly at Minnesota. Though his judgment and tact never quite equaled his energy, Porter spent eight years wrestling admirably with adversity. Never for a moment did he allow the "sinews of his courage" to weaken.

His first act was to persuade the regents to sell the last bits of the old, unprofitable farm and buy a new one. He chose wisely, as the handsome far campus of today testifies. (It is now known as the St. Paul campus.) Enough money was realized in the transaction to enable the regents to equip the new property with "buildings, water supply, implements and stock."

Porter's next attempt to woo the reluctant attention of the farming community was made with a series of lectures on new methods. When this not unfamiliar proposal was offered to them, the regents, thinking that they heard once more the song of an old and rather tried Lorelei, wearily agreed to sponsor the undertaking only if at least thirty persons had enrolled for it. Porter presented them with a list of two hundred fifty-five applicants, herded together by his infectious enthusiasm.

For two years the Farmers' Lecture Course was maintained on a high level of seriousness. Then, unhappily intoxicated by success, Porter tried further to popularize the series by importing mere entertainers from the periphery of the world of domestic science. A giddy woman teacher of cooking brought together eleven hundred Sybarites to hear her coo gently about the delights of "cream of salmon." Her success proved to be calamitous. As Folwell wrote: "So, diverted from its true purpose, ended the Farmers' Lecture Course."

Porter had learned his lesson. Snatching back part of the reputation he had earned, he solidified his relationship to the farming community by launching a pioneer experiment in agricultural extension work. From 1883 on, his series of farmers' institutes carried the latest and most authoritative word on scientific farming into every corner of the state.

But Folwell's troubles—as a man too far in the vanguard of his time to have many close adherents—were just beginning. He had to cope constantly with a board of regents who, conscientious and high-minded though they all were, allowed their effectiveness to be vitiated by busy concern with the trivia of administration. They listened at great length to the complaints of teachers about their salaries; to students who thought themselves wronged in the matter of demerits; above all to the embattled "Bourbons" (as Folwell, for once yielding to impatience, called his academic enemies) when they presented reports designed to destroy the president's prestige. They still wanted a nice little college in which they could teach Latin and Greek and from which all the Folwellian nonsense about the vulgar pretensions of the natural sciences and the social sciences had been banished.

Bewildered by most of what they heard but having a strong predilection in favor of economy, the regents responded to a faculty revolution of 1879 by eliminating the departments of physics and history. An enlightened few protested against

44

this "retrograde movement," but the regents, experiencing the sudden access of stubbornness that often attaches itself to basic insecurity, held to their decision.

A year later, they laid about them, hip and thigh, with even more abandon. In response to another injudicious plea from the faculty that the board "look into the fitness of all teachers" (meaning Folwell), the board exercised the most autocratic of its powers and summarily dismissed all the prominent members of the faculty except Folwell.

It then became the president's unenviable duty to try to attract a new company of experienced teachers into the chaos that dissension had created. The responsibility was made the more exacting by the fact that enrollment had been dropping. There had been a slump of 34 per cent in 1875, but this compared favorably with the 69 per cent drop in the populations of many schools and colleges, caused by the nationwide depression following the panic of 1873. For this the president's enemies reluctantly agreed he could not be blamed. But in 1879, when Folwell insisted on dropping the sub-freshman class, another inevitable decrease was alarmingly evident. The tongues of the Bourbons clucked gleefully.

Despite all discouragements Folwell brought back a fine group of teachers: John Downey (mathematics and astronomy) who became first dean of the Arts college; William A. Pike, creator of the engineering program; Maria Sanford (English and rhetoric) who served to be eighty years old and became known as "the best-loved woman in Minnesota"; Charles Benton, a distinguished exponent of French culture in the United States; and Albert Dodge, a Ph.D. from Heidelberg whose subject was chemistry. The first three of these lived out long academic careers at Minnesota.

In many ways the most remarkable was Maria Sanford, a superbly impressive New England version of Hypatia who loved patriotism, teaching and eloquence, in the order named, and loved them all with an intense personal passion. She took her responsibilities so earnestly that once, after hearing a former student speak in support of his candidacy for the

45

governorship of the state, she walked next day into his office and, without a word of greeting, said: "James, in your address last night you split an infinitive." Then, having done her plain duty, she turned on her heel and stalked out again. Years after her public life was officially over, she walked out onto every platform where oratory was welcome and with no apparent effort at all rolled her fine contralto voice into the rafters. "A retired teacher who never retired," as George Vincent once called her, she sat with magnificent indulgence at the special university convocation called to honor her eightieth birthday and heard another former student, Oscar Firkins, salute her in verses written for the occasion:

> "Praise her vehement and gusty
> Praise her oaken-ribbed and trusty . . ."

But even with this fine access of strength, the university continued to struggle with the crises of the time. Enrollment which had been 381 in 1880 fell to 223 in 1883. Folwell was convinced that the difficulty lay in the competition offered by the denominational colleges. A special sympathy had nourished the infancy of these institutions and, compared with the university, many were rich. The word "godless" flung at the university by those who failed to understand its obligation to be impartial (Folwell had pointed out that a university must be "secular") had injured its reputation. The student publication, *Ariel*, had said discerningly:

"If students who have reached mature years before entering college are liable to be led astray at a university within sight of twenty churches' spires it is a sign that something is radically wrong with the influences that surround the home."

Still the problem continued to throw a shadow over the university's development.

From the point of view of the regents the disturbing thing about Folwell was that he meant to be disturbing. He discovered many embarrassing ways of agitating for change. Such was the occasion when he proposed that the university be moved to a new location. Five lines of railroad track around

46

the edges of the campus already had destroyed its natural beauty. With startling foresight Folwell told the regents that soon the university would be a "thoroughfare of trade and traffic" when "elevators storing grain" must inevitably "loom across our front." At Lake Minnetonka, only twenty miles away, an ideal setting could be found where academic campus and farm campus might conduct their studies side by side. But the regents, some of whom had real estate interests in the university's existing neighborhood, met the suggestion with blank dismay. They filed and presently forgot a vague resolution to look further into the matter.

Folwell's notes on the meeting comment that he had merely done his duty in what he knew to be a hopeless cause. A latter-day observer may permit himself to hope, parenthetically, that Folwell might have come to see certain advantages in a university's occupying a situation in the very midst of the drama of everyday life.

The president continued to be tirelessly active. When he was not designing a theoretical "University of the Twentieth Century" in his mind, he was busy designing buildings for his actual school—on paper. Here, too, he met with frustrations more often than with help. Instead of the classroom space he needed the regents gave him a $55,000 drill hall which had been used very little when its inept construction encouraged a fire that burned it to the ground. He kept asking for a library and, during his administration, got none. When, after his resignation, the campus finally achieved a building that was intended to house books, it proved to be a fancy, outsize Greek temple which Folwell described in despair as "an administration building with a library in the corridor."

Always a conscientious builder, he refused to be bullied into running up professional units overnight. The demand for a medical school seemed to him to be premature. There already existed too many "windmill" institutions which exploited human need with cynical cruelty. These private schools would accept any applicant who could pay his fee without regard

47

for his aptitude or educability. From them there went out, year after year, ignorant quacks who did the incalculable mischief of witch doctors.

With such shabby irresponsibility Folwell would have nothing to do. Instead he created a service which helped to correct the benighted practices of the past. The first medical faculty at the University of Minnesota consisted of five men who acted as a licensing board to pass on the qualifications of the graduates of the private schools. These high-grade practitioners from various parts of the state served without salary and even paid their expenses to travel to Minneapolis where they gave the stiff examinations that protected the community from malpractice.

Still everyone was inclined to look at Folwell and say: " 'Behold this dreamer.' " As the jealous, the lethargic and the reactionary have always known, the best thing to do with dreamers is to put them down the nearest well. And this is what presently happened to Folwell.

An absurd incident of student rebellion touched off the crisis. A group of failing freshmen who had been disciplined by the president were unhappily inspired to stage a demonstration outside his house. An impetuous colleague, rushing to Folwell's side, had been armed by his even more impetuous wife with a pistol. Inadvertently the overwrought professor managed to shoot one of the young men in the leg. Folwell's only share in the grotesquely farcical episode was to give prompt, intelligent care to the boy's superficial wound.

But the kind of observer who, having examined all the evidence available, comes judiciously to the conclusion that there are two sides to every story and that where there's smoke there must be fire, threw the weight of such sage judgments against Folwell. Shamefacedly, the regents found a spokesman to tell him that "a different kind of man was needed as president."

Fortunately, Folwell had a genius for loyalty to match his high talents as a prophet of educational theory. He resigned quite without rancor against anyone. Many other institutions wanted him and all made firm offers. But Folwell preferred to stay at Minnesota for the rest of what proved to be a long life, giving, not merely scrupulous, but lively and creative support to his successor.

His interests were manifold, his humor abundant, his vitality all but inexhaustible. So he had a fine life, helping to expand the horizons of political science and writing history with an incisive, literary skill that was innocent of any exhibitionistic flourish. Though he had suffered at the hands of youth, he continued to find his greatest satisfaction in association with young men and women. Those "in the West" particularly appealed to him and he once listed what he thought to be their assets as "burning desire for good learning, power to work and aspiration towards noble character."

During the rest of his ninety-six years he went daily, even after retirement, to his campus office. It was not venerability that earned the nickname "Uncle Billy." He never thought of himself as old and would refer to men much younger than himself as though they were his seniors. What many generations of teachers and students liked in him was his ability to transform the space around his desk or around his hearth into a forum where the new idea, the new faith, the new loyalty—all values associated with the intellectual life—were examined critically and appraised impartially. And if Uncle Billy found such an attitude worthy he followed it with zest to the end of the course.

Folwell's rueful reference to the opinion of his opponents that he was a "wild educational mutineer" reflected the humorous generosity of a man who had nothing in his temperament of either the hysteric or the rebel. What has proved to be of immense value to those who have chosen to follow his example is the fact that he was a lover of order and a master of discipline. In scores of ways he anticipated the ideas that have become part of the educational philosophy of our time. It was as an architect of the future that his successors—Vincent, Coffman and Morrill—have consulted with him either in person or on the printed page. It is scarcely too much to say that the blueprint of his "University of the Twentieth Century" has become a reality in the University of Minnesota today.

CHAPTER THREE

CYRUS, THE CONCILIATOR

T HE SECOND PRESIDENT of the university was, indeed, a very different kind of man from the first. Cyrus, the conciliator, he might have been called, and his reign, lasting more than a quarter of a century, was one of uninterrupted benignity. No one in the history of Minnesota ever attracted so much admiration or attracted it with so little effort. Genius, if it were to be redefined in terms of Cyrus Northrup's experience, might be called the art of giving no pain at all.

When the regents called on him in New Haven, where he was comfortably established as a teacher of rhetoric and English literature, Northrop was not in the least inclined to uproot his family and move west. He had been enormously popular with each successive generation of the young men at Yale who shared his relaxed and unsurprising adventures among masterpieces. He was successful in other fields as well. Before becoming a professor he had been a newspaper editor and a participant in Republican politics. In a moment of triumphant improvisation he had had two salaries: one from the university, the other as collector of the port of New Haven. Though the political plum had been taken from him in 1882, he still had the memory of affluence and the hope of its return.

But the Minnesota men were determined to have him. They had had the most valuable of all possible endorsements of him—the word of President James B. Angell of the University of Michigan that Northrop was "a ready speaker and a man of good presence."

It is not surprising, yet nonetheless ironic, that the example of the University of Michigan should have meant so much to the regents. Under the administration of Henry Philip Tappan the broad and liberal policies that characterize the program of Michigan today had been solidly established. But the president himself was far less secure in his chair. A famous academic battle had resulted in dismissal. Tappan had to wait, with what patience he could command, the justification of his ideas and the near canonization which a later generation offered him.

Now the regents of the University of Minnesota had done very much the same thing. They had dismissed their liberal leader though with no such bitterness as had characterized the Michigan fight. Yet they found nothing odd about turning to Michigan for advice or about taking it as though it came from on high.

But, despite their urgent pleas, the best that Pillsbury and his associates could get from Northrop was a promise to visit Minnesota. This he did in the spring of 1884, sitting anonymously among the students in chapel and gathering his impressions. They were not favorable ones to begin with. The campus seemed to him a little "dun and dreary"; the prospect for the university's future even less bright. But at a reception in his honor, held in Pillsbury's house (now the official residence of the president) Northrop was warmed by the somewhat naïve graciousness of his fellow guests many of whom told him that he "seemed like a western man."

Even better evidence of their generosity was the offer finally made to him. He was to receive a salary that equaled the sum of his earnings in the time of affluence—$6000, nearly twice what the president of any midwestern institution then dared to ask.

In August, 1884, he arrived in Minnesota, and the general public had its first opportunity to see the man who was to dominate its collective imagination, as exemplar of learning, for a whole generation.

If anyone had had a fancy, in that day, to present a Biblical drama in contemporary dress, Northrop arrayed for the platform would have fitted ideally into the role of the most bland of the prophets. A lively sympathetic eye lighted the face toward which so many were to turn for comfort and encouragement. A full mustache—first, dark, and later, snowy white —drooped over a mouth that always spoke the word of kindness and often gave it the inflection of wit. An immaculate frock coat enclosed a compact figure of medium height. A white bow tie which seemed neatly to balance the unassertive fullness of the mustache, presided over an expanse of starched shirt front in the center of which glittered a diamond stud. Northrop in his very presence commanded awe and yet, at the same moment, wooed confidence. He was, as Oscar Firkins once suggested, the embodiment of reassurance.

And reassurance was the keynote of his administration from the first. It was, by tacit agreement with the regents, the essence of his contract to be as unlike Folwell as possible. Even before he took up his duties Northrop had indicated that this was to be true by announcing that he had "no pet theories of education." The contrast between the two men was complete in this respect. Throughout his career Folwell bristled with theories; Northrop always remained downy with acquiescence.

In his inaugural address (it was not delivered until he had been at his desk a year and it was time for his first commencement) he disposed of all the old thorny issues simply by throwing them out, just as he disposed of the great bulk of his correspondence by filing it in the wastebasket.

Out, first of all, went the Minnesota Plan. It had never been anything but a vision in Folwell's mind. But a vision that casts a shadow is disturbing. It seems like black magic. So it got prompt exorcism from Northrop.

Into the discard, second, went the idea of limiting enrollment to students who were ready for "proper university work." Once more all comers would be welcome. Leaders among high-school superintendents, whose field had just begun to show promise, protested that this would be ruinous to their schools. If that should prove to be true, Northrop answered, it would be proof of the failure of the high schools. For his part, catch-as-catch-can would be the rule.

Third, he laid the ghost of "godlessness." "I am not an agnostic," he said from the platform, "and I do not propose to be the instrument of making agnostics of others." One clergyman was promptly heard to rejoice that, at last, the university had come under the control of "evangelical religion." That interpretation troubled a Unitarian minister who foresaw that "mischievous results" might follow if the university were complaisantly to acknowledge "the taint of that kind of sectarianism." Northrop brought the argumentative elements together and persuaded them to agree that it would be sad to see "the university divorced from Christianity." So the matter was wrapped up decently in ambiguity and laid away on the shelf.

Northrop's assertions of principle in the inaugural address were limited to the suggestions that now there must be stability, "a settling to honest work . . . undisturbed by the perpetual apprehension of change and revolution." Folwell's belief about what constituted proper studies for a university was seriously misinterpreted in the statement: "Those who tell us we must begin with the immediately useful, meaning thereby that we must omit time-honored training in mathematics and languages, exhibit something worse than midsummer madness." (Madness this would surely have been, but quite as surely it was not Folwell's brand.)

However, there was obvious need for Northrop's concessions. Enrollment which during the last year of Folwell's administration had wavered between 250 and 300 took a dizzy and dismaying plunge in 1884. Fewer than one hundred students greeted the new president. Northrop took comfort from the assurance that many more would drop in during the course of the academic year.

54

During the first five years of Northrop's regime, destiny and the community's natural growth collaborated with a kind of patient persistence, not unlike the president's own, to give the institution stamina. By 1889 the student body had grown to a thousand. Within a decade of Northrop's arrival it has passed the two thousand mark.

Northrop once said that he intended to preside over the campus population as though it were "a kind of family," and the paternal tone quietly dominated all his relationships. The president sat at a long table in an office which he shared with the registrar. Anyone might drop in on him without an appointment. He tended to assemble his faculty as though he were adopting sons or foster brothers. At Yale one of his favorite students had been a young man named Frederick Jones. On impulse one day, as he was about to set out for Minnesota, Northrop, thinking of the loneliness he might experience as stranger in a strange land, offered Jones an appointment to his faculty. To teach what? the startled boy wanted to know. "Well," said Northrop, according to his own report of that amiable conversation on the fence, "I suppose you know as little about one thing as another. We will put you on the faculty first and find something for you to do afterward. All I ask is that you do your best and stand by me in my work."

The casualness of this method was only a little less startling than its success. Jones proved to be a vigorous administrator and a man of vivid individuality. He became, first, an able teacher of physics, then a valuable dean of the College of Engineering and, finally, after a return migration to Yale a notable figure there.

In much the same way Northrop acquired a dean for his new College of Law. This came into being almost overnight in response to the public demand that professional schools be created forthwith. Folwell, jealous of the prestige of his "University of the Twentieth Century," had resisted the temptation to work miracles. He wanted a law course, for example, only when there should be applicants who could show records of satisfactory work in a two-year preparatory course. Swank! snorted the old-time lawyers. Why should a frontier institution be more rigorously selected than the well-established eastern schools?

Northrop, with his curious kind of concessive temerity, did square off and work the miracle of creating a law shcool. Then he called in William Sullivan Pattee to attend to the details. The time was 1888, four years after the opening of the new dispensation.

Intellectually, temperamentally and spiritually, Northrop and Pattee were identical twins. They even looked alike. They wore the same kind of frock coat, the same kind of mustache, the same air of paternal grandeur. They spoke the same language of eloquence and even showed the same predilection for being photographed in profile. When Northrop found that he had too many engagements to speak in public he liked to send Pattee to some of them in his stead. He knew that his alter ego would win the confidence of any audience in much the same way that he himself would have done. As "a man of good presence," the president liked to have others of his kind about him. A slightly acid observer once said that, in Northrop's time, "Minnesota had the greatest collection of male pulchritude to be found anywhere in the academic world."

Pattee promptly knocked down the stern requirements of the Minnesota Plan to the point where his college became a safe refuge for football players. All that a young man needed to enter was to be eighteen years old and "of good moral report." An "adequate background" for "new studies" was also asked, but this was left tactfully undefined.

The dean also knocked together a curriculum and a law library. Into an old packing box which he himself fitted with shelves Pattee put his own books. "Done," he sighed contentedly and the College of Law was in operation. The legislature gave him nothing but the use of a basement room in Old Main and the promise of a salary of $2500 if he could make it up out of the $40-a-year fees paid by students.

That Pattee was staunch and faithful no one doubted. His philosophy of the law was similarly rugged and simple. "God wills it," he would say to each entering class; "man's duty is to discover and establish it."

For years Pattee was the law at Minnesota. He could afford no faculty. He brought in as many visiting lecturers like Frank Kellogg as he could woo. For the rest he trudged devotedly on alone, working by day with students of the regular course and by night with special matriculants. It was not until 1889 that the College of Law was thought to have justified its existence. Then, at last, the legislature gave it a building of its own.

The early development of the College of Medicine followed a similar course. In 1887 Dr. Perry Millard, a member of the licensing board created in Folwell's time, persuaded the state itself to take over this function. It is a proud "first" for Minnesota that it established the precedent of appointing an independent board of medical examiners to protect its citizens against the ignorance loosed on the community by products of the poisonous private schools.

With that accomplishment behind him, Dr. Millard moved on to become leader of a cause. This was to bring together, as one authorized school of instruction in medicine, all the struggling ones then in existence. With urgent eloquence he succeeded in persuading four such institutions voluntarily to surrender their charters and accept absorption into a new school sponsored by the university.

There were howls of protest from several sides, all couched in the uninhibited language of the time. "Bribers and robbers," screamed the die-hards of one school while representatives of another looked at the university and sneered: "Unsavory reputation." These came from the men who wished to protect their personal interests. But even the impartial observers were dubious. The requirements for admission to the

57

new school were, they said, "shamefully inadequate." These consisted of: the ability to write an acceptable composition of two hundred words; sufficient knowledge to be able to translate a prose passage from Latin, French, German or a Scandinavian language; and the ability to pass an examination in elementary algebra, plane geometry or botany and another in elementary physics. But if these were inadequate, Dr. Millard answered, Harvard asked no more of its matriculants.

So, the College of Medicine went into operation. A start had been made at Minnesota, however inadequately, toward the establishment of a federation of professional schools.

The problems of agricultural education grieved the conciliator, Northrop, quite as hopelessly as they had outraged the rebel, Folwell. Even the farmers' institutes had not reconciled the man with a hoe to the idea of theoretical instruction in a classroom. In Northrop's first year at Minnesota, one student registered for the agricultural course; the next year there were none at all.

But something of the dogged effort of Professor Porter, sitting alone on the farm campus brooding on research problems, had borne fruit nonetheless. The United States Congress, after debating the matter through many sessions, decided finally to create experimental stations and to support them with federal funds. In 1887 the Hatch Act was passed. The fact that Minnesota was ready to receive its share gave the farm campus an advantage of twenty-five years over the rest of the university in its tradition of devotion to research.

Porter, undiscouraged by years of neglect and derision, set out to assemble a staff for the experiment station. The group of men whom he brought together was brilliant as the names Willet H. Hays, Samuel Green and Otto Luger will serve sufficiently well to remind specialists in their fields. The long-neglected science of veterinary medicine was given the ultimate endorsement of academic respectability by Otto Schwartkopff whose forked beard should have made him look

58

like a Prussian officer but actually made him look even more impressively like Zeus.

To the long history of Professor Porter's calamitous successes, one more was now added. He was so outshown by his faculty that rebellious members of the Grange and of the Farmers' Alliance began to find him a figure of fun. The university itself suffered in their estimation by having supported him so long. It was time, they urged, to separate the Department of Agriculture from the university. Many critics made the quite unjust assumption that the academic twin had been robbing the pocket of the farm twin, forgetting that an agricultural campus existed only because of Pillsbury's conscientiousness. They chose to forget also that Folwell had done everything to bring students to the Department of Agriculture just short of kidnapping them.

It was in such an atmosphere of tension that Northrop's gift as conciliator shone most attractively. He turned away the wrath of all but the most unreasonable by pointing out that, if Minnesota had managed to turn out few graduates in agricultural education, neither had the supposedly model schools at Brookings, South Dakota, and Ames, Iowa. Then, he sat down with the most articulate of his critics, the Grangers, and undertook to develop a new pattern of instruction better suited than any previous one had been to the immediate realities.

Out of these consultations emerged the design for a School of Agriculture that would appeal to "such boys as aspire to become successful and intelligent farmers, overseers of farms, veterinary surgeons, entomologists, agricultural chemists and botanists . . . and who have already had some experience in farm work together with a good common school education." Such young people of high-school age were not to be snatched from their father's farms during the periods of seedtime and harvest when they were needed at home. School began in the middle of October and ended in the middle of April. Boys were permitted to work for their expenses at twelve cents an hour.

59

This scheme was not inherently different from that of Professor Porter's old, woefully unsuccessful school of practical farming. But the new one had the enormous advantage of being able to draw, for instruction, on the superbly able staff of the experiment station.

Still the complaints were not quite stilled. The Grangers, who had helped to design the school, were thought merely to have gone over to the enemy. In 1889 the die-hards were once more able to get the ear of the state senate with a resolution calling for the separation of "the institutions known as the State University and the Agricultural College."

At this moment Northrop's skill as campaigner came briskly into operation. His devoted friend Pillsbury was in the governor's chair. During a noon hour, one day, Northrop led him out of the capitol for a walk around the neighborhood. Pillsbury often had said that he wanted eventually to give a sizable gift to the university. The time had come, Northrop urged. Let the governor give the $150,000 which the legislature needed in order to build a "science hall" and opposition might evaporate into gratitude. The university would be "saved from embarrassment and dismemberment."

The plan worked perfectly. Pillsbury made his proposal to a joint session of the two houses of the legislature, saying: "All I ask is to know that these land grants will be kept intact and this institution firm and strong in its maturity." The legislature made unconditional surrender in a resolution offering "solemn assurance that the unity of the several departments will be preserved." Pillsbury Hall, a splendidly "firm and strong" example of the Richardson school of architecture, stands today as a monument to this moment of triumph when a successful family adjustment was made under the joint fatherhood of Pillsbury and Northrop.

The last courageous act of the irrepressible Porter was to bring together as good a staff for the School of Agriculture as he had assembled for the experiment station. Again his success was complete—and calamitous. Everyone liked W. W. Pendergast whom Porter chose as principal. Everyone liked the Brewsters, too—Henry and Florence, man and wife—who were Pendergast's chief assistants. But still no one was patient with Porter and at last, in 1889, he resigned to go to the University of Missouri.

The fundamental purpose of the regents in creating the "school" of agriculture was to justify the existence of the farm campus by giving it some kind of population. If older young men could not be attracted into the "college" boys would have to do. The college was not dropped from the theoretical design of the department. It merely bided its time.

And the plan worked. By 1890 enrollment in the school had risen to one hundred. Many buildings—a dormitory, a laboratory, a veterinary building, a drill hall—were added to the campus. Samuel Green, employing his doubly green thumb industriously, kept the grounds beautiful with shaded walks and flower beds, each feature of this display properly labelled with both its popular and its botanical name.

Girls were later admitted to the school though only tentatively, at first, while the legislature kept a worried ear open for reports of indiscretion. When coeducation proved that it had only civilizing effects, girls were received on a basis of equality. A dormitory and a full curriculum in domestic science were provided for them.

Important men were attracted to the Department of Agriculture. (Though even the legislature used all terms of administrative design loosely and interchangeably, there existed officially a "Department" under which were bracketed the School of Agriculture for students of high-school age, the College for older students, and the Experimental Station.) None was more distinguished than Theophilus Haecker whose studies in animal nutrition and milk production were so impressively authoritative as to be honored by the permanent acceptance of the "Haecker standards." He was a man of wisdom and wit who used to say to his young men: "Be gentle with the cow, boys; remember, she's a lady and a mother."

But the success of the School of Agriculture, though it put

61

to eminently respectable use the resources provided by the Morrill Act, hardly justified the highest hopes of the law's author. Hundreds of young men went through its course but no more than a tenth of them stayed on to take the college work. Year after year, some twenty young men would enroll for advanced training in agriculture but only two or three of them stayed long enough to receive diplomas. The farm boys still were "standing with reluctant feet" where secondary and university education meet.

It took a new man, Colonel William H. Liggett, to consolidate the precarious gains of three decades. With his appointment in 1892 as first dean of the Department of Agriculture, the farm campus became virtually independent of the academic. Liggett himself had a status equal in authority to that of Northrop. He could speak directly to the legislature.

Liggett supported the vigorous plan of Professor Hays for developing, still further, the work of the School of Agriculture. A survey showed that most of its pupils came from homes that were within a radius of eighty-five miles of the campus. Farmers in the outlying districts obviously found costs too high to send their children to school. Therefore, the school must go to them. Branches were presently put forth at Crookston and Morris. Other projects were begun for carrying instruction to the people. The Summer School at Itaska State Park was one. The Division of Agricultural Extension, created by the legislature in 1909, was another—far the most significant of all in the program of spreading the gospel of scientific farming. Before the end of the Northrop administration the Department of Agriculture had achieved stability, self-respect and a total enrollment of 1500 students in all divisions.

What impresses a latter-day observer of the university's early struggles is, above all else, the idealistic zeal of the builders of all departments. In the face of chilling discouragements, their hopes continued to be hardy and perennial. Frederick Scheetz Jones, having chosen a career so casually at Northrop's suggestion, educated himself at his own expense in Germany and returned to Minnesota to create a physics department that would be ready for the great responsibilities and distinctions that were to come to it in the atomic age.

Dr. Millard, presiding first over a faculty which occupied the quarters of the disbanded Minnesota Hospital College across the Mississippi River from the campus, insisted in 1892 on closer integration. When the legislature was unable to supply funds for a new building, Dr. Millard dipped into his own pocket and brought up $60,000 to complete the project. Standing stoically in the midst of furiously embattled homeopaths and allopaths—equally determined that their paths should never meet—this completely dedicated man clung to his own high standards. The language of enmity still buzzed about his ears. But he managed to be indifferent to it. And, in the end, he had his reward. In 1910 Abraham Flexner made an impartial survey of medical education in the United States. His account was so thorough and so candid that many criminally negligent institutions had, as a result of the bad reports given of them, to close their doors. But of Minnesota's College of Medicine Flexner said that it was one of the most capable and conscientious in existence.

Burly or elegant, bulky or fragile, the builders of all the colleges that came into existence during the 1890s showed the same vein of iron in their creative temperaments. Frederick Wulling, who looked like a diminutive Spanish grandee, stood stalwartly against all the poisoned darts of deprecation directed against a "mere pharmacist" and, almost stone by stone, build a good school. Risking further abuse for the nicety of tastes, he played the violin in string quartets, helped to organize the Minneapolis Institute of Arts, and bought the work of local painters. Risking, most recklessly of all, a reputation for eccentricity, he studied law at night and earned a degree. This neat little package of energy, imagination and intellectual curiosity produced, out of its suprisingly capacious depths, a dedication to duty unequaled in his field. The standards of Wulling's School of Pharmacy were as high as any to be found in an American institution.

Much more on the rugged side, but no less faithful to basic principle, was William Remsen Appleby, creator of the School of Mines. His branch of instruction also sprang out of the Morrill Act but, for nearly three decades, it creaked dismally in all the winds of circumstance, looking withered if not actually dead. During the first fifteen of these years— 1870 to 1885—the classes in civil engineering and mechanical engineering, which acceptance of the bounty of the Morrill Act bound the university to offer, were able to produce just sixteen graduates, a pitiful average of one a year with a bonus of one more "for effort." Everyone agreed that the situation was absurd, particularly for a state that had great mineral wealth. With weary determination to do its part, the legislature had provided a Mechanic Arts building in 1886. The regents had established a School of Mines in 1888, but it continued to exist only on paper. "The university was at a loss to know what to do," Northrop wrote in his *Reminiscences*, "because the school must be fashioned by one man, it being impossible to provide a complete faculty at first."

It was time to work another miracle, and Northrop did so by discovering the one man to do the job, Appleby.

But still the realm of "the mechanic arts" was not at peace. For seven years, "engineering" and "mining" wrestled together for supremacy while Northrop stood on the side lines, and grieved over "the seeming chaos in this college."

Then, in 1897, the regents, precipitating a revolution of their own, separated the embattled elements. The School of Mines and the College of Engineering became distinct entities. Playing the role of a somewhat perverse Solomon, Northrop dismembered the baby still further by lopping off chemistry from the main body. Part of its work was given to the Arts college; part set up in a new School of Chemistry. Able men took over each division. Appleby became dean of Mines. Frederick Jones, still "doing his best and standing by

William Watts Folwell, President 1869-1884. "Crusader of Education," "Uncle Billy" to many generations of students. (Courtesy of the University of Minnesota News Service)

Main was the university when Folwell came. He called it a fire trap, and it burned he ground on September 24, 1904.

The statue of John Sargent Pillsbury, "Father of the University." He presides permanently as he longed to do over the "old campus."

Pillsbury Hall—A gift from John Sargent Pillsbury made possible its erection and "saved the university from dismemberment."

Folwell Hall on the left, Jones Hall on the right. Contrary to legend, Folwell never had gargoyles on its many chimneys.

Cyrus Northrop, President 1884-1911. He "sanctified the whole place," and humanized the University community as well.

Northrop Memorial Auditorium. (Courtesy of the University of Minnesota News Service)

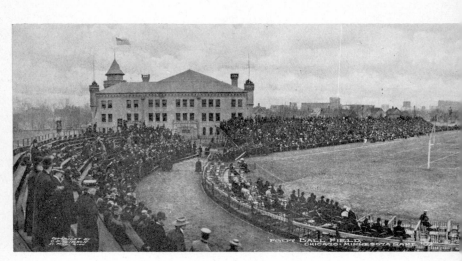

The old Northrop Field where the second president waggishly acknowledged

The "old campus"

imself to be the "grand old sport." Scene of the Minnesota-Chicago game, 1907.

s it looked in 1909.

George Edgar Vincent, President 1911-1917. "Refounder of the university"—"statesman of education." (Courtesy of the University of Minnesota News Service)

A glimpse of the medical buildings of the university today. Vincent's dream is fullfilled in the Mayo Memorial which towers above the other units.

rion LeRoy Burton, President 1917-1920. He was
ed-haired giant of whom one Minnesotan said: "He
cost the legislature millions of dollars. Everytime
asks for anything the members will tumble over
h other to give it to him." (Courtesy of the Uni-
sity of Minnesota News Service)

rton Hall. Folwell called it "an administrative
lding with a library in the corridor." Today, re-
ned for the 4th president, it is neither library nor
ne of the administration but a classroom building.

The mall of the "new campus" that Burton ordered. Cap and Gown
Day, May 1949. Coffman Memorial Union in the background. (Courtesy of the University of Minnesota News Service)

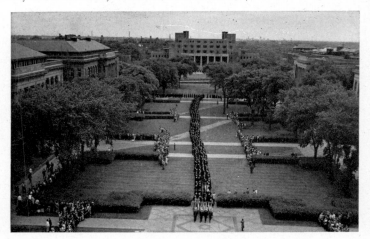

Lotus Delta Coffman, President 1920-1938. "Scientist of education," creator of "unique educational experiments." (Courtesy of the University of Minnesota News Service)

Coffman Memorial Union. It presents daily a successful dramatization of the well-ordered student life of a huge university.

Guy Stanton Ford, President 1938-1941. Co-creator with Vincent and Coffman of the University of Minnesota as a modern institution. (Courtesy of the University of Minnesota News Service)

Theodore C. Blegen, dean of the Graduate School. Guy Stanton Ford's student, disciple and successor. Together these two men have presided over the whole history of the Graduate School of the University. (Courtesy of the University of Minnesota News Service)

View from the Mayo Memorial Tower. (Courtesy of the University of Minnesota News Service)

Walter Castella Coffey, President 1941-1945. "Master of crises," "as cool and disciplined in the conduct of affairs as he was warm and convivial in human relations." (Courtesy of the University of Minnesota News Service)

A glimpse of the St. Paul campus, home of the Institute of Agriculture. (Courtesy of the University of Minnesota News Service)

A glimpse of the 3rd large campus . . . Olcott Hall at the Duluth branch. (Courtesy of the University of Minnesota News Service)

James Lewis Morrill, President 1945—. "Devoted exponent of the land grant idea," who has opened the door ever wider on educational opportunity. (Courtesy of the University of Minnesota News Service)

Malcolm M. Willey, Vice President, Academic Administration. (Courtesy of the University of Minnesota News Service)

William T. Middlebrook, Vice President, Business Administration. (Courtesy of the University of Minnesota News Service)

THREE DEANS WHO PRESIDE OVER MICHIGAN'S LARGEST RESEARCH PROGRAMS:

Harold S. Diehl, Dean of the Medical Sciences. (Recently resigned but still advisor) (Courtesy of the University of Minnesota News Service)

Athelstan Spilhaus, Dean of the Institute of Technology. (Courtesy of the University of Minnesota News Service)

Harold Macy, Dean of the Institute of Agriculture. (Courtesy of the University of Minnesota News Service)

Comstock Hall, one of the dormitories for women.

Centennial Hall, one of the dormitories for men.

dmond G. Williamson, Dean
Students and Professor of Psy-
ology. Interpreter of Minne-
ta's unique "Magna Carta" of
udents' rights and of the "Min-
sota point of view."

A group of incoming students on an orientation
tour during Freshman Week. (Courtesy of the
University of Minnesota News Service)

. huge graduating class and its parents at a night commencement
eremony held in the football stadium. (Courtesy of the University
f Minnesota News Service)

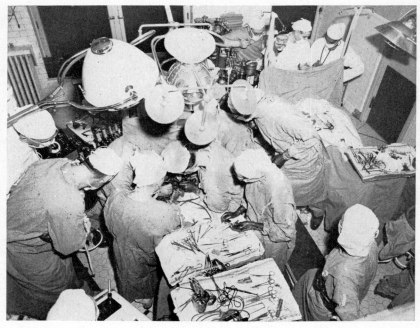

The famous team of Minnesota surgeons performing the unique "cross circulation" operation. (Courtesy of the University of Minnesota News Service)

The Heart Hospital, a project launched by the Variety Club, a group of showmen in the region.

Solar energy at work in Korea. Vice Presidents Malcolm M. Willey (left) and William T. Middlebrook (second from left) of the University of Minnesota watch the operation of this solar energy unit at the College of Engineering of Seoul's National University on their visit to Korea this summer. Reflecting the sun's rays, the unit was used to boil the water in the tea kettle in about 15 minutes. Korean engineer at right is shown igniting a piece of wood at the focal point of reflection as the tea kettle perks.

The University of Minnesota and Seoul National University are taking part in a $1,800,000 U. S. Foreign Aid contract involving an exchange of professors and technical assistance for the Korean school.

A late addition, the new library to the St. Paul campus.

A view from the air of the Minneapolis campus today.

the president in his work," brought to engineering three assets; his own taste for learning; an ability to get on with young men; and a fine, authoritative pair of lungs. George Frankforter, to whom a test tube was man's best symbol of high adventure and research the only proper goal of a thinking man's life, assumed responsibility for chemistry.

Like Wulling, Frankforter lived close to the cultural life of the community. He was instrumental in bringing his friend Emil Oberhoffer to Minnesota as a teacher of music. Later, he helped to create the Minneapolis Symphony Orchestra and to install Oberhoffer as its first conductor.

Appleby proceeded promptly to the task of building up one of the best-equipped departments in the university. His work recommended itself so heartily to the people of the state that he became an important adviser not merely to the university but to government and industry as well. Appleby may be said to have put one of Folwell's pet theories actually to work, in overalls. At the request of the mining companies, he and the faculty of the School of Mines began to make studies of the "benificiation of low-grade ores." So the university became, in this instance, what Folwell had said it should be, "a resort for resource, for counsel and for information." The dramatic story of the development of taconite (to be recounted later in these pages) brought that effort to rewarding fulfillment.

Another one-man department of fine distinction was that of dentistry. Alfred Owre was the man. In 1905 when he became dean, this modest, gentle little devotee of science set for himself the astonishing task of becoming the prophet of a new day for his branch of learning. Dentistry, he knew, had lagged disgracefully behind medicine in the search for knowledge and in the development of techniques. Owre was determined to see it catch up. That he did so triumphantly, witnesses will rise up, all over the world, to testify. Dentists in Paris have been known to look into an American mouth and, after a moment of inspection, pronounce the name Owre in tones that blend reverence with rhapsody.

He was a magnificent oddity: a pacifist . . . a lover of poetry . . . a gourmet who knew all that there is to know about such things as Persian honey but who lunched on water and allowed himself only two thousand calories of food each day . . . a bachelor, until he was forty-five, who built himself a uniquely beautiful house near the campus and filled it with art objects of his own fine selection. His tastes were fastidious and they were his own. The result: he had an enormous influence in elevating the standards of students not only within his own specialty but also wherever he could touch the periphery of the educational process.

Born to naturalized Norwegian parents, Owre had worked in a Minneapolis hardware store to put himself through high school. At nineteen he was able, at last, to go to college and he planned to become a surgeon. (Actually he took an M.D. degree just to satisfy his own exacting idea of what a servant of humanity should be.) But his awareness of the great need to lift the level of dental training deflected him. He became a graduate in dentistry and set about the job of performing his miracle of levitation.

Most dental schools of the time were, as he once wrote, nothing more than "commercialized diploma factories." Someone must create a new program, one that would be at once practical and thorough. This program, he saw, must "start with what was at hand and proceed toward the ideal." He would settle for nothing less than the ultimate recognition of dentistry as "the equivalent of an oral specialty of medicine." Having surrendered himself to his convictions, Owre allowed their strength to support him in the struggle against a tendency on the part of medical men to be patronizingly dismissive of his rights and with the equally distressing tendency of his own profession to settle for second best. Owre insisted that dentistry fight to achieve "professional self-respect." He did so by steadily improving requirements for admission to the College of Dentistry, steadily broadening

66

its curriculum, steadily advancing technical facilities. He urged his students to become men of broad interests and he worked at making himself a proper guide by returning, each year, to one or another classroom to study educational method, English literature, literary criticism. Before he left Minnesota to go to Columbia, Owre had transformed the College of Dentistry from a "refuge for butchers" (as one of its more acid-tongued critics had called it) into something that had been recreated in his own image of idealistic pride.

It was Alfred Owre who once offered the best possible description, uncluttered by academic reservations and complications, of Northrop in relation to his task as president.

"Your true paternal attitude toward me," he wrote, "toward my faculty and my cause has been and will be an inspiration as long as I live. We are all your boys."

In that ability to attract devotion lay Northrop's strength. His interest in academic theory took its direction chiefly from a desire to satisfy, or at least to still, the clamorous demand. The articulate public, in so far as it was at all concerned with the university's affairs, wanted large enrollment. Northrop bought it with many compromises. Each profession wanted its prestige acknowledged in the form of a school or college of its own on the campus. Northrop created these units, knowing that his deans would need to be men of heroic strength in order to keep them alive. It was his placid habit to look the other way while the struggle went on and then generously to share the credit if it succeeded. His genius for adoptive parenthood enabled him, again and again, to select exactly the man who would be willing and able to face the appalling effort of holding the jerry-built institution together.

In his *Reminiscences* Northrop wrote: "Year after year passed peacefully—one very much like another." If, actually, there was no such peace as he liked to believe but rather a great convulsive ferment of intramural jealousy among his professional schools, at least the fact that Northrop made no disquieting demands of his own (as Folwell would certainly

67

have done) provided a much-needed tranquilizing drug. Agitation might have killed the patient. Northrop's treatment gave the university a long period of rest—a protracted infancy—during which it grew physically of its own inner strength. Enrollment increased from a few hundred students to nearly six thousand. The plant expanded from five small buildings to forty scattered over two campuses.

Among Northrop's "boys" (and girls) there were many who achieved the highest distinction in the academic world. Looking at a list of teachers who belonged, at one time or another, to Northrop's faculty, a Columbia professor once exclaimed: "Is there anyone who hasn't been at Minnesota? Is it some kind of divine law?"

Many of these men moved on to assignments at other universities all the way from Harvard and Yale to California. But they left their signatures to many statements of what they believed academic responsibility to be. Wallace Notestein, for example, before he went on, first to Cornell and later to Yale, was a member of Northrop's faculty long enough to increase the prestige of the history department immeasurably. To the Minnesota library his efforts added a collection of materials for the study of seventeenth-century parliamentary history the equal of which is to be found only in the British Museum. Ever eager to advance scholarship wherever it had made a start, Notestein was instrumental in attracting many brilliant minds to Minnesota.

Others of Northrop's young men stayed on to become venerable ones in his service. Frederick Klaeber brought out of Germany a knowledge of philosophy so thorough and precise that for many men in his field Minnesota existed, during the 1890s, as an otherwise nebulous point in the midst of *terra incognita* from which that great man sent out his messages to the learned world. (The regents did not quite share this generous view. They once passed a solemn resolution urging Professor Klaeber to give up dabbling in research and to get on with the honest business of teaching Beowulf and Chaucer to undergraduates.)

68

Joseph Warren Beach, a student of the classics, first at Minnesota and later at Harvard, returned to the West and spent nearly half a century on the Minnesota campus. Bringing the authority and discipline of rich scholarship into an unworked field, he made the first serious appraisals of contemporary poetry and fiction. Himself a poet of high distinction, he looked in his youth like a lineal descendant of Shelley but his durability proved to be impressive. Before he died at the age of seventy-seven, he had imparted to many generations of students his fine gift for what an eastern sage has called "right rapture." The brilliance and originality of his critical approach illuminated the widest possible reach of the creative impulse not merely in his classroom but in his many books. Seeking outlet for its inexhaustibility, the same spirit of sober, searchingly humanistic inquiry flowed into his private relationships. Professor Beach's salon on University Avenue became for all his associates a place that was dedicated to ideas; indeed, to all the graces of the mind—knowledge, insight, curiosity, wit, tolerance and, as Beach's own phrase expressed it, "the courtesy of the heart."

David Swenson, product of undergraduate training at Minnesota and graduate work at Columbia, taught philosophy at his alma mater, adding to his local reputation as the friendliest of teachers national fame as the leading American interpreter of Kierkegaard. Indeed, his lucid amplifications of Kierkegaard's paradoxes served to make the most difficult of modern mystics intelligible even to stubborn unbelievers. Man, Swenson suggested (in expounding Kierkegaard's central thought) has darkened his days by shutting out wonder; he must "confront God rather than His gifts" and learn to recover "an amazement so profound that every suggestion of an imperfectly realized idea is excluded. It is only for the religious man that all things work together for good—science and art, sorrow and joy, success and frustration, life and death." Swenson, too, was, in his way, one of Northrop's "boys." It was the president's self-assigned task, as a half respectful, half impertinent observer once said, to "sanctify the whole place." No one ever seconded Northrop's efforts to offset the charge of "godlessness" with more of illuminated dignity than David Swenson was able, by his word and his example, to do.

Another Minnesota product, long a member of its faculty, was Oscar Firkins, the witticist of moralists in his studies of comparative literature. Purblind, shy, acutely sensitive both as critic and as human being, Firkins overcame all handicaps with an almost unexampled hardihood of spirit. He read omnivorously (through the eyes of student assistants), was in command of a half-dozen modern languages, and became the author of more thousands of elegantly phrased, Rhada-manthine judgments than any critic of our time. Writing once of a drawing-room comedy which displayed a peculiarly offensive kind of irresponsibility, Firkins suggested that its tone was as vulgar as its morality was murky. Throughout the play's length a woman seemed constantly to be about to surrender to a lecherous lover but, at each crisis, she saved her dubious virtue by a trick. The outraged Firkins wrote: "If a woman is to sell herself, let her sell herself; if she chooses to remain pure, let us be clear about that, too." And he added: "I speak with the coarseness which is the sanative retort to this spurious delicacy."

Northrop offered his own lively description of another of his "boys," the spirited Dr. "Dickey" Burton who "rode his aesthetic hobbies like a cavalry leader." Indeed, as he ordered his indefatigable charges upon Olympus, Burton was the aca-demic equivalent of Teddy Roosevelt, complete with energy, audacity and pince-nez. He progressed steadily through many years at Minnesota in the estimation of the Women's Clubs of America and became, at last, their favorite high priest of culture.

In 1910, at the age of seventy-six, Northrop reached the firm decision that he must resign. For two years he had been making tentative plans to do so, but each time his "boys" had urged him to stay on a little longer. But the sticking point came, at last, when he wanted no longer to be in the public eye.

Throughout the long years since 1884 he had recommended himself tirelessly to every sort of audience. In this he had been particularly successful with students. Once when the campus was threatened with the indecorum of a parade in nightshirts, he had been able to quell the outbreak of impropriety with a single word to its leader. The boy stood up to his followers and said, with the air of a junior conciliator: "About those nightshirts—we can't do it. I proposed the plan. But Prexy doesn't like and what he says *goes.*"

And he had recommended himself to the general public with such genial authority that he was saluted everywhere as "Minnesota's grand old man." Even after his retirement from the presidency an effort was made to lure him back into public life. The suggestion that he run for the governorship was made by the Democratic party though Northrop was known to have been a Republican all his life. But Cyrus, the conciliator, was not nonplused. "Gentlemen," he said, "if you will get me the unanimous endorsement of both parties, I'll be glad to make the run."

Underlying all his gifts of reconciliation and peaceful adjustment ran a vien of perennial boyishness. He loved a practical joke. It did not embarrass him to be caught lying on the floor of his library blowing the smoke of a forbidden cigar up the chimney.

Once, midway of his career, he dramatized this playfulness memorably. Northrop Field was being dedicated to the future of sport at Minnesota. The mayor of Minneapolis gave the address of the occasion. "We are here," he began, "to honor a grand old sport." The intended reference was, of course, to football. It brought forth so tumultuous a burst of applause that the mayor was thrown a little off balance. His bewilderment increased when shouts of uncontrollable laughter followed. He understood only when he turned to find that Northrop was on his feet bowing ceremoniously and saluting the crowd with the extravagant gestures of a Touchstone.

The president had been inspired to pretend that the "grand old sport" was himself.

After twenty-five years of making benignity an art, a science and an administrative technique Northrop was tired. As he said, he had done all that it was possible for a man of his temperament to do. And he had accomplished his mission. He had enabled the university to survive. He had "sanctified the whole place" and humanized it as well.

CHAPTER FOUR

THE WAY OF THE PERFECTIONIST

AND THE THIRD PRESIDENT of the university was a very different kind of man from the second. Only in his ability to excite intense admiration and respect was George Edgar Vincent like Northrop. Otherwise the contrast between the two men was complete.

Northrop was paternalistic, a benevolent dictator who was used to praise and to having his word go. Vincent was a typical believer in the democratic process. He seemed to care little for adulation if only he were allowed to get on with the job of building up a monument to the democratic spirit.

Northrop had no taste for detail. When a department head sent him a long report about his needs, the president would summon him to the office. "My boy," he would say, "when you want to communicate with me just come in and talk." Dropping the report into the commodious wastebasket at his side, he would banish the grim formality of the conference in favor of the atmosphere of the family chat.

Vincent was an administrator for whom organization had all the attraction of a work of art. The disciplines of the academic world were not hardships to be endured but techniques to be used gratefully for the realization and fulfillment of creative potentialities.

Northrop had no "pet theories of education." To him improvisation, rather than mutation, was the way of evolution. Vincent had a brilliantly clear idea of what a "true university" should be, namely, an expert adviser to the state. Northrop was content to preside over a "loose federation of disparate colleges." Vincent saw that a university must have unity of purpose. He made it his task to develop at Minnesota a disciplined educational body, capable of fulfilling many functions, neatly articulated in all its parts. The systematic and harmonious working of this social organism, in the service in the community as a whole, was the ideal toward which the educational process must strive.

With Vincent's appearance on the campus, the university returned to the purposes of Folwell to whom this obligation of the true university had also been luminously clear. But Vincent had the enormous advantage over his predecessor of having something more than a vision with which to work. Years had intervened and a body had been formed to the further development of which discipline could be profitably applied. Vincent's work, as Guy Stanton Ford once said, amounted to "a second founding of the university."

To this exacting assignment Vincent brought a glittering collection of assets. His physical handsomeness was not of the kind to which the slur "male pulchritude" could be applied. The face was of the classic style associated in the imagination of many a man with the portrait bust of a Roman senator. The lively play of expression flashed messages of sensibility and strength so rapidly, one after another, that they merged into a single effect, one which only the finest product of the civilized way of life can convey.

Imagination and integrity were traits that seemed also to be interchangeable, almost indistinguishable, in the flexible play of Vincent's thought. He could no more have compromised with an ideal than he could have failed to recognize the ideal when he saw it. It delighted his associates to watch the practiced and disciplined movements of his mind; it leaped at an idea with the expertness of a highly trained athlete. The completely alert, yet relaxed, control of his intelligence in action was as exhilarating to watch as a high dive.

74

Wit was as much Vincent's native language as was English itself. The dexerity with which insight and verbal inventiveness were made to collaborate on a platform constituted one marvel of articulateness; the speed with which he spoke constituted a second. He was completely intelligible at two hundred fifty words a minute, and the intoxicating ease of the whole performance tended to stimulate a hearer with the feeling that he was somehow part author of the wit. Vincent flattered an audience with the assumption that it could participate at his pace; the result usually was that the most casually assembled company managed to take the hurdles of sly reference and the pole vaults of epigram as though everyone were at the height of training for the Olympic games.

As a teacher of sociology at the University of Chicago Vincent had managed even to administer a rebuke with a convivial gaiety that underscored the protest and made it memorable even while it deftly removed the sting. To a student who had struggled through a haze of improvisation Vincent once said: "The variety of your misinformation is almost an excuse for its being." A charming, but slightly vague woman on whom Vincent once had occasion to call kept referring to the three children who sat with her for exact data: a date, here; a name, there; a quotation, from a third. "To an academic like you," she apologized at last, "I must sound like an idiot." "Not at all," Vincent answered. "You work in the best academic tradition. You see your children as your footnotes." A meeting at which Vincent presided had suddenly turned both acrimonious and discursive. Vincent cut it short, saying: "Gentlemen, I'm sure you will all agree with me that this argument has degenerated into a cat fight. I shall end it by putting the question to a vote. All those in favor say: 'Miaow.' " He delighted his first audience of undergraduates at Minnesota with an inspired, spontaneous greeting. The occasion was the chapel exercise at which he was presented as president-elect. There were more young people who wanted to hear him than could find seats and many were perched on the ledges of the open windows. Vincent

75

got to his feet with an air that was to become familiar at Minnesota, that of seeming to have been shot from a cannon. "Mr. President," he said, acknowledging Northrop's introduction, "members of the faculty, students—" and then, seeming for the first time to be aware of the overflow in the windows, he added, "and incoming students."

But Vincent's witty inspirations never seemed frivolous. As an undergraduate of his time recalled long afterward, on the occasion of the twenty-fifth reunion of his class:

"To hear President Vincent begin an address: 'Men of Minnesota,' was to have conferred upon one, all at once, the privileges of manhood, a prideful awareness of one's position as student and a sense of responsibility toward both."

Even before Vincent delivered his inaugural address—this was delayed until the fall session had begun, after the official opening of his administration in July—the new president had established many reforms. "I feel like a man who has an unknown number of blank checks out against his account," Vincent said as he studied the university's finances. He called in an expert to create a budget, the first the university had had. It replaced a curious kind of cafeteria system of self-service which permitted the first and the most acquisitive of the deans to gather up all the best nourishment while the late-comers took what was left. (Worse than this, a small inner circle of deans were thought to be favorites of the administration in Northrop's time. "The robber barons," they were called by the less privileged.)

For the old routine of daily chapel, Vincent substituted a program of triweekly convocations to which Howard Taft brought his chuckling awareness of the infinite variety of the human comedy, Georg Brandes testified, with his peculiar kind of cool Northern zeal, that Flaubert and Ibsen were no aloof, unapproachable gods of literature but had once been living men, and others, like Shailer Matthews and Louis Brandeis, came with the news that the twentieth century was

76

in a fine intellectual ferment. The campus became an exciting place.

It became a gay place, as well. The president and his wife, still in their forties, loved the theater, music, dancing and sport. (Mrs. Vincent was rather more active in the last of these interests than was her husband. Sometimes they would separate for the summer and Mr. Vincent would travel in England while Mrs. Vincent shot mountain lions in the Rockies.) Their social exuberance flowed over spontaneously into an endless succession of fairs, fetes, parties and pageants. Pillsbury had lent his old house to the president (even before his heirs made it university property) and it became the scene of liveliness for people of all ages and of all academic groups. On the ballroom on the third floor Mrs. Vincent would bring freshmen together to dance the Texas Tommy to the throb of a player piano on a Friday night; early the next morning she would be resolutely herding faculty wives into it to play basketball or to attitudinize delicately in the modish manner of Delsarte. Vincents of two generations rode horseback together regularly and looked very handsome doing so. At eighty Mrs. Vincent uttered one of the rare complaints of her crowded, fortunate life against "that old fogey," her doctor, who had forbidden her to ride any more.

In Vincent's subtle mind a second purpose for all this gaiety supported the primary one of making the university atmosphere pleasant. It was to blow away old hostilities with a fresh breeze of good will. Vincent was the first president to offer himself successfully as a liaison officer between the academic campus and the farm campus. His unaffected pleasure in association with men whose gifts he respected made him a welcome guest on the farm. His contagious enthusiasm spread to many on the main campus. A new era of ready communication between the two faculties began with a fair, planned by Vincent, at which they met under Professor Green's magnificent trees.

If anyone had failed to understand that Vincent's purpose

was clear to him, or to believe that he was prepared to put a bold new program into operation, his inaugural address swept all doubt away. In a passage displaying all the diamond luster of his style as well as the earnestness of his faith, he described what a modern institution of higher learning must be prepared to do and be.

"We are coming to realize that good farming is not a robbing but a compensating of the soil; that it costs as much to plant bad seed as good; that cows are sometimes pensioners instead of producers; that bad highways are the heaviest road tax; that public health is national capital; that juvenile delinquency comes less from depravity than from deprivation; that industrial accidents are not lawyers' perquisites but costs of production; that all idleness is not due to indolence; that social legislation is not an amiable avocation but an exacting profession; that municipal government should not be so skillfully designed to keep bad men from doing harm that it keeps honest and efficient men from doing good; that the United States must trust less to 'manifest destiny' and more to constructive purpose. In these changes of theory and method there is need of accurate knowledge, carefully interpreted experiment and authoritative advice. If the University is true to its mission it will put all of its resources at the service of the community. Amid the conflicts and rivalries of many interests, parties, sections, professions and groups, the University must never waver from the position of the unimpassioned, unprejudiced seeker for the truth, all of it and that alone."

Here, once more, was Folwell's "University of the Twentieth Century," a vision that had been clear to Tappan in the early days at Michigan and that Van Hise had recently been transmuting into a blueprint plan for Wisconsin. Vincent had stepped confidently into the vanguard of leadership.

In his inaugural Vincent quoted a passage from Francis Bacon's *The New Atlantis*, describing how the "College of the Seven Day Works" sent out its "merchants of light" to travel the world over and bring back its latest discoveries.

It was to summon back such merchants of light and assemble them, in even greater numbers than before, on the Minnesota campus that Vincent took to be his chief job as administrator. Believing intensely in the democratic system, he wrote finis to the old paternalistic regime by creating the University Senate in which the faculty could make its voice heard and the All-Student Council, intended to make undergraduate opinion clearly audible. He wanted nothing better than to delegate to competent men the tasks of rejuvenating—or in instances where inertia had set in of vitalizing—the departments of law, medicine, graduate study, arts, extension and agricultural science. In several of these he had the good fortune to be able to make new appointments shortly after his administration began. Each of these new men proved to be the merchant of light that he needed.

The charge was sometimes brought against Vincent that he was autocratic. Seldom has it been less deserved, as an intimate associate, William Reynolds Vance, would rise to testify.

It was to Vance's care that Vincent entrusted the reform of the law school, leaving him quite free to work as he thought best. The dean's response to this challenge was to build up so distinguished a faculty that, within half a dozen years of its assembling, Yale had kidnaped it bodily and almost en masse.

The turn of the century brought a sharp break with tradition as far as the teaching of law was concerned. Up to that time all a young man need do to become a lawyer was to "read law" in the office of an established practitioner. This procedure—it could hardly be called a system—had the precedent of Abraham Lincoln's experience to support it. Wherever anyone rose in a session of the American Bar Association to suggest that this sort of loose instruction was no longer good enough, some product of the same kind of education would retort eloquently (or tearfully, or both) that what was good enough for the "rail splitter" must not be brought into disrepute by modern hairsplitters. As William Howard Taft made bold to tell the association, at last, the ghost of Lincoln had been forced to stalk the halls of justice far too many years. He must be allowed to rest while a more exacting program for a more complex society—one which Lincoln, as liberal and progressive, would certainly have endorsed—superseded the old way of improvisation. Taft won his point. The perfection of his finesse simultaneously saved the faces of the old die-hards and the prospects for reform. The Bar Association endorsed the high standards for legal training which Taft advocated.

Vance brought with him to Minnesota the same sort of high principles. A man of rare cultivation, he had taken a Ph.D. in English at Washington and Lee University and taught that subject at his alma mater while he studied for his LL.B. Before coming to Minnesota he had taught law at George Washington University in Washington, D.C. and at Yale.

Fighting all the old compromises that tended to make the law school safe for mediocrity, Vance gradually ridded his classes of football players and night-school students. "There is," he said, "only one justification for a law school: the expectation that by reason of its activity the laws would be better made and better administered." It was, in his estimation, always unsound policy to temporize with principle. "The cheaper value will always drive out the dearer."

So, with the poise and urbanity of a well-trained humanist and, at the same time, the rigor of a specialist in an exacting discipline, Vance proceeded to do the law school over from entrance examination to awarding of degree. He began with the faculty. At George Washington he had been associated with two men whom he trusted implicitly. The first, Edward Sampson Thurston, was a man of great learning and dignity whose lectures were regarded as models of lucidity. The other, Ernest Gustav Lorenzen, was a unique product of the German-American tradition. Born in the old world, he had been brought to the United States as a child. Then, in his young manhood, he had returned to Germany to study, first at Heidelberg, later at Göttingen where he had taken his degree

80

as Doctor of Laws "with the highest distinction." Lorenzen was just German enough to be a slave driver and just American enough to know that his fellow countrymen could not be expected to be slaves. His classes were wonderful arenas of intellectual struggle. Lorenzen himself was always the most ardent and tireless fighter of all.

Vance brought both these men to Minnesota to help him work the reforms that together they had worked at George Washington.

To this inner circle of the new law faculty was added another vivid figure. Edmund Morris Morgan was chosen, in part, because he was a citizen of Minnesota. After several importations, Vance tactfully decided it would be well to give "the broad West" (as his correspondents liked to call their region) one of their own men. A safer gamble could hardly have been taken. Before entering private practice at Duluth Morgan had earned A.B., M.A. and LL.B. degrees at Harvard.

A brilliantly dramatic rivalry immediately sprang up between Lorenzen and Morgan. The first of these men was big and powerful. He drove himself even more relentlessly than he drove his students. After his late marriage, made during the Minnesota years, Lorenzen still took home, night after night, a great green bag full of books. A colleague once dared to ask him if he meant to continue this regime indefinitely.

"Every night," said Lorenzen sternly. Then he added with a flash of Olympian humor: "This year, in honor of my wife, I do not work Sundays."

Morgan was small—so small, in fact, that when, during World War I, he served as major (finally, colonel) in the judge advocate's office, the reckless and the gay among them called him "the boy scout." But he was also a man of unremitting energy and intellectual voracity. "That little octopus," Lorenzen used to say, "he is so little—so little!—but he manages to be everywhere."

The difficulty was that both men were insatiable devourers of the time of students. Each wanted his young men to read an incredible number of cases and each thought the other unreasonable in his demands. All the undergraduates in law had to wrestle not with one angel but with two. And behind their backs the angels wrestled unrelentingly together. It was as different an atmosphere as possible from that of the old footballers' rest home. The young men who survived it were formidably educated young men, indeed.

Another man who added enormously to the prestige of Vance's school was Arthur Pulling. He built up one of the "five best law libraries in the country," partly by raiding the desks of his colleagues to collect pamphlets and offprints which, without his intervention, might have gone into the wastebasket.

And there was James Paige, "the last of the covenanters" as his colleagues called him. He did a magnificent job of editing the *Law Review*, another of Vance's creations. "Jimmy" Paige was also a severe taskmaster. It was said that his former students, when they had been out of school only ten years, still hated him. During the next decade they began to forgive him. But if they survived more than twenty years of practice, the rich deposits of integrity that he had put into their minds began to prove their worth and, half reluctantly, all Minnesota men woke to a kind of reverence for "Jimmy" Paige.

Paige, for all his Scotch rigidity, was capable of strange gestures of gallantry. His wife, Mabeth Hurd Paige, was for years a hardy perennial of the state legislature. Her Minneapolis constituency included, besides part of the sedate East Side, the anything but sedate Bridge Square section. Jimmy Paige uncomplainingly made the rounds of the saloons and flophouses, campaigning on his wife's behalf, enduring as well as he could an occasional salute from a raffish student: "Jimmy, fancy meeting you here!"

Basic to Vance's philosophy in building up the law school was a concept completely in sympathy with Vincent's and with Folwell's view of the university as servant to the state. The dean found precedent for the idea in the writing of a much earlier theorist of education. Thomas Jefferson, in an address called *Law and Politics*, had once set forth what he believed a "real state university should be." As Vance paraphrased his ideas:

"In the University of Virginia young men should be taught law in connection with the science of government so that they might be qualified not merely to care for clients but be fitted to lead the people wisely and well in the never-ceasing struggle that man is making to give better expression to the highest rules of social cooperation in the rules of society."

Acting on that principle, Vance worked closely with the Bar Association to give its will a wider forum and a more immediate kind of authority with young men. Even more expressive of his impulse to make the school serve the community was his creation of the Legal Aid Bureau to which the poor, the ignorant, the bewildered could apply for legal advice, offered by senior students of the law school. While he remained at Minnesota, Vance was, as Morgan once said, "a chief citizen of his city and a power on the bar of the state."

This period in the law school—the time of Vance and his associates—ended when Yale began its raids. In 1917 Lorenzen and Morgan were both invited to go. Morgan accepted immediately; Lorenzen hesitated. "I had a dream last night," he told a colleague. "I was in New Haven and everything was wonderful. Students filled my classes. They read all my cases. They read whole series of cases for me without complaining. I woke up. I was happy. I whistled. I sang. I said: 'I will go.' Then, while I was shaving, the truth came over me. I said out loud: 'But damn it, Eddie will be there.'"

Nonetheless the wrestling angels set out together in 1917. In 1919 Thurston followed. So eventually did Vance himself. Once more the team which had been together at George Washington and at Minnesota was reassembled at Yale, with Morgan added. It was broken again when the youngest member went to Harvard.

But Vance left a good man in his place at Minnesota, Everett Fraser (A.B., Dalhousie; LL.B., Harvard) who had been on Vance's team at George Washington. As subsequent

83

events were to prove, Vance's dedication to the highest standards lived on in Fraser and the distinction of his school was made secure by the work of his successor.

The refounding of the law school had proved to be so painless an operation that Vincent was not prepared for the violence that resulted when he touched the machinery of the medical school. To an intimate he confided that he wished it had not been necessary to put his fingers into "that buzz saw."

Still his sense of responsibility was such that he had to risk it. He wanted to create there another unit that would serve the state effectively. To do so, he must accomplish three things: build up a distinguished faculty; establish the principle of full-time teaching; and encourage research by creating a graduate school with something more than titular existence.

Each of these problems had the sharpest of buzz-saw teeth. The College of Homeopathic Medicine, having surrendered its charter voluntarily in order to bring the university's unit into existence, felt entitled to immortality under the shelter of the new arrangement. This was extremely difficult to manage. The popular following for this branch of sectarian medicine had begun to fall away. In 1908 only three students applied for admission to classes in homeopathy.

Still the leader of the homeopaths demanded special privileges. He wanted to keep twenty-seven teachers on his staff and add further expense to the training of his students. (This, as a rebel estimated, had risen already to $7500 a year.) But, at last, the regents stiffened their collective back. In 1911 twenty-five homeopaths disappeared from the faculty list, leaving just two "professors of didactic homeopathy."

These unfortunate men became central figures in an absurd comedy that was like a sequel to Molière's *Doctor In Spite of Himself*. This one might have been called: *Sphinxes In Spite of Themselves*.

The regents had ruled that students studying for degrees

84

in homeopathy must take the same thorough preclinical courses as other students took. Since homeopathy no longer offered a short cut to graduation, no one elected to take its offerings. Class schedules scrupulously kept the lectures of the professors of didactic homeopathy free of conflict. Week after week, the doctors appeared in empty halls and were allowed to keep their professional secrets. This policy of what might be called *inimical cooperation*, instituted by Vincent and the regents, hastened the death of the College of Homeopathic Medicine. In April 1911, less than a year after he had taken office, the president was able to speak unregretful obsequies over its grave. Another ghost had been laid to make room in the medical college for help to the living.

One reason why Flexner had described Minnesota in his 1910 report as one of the most conscientious schools then in existence was that it had a nucleus of full-time teachers instead of depending entirely upon the medical profession of the community to provide instruction. These full-time teachers had concerned themselves with problems of research. Dean Frank Wesbrook, for example, had done work on the bacteriological diagnosis of diphtheria and his efforts were credited with having freed Minneapolis from the curse of "winter cholera." Dr. Thomas G. Lee had studied the placentation of rodents. His more sporting students had forced Minnesota's mascot, the gopher, to serve the state, just a little ironically, by shooting many of its kind for use as specimens in Dr. Lee's experiments. Much the most active of all was Dr. John Black Johnston who poured, from an intelligence that teemed with ideas of every kind, a series of important papers for the *Journal of Comparative Neurology and Psychology.*

To this number there were added, in the first years of Vincent's administration, other men of the same type. Among them was Dr. Elexious T. Bell who began a crusade to establish the importance of autopsy in the development of medical knowledge. Dr. Richard E. Scammon, soon to gain national reputation for his important studies of growth, was another. Vincent wanted more men of like stature.

But in his effort to broaden the work of the medical school and to deepen its prestige, Vincent had to fight the kind of impulse which he regarded as immature. He could never bring himself to say: "See how big we are!" and then point proudly to the university buildings. Though Elliot Hospital was then quite new, many insisted that it must be rebuilt to provide more space. In January, 1913, Vincent began to take a firm hand in medical school affairs. To the astonishment, and somewhat to the alarm of the faculty, he appeared regularly at staff meetings. Physical space, he said firmly, would, for the present, be no further expanded. He had not come to Minnesota to "act as a construction engineer." The several departments must "apply the alum treatment" and shrink themselves back to normal size. The success of each was to be measured in terms of the distinction of its teachers and the importance of work done in research, not in terms of brick and mortar.

Vincent talked so much about research that it became a fighting word. Dean Wesbrook, despite his own interest in original work, had always held that it represented a kind of polite indulgence. It was even a creditable one if it were not permitted to interfere with a man's teaching schedule. Northrop had not been willing to go even that far. He had once forced the resignation of a German-trained teacher of psychology who had anticipated the psychoanalytical method by encouraging his friends to write out for him the secrets of their psychic development. "You have become a stench in the nostrils of this community," said this stanch New Englander who knew—even if his psychology professor did not—that a decent man kept himself to himself.

Once, at a meeting of the regents, Vincent talked fluently of research, speaking the word with the accent on the second syllable. Each time that a regent used the word he pronounced it re'-search. Vincent, as persistently, pronounced it re-search'. When the session was over, one member of the board said to another: "Well, I suppose this is the end of re'-search at Minnesota."

It was even more certainly the beginning of re-search'.

Within a month of faithful attendance at faculty meetings, Vincent realized that he had reached an impasse in his struggle with a group of resolute men. His objection was that the organization of the medical school had become top-heavy with comparatively inactive men. Practitioners of the community clung to professorships in such great number that, as Vincent said, "the faculty roll read like the classified section of the telephone book." He decided that, since the alum treatment had not been applied voluntarily, he must take drastic action of his own.

In January, 1913, every member of the medical school faculty was asked to resign.

Chronic viewers-with-alarm were outraged. Vincent, they said, had assumed the arbitrary power of a dictator. To satisfy his own whimsical ideas, he was prepared to build a new school from the bottom up.

Nothing could have been farther from the truth. All he wanted was to be rid of the "feudal lords" of the faculty who, in the opinion of the career men of the school—the "young Turks," they cheerfully called themselves—were "making it impossible to get things done."

Vincent's way of reform was entirely democratic. He appointed a reorganization committee, headed by Dean Wesbrook. Acting on the advice of the medical profession itself, this committee was to name heads for each department. In some instances the former heads were renamed, in others they were not. Sensibilities were bruised in the process, but no one could contend seriously that the blood of martyrs had been spilled. Two sensible men of the old regime, though they lost their headships, kept their heads and stayed on as staff members to have long and honorable careers under their successors. In all details the recommendations of the reorganization committee were accepted by the president.

At this moment the crisis was unexpectedly eased as though

87

by the appearance of a god out of the machine. Dean Wesbrook resigned to become president of the University of British Columbia. Two of the most knightly opponents ever to meet in a faculty contest parted with the greatest amiability on both sides. When Vincent, several years later, left Minnesota, one of the first men to comment on his resignation was President Wesbrook, whose admirable letter speaks of "the recognition the University of Minnesota has had through you."

So Vincent had an opportunity to name a new dean. He wanted a man of eminence in every phase of his job, as teacher, executive and investigator. Dr. Clarence Martin Jackson seemed to be just the man. He was then dean of the medical school of the University of Missouri. Also he was deeply immersed in the studies which led to the publication (in 1925) of the book called *The Effects of Inanition and Malnutrition upon Growth and Structure*, of which Dr. Ancel Keyes wrote, two decades later, that its analysis was so complete as to stand today "without essential alteration."

Dr. Jackson wanted to join the faculty at Minnesota but not as dean. Headship of the department of anatomy satisfied him much better because he was promised time in which to develop his work in research. He gathered about him, in his new post, men who shared his investigative interests. Richard Scammon, Hal Downey, A. T. Rasmussen—so many, in fact, that research men have often wondered why so many scholars of distinction (crowned with the special stars then conferred by the editors of *American Men of Science*) had come together at Minnesota. The reason was simply that Vincent and Jackson, between them, managed to give such men satisfying conditions of work.

Having refused the deanship himself, Dr. Jackson was ready with a nomination for the job. His friend Elias Potter Lyon was then dean of the medical school at St. Louis University. Lyon was a man of exactly Vincent's type. He, too, was determined to make the teaching profession safe for teachers, not merely a polite avocation for busy practitioners. At St. Louis he had fought and won the battle for the "full-time" principle. Vincent wanted him to do the same thing at Minnesota. The struggle took longer in the new setting than it had taken at St. Louis. But eventually the point was established, and Lyon had the satisfaction of creating a pattern of administration that endured under his appointees long after both he and Vincent were gone.

Lyon was a brilliant physiologist. He liked to quote his teacher, Jacques Loeb, who in turn quoted his teacher, Pasteur, as saying: "Any man is fortunate who carries within himself a god, a *beau ideal*, whom he obeys." A kind of apostolic succession seemed to have passed from man to man with this formula. Lyon communicated to his students the same desire to obey the god, science.

He was not a doctor of medicine and this fact was to give him much trouble. But he appears to have lived above the storm clouds in a region of unassailable serenity. When he ended his administration of the medical school, he was able to forget its many fights and say in his valedictory, without discernible strain of irony, that its accomplishments must be attributed to the teamwork of his associates among whom there had been "no cliques, no schisms." Fortunate the man whose inner god makes him invulnerable to slights.

Lyon and Jackson walked side by side through a long series of accomplishments. They were in complete sympathy as reorganizers of the medical school, as men who were devoted to research and as neighbors who played bridge together almost nightly. Something may perhaps be learned about reticence, as shield to the values of the mind and heart, from the fact that throughout their long intimacy these men continued to be "Dean" Lyon and "Dr." Jackson to each other.

Perhaps the most significant, as it was the most dramatic, struggle of Vincent's administration had to do with the affiliation between the medical school and the Mayo organization at Rochester.

By 1914 that extraordinary phenomenon, the Mayo Clinic,

had sprung into full strength as though from the brow of Jupiter Medicus. It was known all over the world and drew its patients quite as regularly from the palaces of eastern potentates as from Iowa farms and Hollywood studios. This did not wholly endear it to the physicians of the Twin City fraternity who were, not infrequently, identified on their travels as people who must live somewhere near "the Clinic."

In Vincent's mind three facts converged to suggest a fine opportunity for the university. First, Dr. Will Mayo was one of its regents. Second, the clinic had built up a surplus of a million and a half dollars which the grateful founders—Dr. Will and his brother Dr. Charles Mayo—wished to turn back to the public, regarding it as a kind of trust put in their care. Third, the clinic had been forced by circumstance to create a kind of graduate school of its own. Staff members had asked for time and facilities to do research. The clinic had provided both, first informally, and then in a thoroughly organized way. A full three-year program for graduate study in pathology, clinical medicine and surgery had been established. In 1914 the clinic had twenty-eight students in this course. In the same academic year the University of Minnesota had only six men working on the graduate level in medicine.

Indeed, the university was forced to make the candid confession that it was groping its way through frontier country as it undertook to create a training program for specialists. As Vincent said:

"The truth is that a man is a specialist when he says he is. Many of the best specialists have been by force of circumstance self-made. Success has depended more upon native ability than systematic training. Not only does the profession lack standards but the public has no way to judge as to the competency of special practitioners."

Because they had already done pioneer work of great importance, the people of the clinic were, Vincent felt, the best possible guides. Dean Lyon agreed that university students would profit greatly by going to Rochester for graduate study.

So did Dean Guy Stanton Ford, new dean of the Graduate School. Rochester offered "a large volume of clinical and laboratory material." By affiliation with it the university could create a graduate school that would "stand absolutely alone in the sphere of medical education in America today."

Moving discreetly, so as not to frighten traditionalists who were bound to distrust association with a private organization operated for profit, the regents suggested the formation of a Mayo Foundation for Medical Education and Research. This unit would be independent of the clinic though closely related to it. In each successive modification of this plan—made under fire from critics—the Mayos proved themselves to be idealistic and unselfish. In the end they agreed to provide an endowment of a million and a half dollars for the Foundation and to allow the university, through the board of regents, to handle all administrative matters including appointment of staff.

For nearly three years the two forces in the battle of affiliation "raged furiously together." Among opponents of the plan there were three chief groups. One feared that the university was selling its prestige into private hands. Go slow, warned Folwell. Don't move at all, urged Northrop. Let the Mayos come to the university if they want to advance science; the dignity of the university might be impaired if it were to go to the Mayos.

A second group was made up of the doctors who had been edged out of their posts in the reorganization. It was for them the night of the long knives.

A third group merely joined the free-for-all because it was free. A strange company of dissidents urged that this was all a plot to inflate real estate values in Rochester. Another said that the insidious purpose was merely to provide free labor for the clinic. (Graduate students would find themselves washing bottles in the basement, presumably chained to the wall.) A few people hinted that a new kind of diploma factory was being created.

Through the war of words the Mayos kept their poise

admirably. "Dr. Will" who had a lively way of his own with words spoke of these flights of moral indignation as "balloon ascensions." He himself resolutely refused to leave the ground.

An organized campaign against affiliation reached its height with presentation to the legislature, in the spring of 1915, of a bill to destroy the plan. Though Vincent urged at a public hearing that opponents of affiliation wished to keep the university in a cloister while its advocates saw the institution as "the center of state-wide life and movement," the bill was passed by the senate. However, action came too late in the session for the house to vote on the measure. There was no official decision when the legislature adjourned.

Before the legislature could convene again, there was time for a vigorous campaign to overcome opposition. First, the regents, having received no final instructions from the legislature, signed an agreement with the Foundation which made its students members of the graduate school of the university, subject to its regulations as candidates for its degrees. Dr. Will Mayo, cool and confident in the knowledge that his purposes were honorable, wrote to a member of the board of regents that all the disturbance had really been for the good. It had "focused attention on the value of advanced work and brought the faculty together in defense of the school."

As the legislature was about to meet in April, 1917, a second bill opposing affiliation was drawn. Before a public gathering, arranged by the St. Paul Association of Commerce, Dr. Mayo spoke so simply and directly of what "my brother and I" hoped to accomplish that all doubts were suddenly dissipated in the fresh air of his honesty. The second bill found few supporters and died on the committee-room table.

With the fight for affiliation won, everyone seemed to troop to Vincent's side in support of all his purposes. One of his teachers—head of the department of surgery—volunteered to give up his private practice and accept the full-time principle, expecting "no increase in salary." A new appointee to an important department entered the faculty with the understanding that he was to give full time to the university though he was allowed to retain "the privilege of private consultation." This became the new formula: full-time members of faculty might "accept, with the permission of their department heads, a limited number of private patients for whom they cared as consultants."

So Vincent escaped the buzz saw deftly. He had won all his points. Four decades after the battle for affiliation had become history, everyone was ready to agree that it had brought distinguished men to Minnesota; that the university's work in research had received the immense stimulation Vincent had predicted it would feel; that the unification of practices and procedures had given the university a medical school that was closely integrated with the work of the institution and, more than that, with the life of the state.

In refounding the university, Vincent had fashioned a new design for the law school by friendly persuasion and a new design for the medical school by moral force. What he did for the Graduate School amounted to an act of original creation, for there was nearly everything to do.

In a volume called *Great American Universities*, published at the moment when Vincent came to Minnesota, the author, Edwin Slossen, had many good things to say of what Northrop had accomplished but he added this critical comment: "Comparatively little has been done in research except in agriculture. The Graduate School was first organized in 1905 and then the regents permitted it only on condition that it was not to cost anything."

What he tactfully did not say was that the regents actually distrusted research as the purloiner of a teacher's time. Dr. H. T. Eddy, who came to Minnesota in 1894 to teach engineering, gave part of his time to the Graduate School as its first dean. But it was the tacit understanding with the regents that he was simply to sit on the lid and let as little fermentation as possible go on under it.

However, the short and simple annals of the Graduate School (first Master's degree, 1880; first Doctor's degree,

93

1880) had moments of distinction. In Northrop's time Minnesota awarded Ph.D. degrees to Edward M. Freeman (plant pathology), Hal Downey (hematology) and Henry A. Erikson (physics), all of whom were to serve science with distinction at their alma mater, and to John Zeleny and Anton Kovarik (both in physics), who were to become important teachers at Yale.

But now Vincent proposed to pry off the lid and stir up the Graduate School. Again it was his good fortune to have a new appointment to make shortly after his arrival. It was shown again to be his gift to choose exactly the right man.

When he came to Minnesota at the age of forty, Guy Stanton Ford already looked "venerable" to the young reporter sent to interview him. This was perhaps because he wore a crest of vigorous but prematurely gray hair. Actually, he was irrepressibly young in temper. From earliest youth he had been a brilliant student. As undergraduate at Upper Iowa University he had often received grades of 100. He bravely refused to become discouraged when his professor of logic had given him only 99½. In 1892 he had transferred to the University of Wisconsin. There he thoroughly enjoyed the fresh air that President Adams was letting into the university as a whole, that Richard Ely with the active collaboration of Robert La Follete was letting into state politics and that Frederick Jackson Turner was letting into theories of the meaning of American history.

History became Ford's own field. After doing postgraduate work in Berlin, he returned to Columbia to take his Ph.D. When a professorship in modern European history was created at the University of Illinois President Edmund James decided that Ford was the man to receive it. Again, he was in an educational world where new attitudes were coming to life. Ford entered so enthusiastically into this lively realm of ideas that, as a colleague was later to say of him, "he left at Illinois a definite mark on the department, on the college and on the university."

It is the way of presidents to choose alter egos as lieutenants. Ford was Vincent's kind of man—a statesman of education, a fastidious yet strenuous collector and distributor of convictions, a fluent, graceful speaker. Added to these assets was an ability to work three-fourths of the hours of the day at teaching, writing, editing, administrative work and, above all, at the germination and nurture of ideas.

Ford believed and said that the Graduate School of a university must declare itself to be "no parasitic institution living upon the scientific productions of others but a contributing member in the advancement of science." He proposed to accomplish this by encouraging research in every possible way. Scholars were to have their creative energies freed by easing of the teaching load which, until then, had averaged from fourteen to seventeen hours a week. Ford appointed a committee of seven men to advise him about ways of stimulating independent investigation. Each man represented a large field of study: (1) the special sciences and law; (2) physical science, mathematics and engineering; (3) the biological sciences; (4) philosophy, psychology and education; (5) language and literature; (6) medicine; (7) agriculture.

The lid had not merely been lifted; it had been pried off and carried away as though to become an oddity of the archives. The Graduate School became, almost overnight, the center of university activity. In medicine, Scammon, Bell and Jackson stepped up the pace of their investigations. In history, Notestein and Albert Beebe White felt the impetus offered by Ford who was their colleague in the department as well as dean of the Graduate School. In dentistry, Alfred Owre and Thomas B. Hartzell set about the original work that was to make important contributions to the advancement of science in their neglected field. In literature, Klaeber no longer needed to fear reproach for being a distinguished scholar; he saw the promised land.

Many years later a Minnesota man was to write a stimulating essay on "the value of useless research," pointing out, as Folwell had done long before, that the great discoveries rise luminous and clear out of decades of what has seemed like

95

misty speculation. Under Ford, basic research became not merely respectable but honored. Yet many of Minnesota's men addressed themselves to tasks of immediate usefulness—everything from the control of wheat rust to "problems of reinforced concrete in floors." The Graduate School made its direct contribution to the idea that a university exists to serve the state. And, like Folwell, it was interested in everything from Plato to hog cholera.

The results were immediately evident. Between 1912 and 1917 enrollment in the Graduate School rose from one hundred fifty-nine students to four hundred sixty-four. In the early years of that period half of the candidates were Minnesota graduates; the rest came from small colleges of comparatively low academic rating. In 1917 only a third of the candidates were Minnesota A.B.s; the others were from Harvard, Chicago, Columbia, Michigan, Pennsylvania, Johns Hopkins and other major institutions.

Johns Hopkins, in particular, sent many students to the Mayo Foundation for advanced work in surgery. At Rochester a program had been worked out which the young holders of fellowships found both practical and stimulating. Each had regular duties in the clinic; each received instruction in clinical studies by conference with Mayo experts; each was required to support his major in medicine or surgery with a minor in a laboratory science. Committees, drawn from the university and the Foundation, conducted all examinations, and it became a sacred cause with them to make sure that these were ruthlessly searching. As Ford said, this development of a new formula of instruction was "accompanied by better teaching and by more definite attempts to see that the peak of pyramidal specialization had a sufficiently broad base."

Under the new dispensation many of the old practices went into the discard. Minnesota had not been innocent, in the past, of the old vice of buying graduate students by offering them jobs as instructors. Ford refused to allow the Graduate School to serve as a kind of employment bureau. His influence raised standards for teaching posts. Even an instructor must be "free of the guild" before he could be considered for appointment to any important task.

He also increased Graduate School enrollment by enlarging the services of the summer session. As early as 1915 Minnesota, through Ford, had started a crusade to improve teaching on the high-school level by offering every kind of encouragement to members of the public school system to do advanced work.

With a mercurial readiness to follow any legitimate opportunity, Ford—all at once—invited the new, protected the traditional, raised standards by force of his own integrity, broadened opportunity in the light of his own vision and, within six years of his arrival at Minnesota, had created out of nothing a Graduate School that was strenuously busy and productive.

Circumstances played many times into Vincent's hands as he struggled to reorganize the university. Each time, when he was ready to start the job of vitalizing another college, he had the good fortune to be able to appoint a new dean. His sharp eye always discovered, sometimes in unexpected places, the men who could help him best. In law, medicine, and graduate education he had fished from the academic pool men of established reputation as administrators. But when, in 1914, he asked the regents to name Dr. John Black Johnston dean of the Arts college, he followed the instinctual impulse of a man who could recognize creative originality no matter what curious disguise it might wear.

Dean Johnston, as academic demigod, gave off different auras to different approaches. Some observers saw the pale blue of his eyes as arctic and forbidding while others thought he looked mild to the point of needing to be given protection and assurance. But to nearly everyone it looked like an act of black—or, perhaps, pale blue—magic to transform this professor of comparative neurology into an explorer of new, uncharted country in the Arts college.

But it did not seem strange to either Vincent or Johnston.

They had watched each other through several years of growing mutual admiration. Johnston certainly had made no secret of his interest in general theories of education. By more than forty years he had anticipated the discovery which has just begun to worry many educators that the public schools have been doing a sadly inadequate job of training the citizens of tomorrow. He had said so to every audience the attention of which he could attract.

During one of the periodic crises of the Northrop administration over the problem of admission requirements, Johnston had told the members of the honorary fraternity, Sigma Xi:

"Our system of public instruction instead of being alive to the needs of the young is the most antiquated of human institutions. It disregards the needs of the young and fills the minds of all with a pablum that is supposed to make every man a king, a great artist or a king of high finance. The schools rebuff young curiosity and stifle youthful enthusiasms —the two prime movers in human achievement. Then the university faculty accepts this dwarfed and misshapen child and sets about the impossible task of making a man of him."

Johnston was dealing with essentially the same theme when, in November, 1913, he spoke before a faculty dining club on "University Organization." He said: Institutions, supposedly devoted with impartial magnanimity to the values of higher education, had settled into a deadly routine of instruction. Bureaucratic department heads were chiefly concerned with making their realms safe for their own occupancy. Young men with ideas could not make themselves heard in such an atmosphere of icy hostility to the new. He concluded boldly:

"The university never adjusts its ideals to the times but is forever denying itself the information which its individual members could supply."

He had spoken that evening with the fatalistic air of being one who cries in the wilderness. With what proved to be dramatic irony, he characterized himself as a man who has "passed the time when he can be expected to produce new ideas." But within six months the dean of the Arts college had resigned and Johnston sat in his place. For the next twenty-three years he produced new ideas at an astonishing rate not merely for the University of Minnesota but for the use of the whole world of American education. Indeed, he reformed the Arts college throughout its design, from entrance regulations to standards for graduation and from top to bottom of its curricula.

It was his basic philosophy that "everyone should be educated in proportion to his capacity, limited only by the economic resources of the country." In return for its investment, society could expect to get manpower to do the work of the community. These workers would not operate all on the same level. There would be, first, the learned men, trained to improve the standards of the professions. There would be, second, the army of teachers who would carry on the functions of instruction in the primary school, the secondary school and the college. And, finally, there would be the men and women whose place was "the large-scale laboratory of social intelligence" in which "the everyday work of the world is conducted."

These groups had unlike needs and aptitudes. They should receive instruction according to those needs. To solve the problems of "differential treatment of students" became Johnston's lifework. In his disciplined and orderly confrontation of these problems he made distinguished contributions to theory. Following Vincent's principle that the university "must adjust traditions to new situations," Johnston evolved his "techniques of estimating native abilities" so that the individual's "fitness to profit by training" might become the realistic guide in providing an education for him.

Vincent and Johnston wanted the same three things: first, to provide a stimulating cultural background for the average student; second, to put the proper tools into the hands of good students with specialized interests in the professions, and third, in Vincent's lively phrase, to "throw out a dragnet" for

99

the superior student so that the high potential of his intelligence might be realized in special services to society.

The university must give—and wishes to give—a chance to all young citizens. But they must not be thrown into the same mill. That would be not merely to grind all intelligences exceeding small but actually to pulverize some. Johnston introduced many modifications of old procedures. Entrance requirements were made more flexible. With a high-school diploma in his hand anyone might apply for admission to the university. Strait-jacket regulations with regard to languages were removed in order to give the potential engineer or business executive his chance without having to pretend to an interest in the conjugation of Latin verbs. The propriety of a student's interest in the social sciences or even in vocational subjects was recognized. An indirect result of Johnston's reforming zeal was that Minnesota assumed leadership in the development of good schools of Social Work and Business Administration.

Only three years after he had assumed the deanship of the Arts college, Johnston had evolved a formula for admission to the university which is realistic enough and adaptable enough to have endured until the present day. It requires an entrance examination which is designed to test, not knowledge of specific subjects, but general aptitude for college training. Students in the top 10 per cent of graduating classes may be admitted by certificate. All others must achieve a college aptitude rating of 40 or higher, that is, they must be among the top 60 per cent of candidates for admission. The aptitude rating which is a composite of high-school grades and special examination scores, offers a screen for sifting talent. Even students without high-school diplomas may be admitted if they show high aptitude in special examinations.

Johnston's purpose from the beginning was to put the right student in the right place. "Differential treatment" has helped to divert young men and women of average abilities into channels of instruction suited to their needs. It has kept standards for admission to the professional schools high. It has served well to identify the potential scholar and the genuinely creative intelligence. Few students who are foredoomed to failure now endure that humiliating experience. Brilliant students are no longer allowed to hide their lights under the old academic bushels.

Despite his preoccupation with the administrative reform of the Arts college, Vincent was by no means indifferent to the job of giving it men—as teachers—to match his high ambitions. During his administration the most vital scholarly spirit flourished. To the English department came Elmer Edgar Stoll. Tall, gaunt, witty, contentious and uncompromising, he became a striking figure on the campus, long before the world recognized him as the leading Shakespeare scholar of our day.

After taking his Ph.D. at Munich, Stoll returned to America to begin his one-man campaign against the "psychologizing" of the great works of literature. His deft stroke has, as Logan Pearsall Smith once said, helped to "brush much cobweb from academic criticism." Stoll's studies, which insist on a sensible acceptance of the artist as a man of his time—complete with national prejudices and the limitations imposed by the temper of his hour—have all shown, simultaneously, the severity of his intellectual temper and the urbanity of his style. At Minnesota he became a scourge to sentimentalists and doctrinaire Freudians but to its campus he attracted adherents of sound scholarship. In an atmosphere curiously blended of grace, challenge, hospitality, formidability and aloofness, he lived a unique drama, neatly corresponding to the unique position he has occupied in the world of scholarship.

Joseph Beach, as the century moved through its teens and on into its maturity, continued to explore, ever more and more widely, the values of contemporary literature. Long before the great Henry James revival of the last few years had begun, he wrote brilliantly to show how the dramatic method in the novel had been anticipated fully and consciously in

The Wings of the Dove and *The Portrait of a Lady*. His intense interest in poetry, as spontaneous expression of the genius of an age, inspired his close analytical studies of twentieth-century man in the writing of all representative figures from Frost through Eliot to Auden. The presence of men like Beach on the campus of the University of Minnesota attracted many students in the 1920s, 1930s and 1940s, making its English department, in the opinion of Bernard De-Voto, "the best in the country."

Ever confident of his own judgment, Vincent was quick to recognize special talent and to honor it in men like Oscar Firkins. He did so in the face of forbidding oddity. Firkins had no talent for tact and no respect for circumspection. Yet, though he was a thorny man, Vincent did not hesitate to accept him as he was, nettles and all. This the president and his wife, between them, once demonstrated with delightful graciousness.

Mrs. Vincent, an enthusiast of the theater, had written a play which a group of clubwomen planned to present on their stage. Before allowing it to go into rehearsal she sent it to Firkins for critical comment. The professor returned the work of his president's wife with the succinct, but not very helpful judgment, that it was the worst play he had ever read.

Not in the least nettled herself, but understandably disturbed, Mrs. Vincent hurried to Firkins' house to ask how the play could be improved. She was met at the door by the small standing army of sisters maintained by Firkins for the protection of his privacy. The captain of this company told Mrs. Vincent that her brother was not at home.

Her anxiety not yet soothed, Mrs. Vincent stood in the hall, asking urgently if she might not have a later appointment, and as she did so, she saw the professor at the head of the stairs. Impetuously she dashed up half the steps, calling: "Mr. Firkins! Mr. Firkins, I must see you."

At that, a terrible image was turned upon her. Not even the thick lenses of Firkins' glasses could dim the look of indignation. "Mrs. Vincent," he said, "you have been told that I am not at home."

"I understand! I know," the president's wife said, suddenly reduced to the status of an undergraduate pleading for a make-up examination. "But if you are not at home now when will you be at home?"

"Mrs. Vincent," spoke the voice of doom, "I shall never be at home to the author of that play."

It was shortly after this incident that Vincent created for Firkins, in order to give him the prestige and the isolation that he craved almost equally, a one-man department of Comparative Literature.

A Minnesota man who became a kind of living monument to the spirit of free interplay between teacher and student was Joseph Morris Thomas (Ph.D., University of Michigan). His striking gift for unexpectedness gave him an influence with undergraduates which uncompromising predictability seldom attracts. As teacher of English rhetoric, creative writing, "Tommy" had an enormous personal following, and his influence was always stimulating. He liked to tell the story of a bright girl who had been getting the mediocre grades of a dilettante until he taunted her into working on a level with her talents. On the day when she was awarded a Phi Beta Kappa key the young woman's father said to Thomas: "The credit is really yours. How did you do it?" "I did nothing," said Thomas, "except to give her a kick in the pants now and again." Then he added soberly: "Of course, it was only a metaphorical kick." Equally sober, the father said: "The pants were only hypothetical." To an address for which he became famous among students, Thomas gave the title: "A Metaphorical Kick in the Hypothetical Pants."

Of Vincent, Thomas once said that he was one of the two or three men to whom, in a lifetime, he had given unreserved admiration. His admiration for Dean Johnston did not preclude disagreement with certain policies. But the resulting bouts in the academic arena were not allowed to disturb the temper of either man and, when affairs of the college had become so complex that an assistant dean was needed, it was for Thomas that Johnston asked. The dean valued his "loyal opposition," a fact which says much about the temper of the time at Minnesota.

A fresh current was let into the psychology department when Karl Lashley came to it, in 1917, elegantly tousled as though wind-blown by the powerful new doctrine of behaviorism. At Minnesota, Lashley introduced the fortunate company of his students to laboratory method. He introduced them also to chamber music and, in all-night, off-campus seminars, to every possible challenge that a liberal, searching intelligence could toss off. From his desk at Minnestoa went the important research papers on which Lashley's later work at Chicago and at Harvard was based.

Another indefatigably creative man who came in Vincent's time was Solon Justus Buck. He taught history and created the Minnesota Historical Society before Washington called him away to become archivist of the United States and curator of manuscripts of the Library of Congress.

Arthur Compson, en route to Nobel prize eminence, paused at Minnesota to give fresh impetus to the physics department, sustained too long, as Vincent pointed out, by the vitality of the university's own graduates.

William Emmons became the embodiment of the conviction that a university must serve the state. He trained some six hundred geologists to become leading research men for mining companies of the state and of the nation.

Vincent and Johnston together kept the Arts college a place in which academic news was made. That their experiments were sound the world of educators generally agreed. Many other institutions followed their lead in matters of admission policy. Thirty years later the University of Minnesota was to build some of its own innovations on the new ideas which sprang out of the readiness of Vincent and Johnston to try the untried.

"The merchants of light" to whom Vincent had referred in

his inaugural address may well have stood, in his mind, for imaginary precursors of the extension movement in education. But there was a difference: Bacon's merchants of light went into the far places to bring back light while it is the task of the extension expert to carry light into far places.

Vincent was an enthusiast for this kind of service to the community, and had been from his young manhood. His father, Bishop John Heyl Vincent of the Methodist church, was the founder of Chautauqua, that still unique, still brilliantly successful experiment in adult education, conducted each summer on the banks of Lake Chautauqua in New York State. Begun as a training program for Sunday-school teachers, the mother Chautauqua soon broadened its purpose and brought together the best of contemporary thought, the best of contemporary entertainment, for the stimulation of its followers. Unlike the abortive efforts at imitation which assumed the name and roamed the Midwest in the teens of the century, the mother Chautauqua was of a dignity and sobriety so great that William James once said its world offered "a foretaste of what human society might be were it all in the light with no suffering dark corners."

What the middle-aged citizens of the Middle West remember as "the Chautauqua movement" is a dreary caricature of what William James knew. One thinks of sweltering evenings spent under tents in the course of which one was exposed to a bizarre jumble of attractions—the improving oratory of William Jennings Bryan, a vaudeville act in which a woman was sawed in half, a performance by a barbershop quartet, and a foretaste (actually) of the art of Edgar Bergen. But at the mother Chautauqua one heard the great voices of the day, those of Phillips Brooks, Charles Eliot, Jane Addams, Julia Ward Howe.

Vincent used to boast, whimsically, that he was the founder of Chautauqua. The justification of his claim lay in the fact that when his father had gone to look for a camp site for the Sunday-school group, he had gone along, a boy of nine, and

105

been the first to leap from the boat onto what became historic ground.

It is literally true that Vincent had grown up with the movement. He had sat at table with the demigods of its platform; became, at twenty-three, the vice-principal of the system and, at twenty-five, its principal.

Often it became his job to introduce speakers. In later years he liked to tell an anecdote of one such occasion when he had been bested in pleasantries. With youthful eloquence he had described himself—too long and too ingeniously—as the tugboat that leads the great ocean liner out of the harbor and into the open sea. When, not displeased with himself, he had finished his introduction, the great man of the evening rose. "I read just the other day," he said, "an account of such a tugboat. Before it could get its companion out to sea, it—blew up." And he looked with sly reproach at Vincent.

By the time he reached Minnesota, George Edgar Vincent had long since developed a technique for making up neat parcels of education to be handed to adults. He proposed to create a university system for state-wide adult education that should be modeled on that of Chautauqua.

Again, there was nearly everything to do. Few institutions of the time offered extension service. Except in the Department of Agriculture Minnesota had only scattered traces of effort. No centralized authority existed. The final report to the regents made by President Northrop had said: "It is scarcely possible that regular university courses ever will be demanded by large enough groups [of extension students] to make them self-sustaining."

Nonetheless Vincent went to work on the theory that only snobbery had prevented the development of extension work. The well-established teacher thought it beneath him. But this attitude, he was sure, could be broken down. In creating a General Extension Division, as the legislature of 1913 authorized him to do, he chose as dean to head it a man of immaculate academic standing. One candidate was dropped because, as Vincent told him candidly: "I cannot appoint a man who does not have a classical education. The director I want must be in a position to stand up to any dean and talk back to him as an academic equal."

Richard Price was his choice, a man of eminent respectability from the academic standpoint. He had taken a Master's degree at Harvard in classical philology. Later, he had been drawn into extension work and had organized the division at Kansas State University. A driving man, Price made assets even of his nervous disposition and his stomach ulcers. When these gave him no rest at night he spent the time planning further conquests for his department.

His first budget was far from princely. He was given $40,000 with which to make a start. It was his task to build up night classes in English literature, Greek literature, French and German. Regular faculty members had to be persuaded to take these on, and Price developed a fine technique for enticing, cajoling or appealing to the sacrificial natures of his colleagues. He was responsible also for correspondence courses, lectures and all entertainments sponsored by the university.

He found, almost immediately, that the demand for extension work had been underestimated. Within a year enrollment in the offerings of his division had doubled. Within four years it had reached four thousand.

As merchant of light he carried the benefits of education ever farther and farther into the distant areas of the state and into its least promising alcoves. Night courses were created in half a dozen towns. Short courses, like one for retail merchants, brought together a new group of students who had thought of the university as aloof and austere with nothing to offer them. The lyceum bureau provided lectures for communities which, in that pre-radio era, would otherwise have had little stimulation besides what the movies could supply. Prisoners in state institutions were offered correspondence courses. One of Minnesota's famous murderers (as a suggestible youth he had obliged a friend by getting rid of an unwanted wife) turned genial and contemplative in solitude.

He took every course the extension division had to offer and got A's in all but one in which he had to be content with a B. Price met every crisis with the kind of resolution that Vincent had expected of him. He fought only one battle unsuccessfully. That was to get for the extension division a separate faculty such as the University of Wisconsin had brought together. Here Price had to yield to considerations of economy and go on cajoling regular faculty members into teaching his courses.

In the matter of credit for work done in his division he stood up and talked back to all the deans with the greatest firmness. These gentlemen persisted in the idea that work done in extension courses must not be allowed to count toward a degree. With the noble defiance of a Cicero, Price rose in the university senate and said:

"Is education, then, a matter of astronomy? Does it derive its authority from the movements of the sun? According to the principle just set before you, if a class meets in a particular university building, under a particular instructor, at four o'clock, that is education. If it meets in the same building under the same instructor at seven o'clock it is not education but something inferior upon which the university dare not set the stamp of its official sanction."

The senate blinked, admitted the absurdity and changed its mind. In theory, at least, it is now possible for a student to earn a degree entirely in the extension division of the university without having ever been in residence on any of its main campuses.

Perhaps Price's best achievement was the creation of the League of Minnesota Municipalities. This agency implements another phase of the job of serving the state. The League's office on the campus serves as a laboratory in municipal problems. Town officials may apply to it for advice on such problems as those of taxation, assessment, the relationship to railroads or to public utilities, planning of plant or scheduling of pensions. Once more the university had fulfilled Folwell's purpose of making its agencies serve as counselors to the people of the entire state.

*

What Price actually accomplished was to make his division a microcosm of the university as a whole. As a result people on the range, on the prairie, in the lumber camp and the isolated border town came to know its work and to respect its purposes. Vincent himself became a merchant of light to carry the general news of university activites to the people. He created the institution "University Week" and became one of its chief attractions. This was an extension course in miniature made up of debates, lectures, recitals, plays—all drawn from the university's best resources. This troupe of peripatetic scholars, headed by the president himself, traveled from community to community for several weeks each spring, offering a taste of the university's quality. And the citizens found it good.

One of the chief purposes of University Week was to break down the last of the old feeling of hostility between town and gown. Vincent, always the most energetic of the caravan, showed the kind of authority in the doing of the showman's job that Chautauqua had taught him. When he loosed the machine-gun bursts of his wit upon an audience, the attention of even the least responsive member was arrested. When he allowed his brilliant intelligence and animating individuality to carry a theme from climax to climax, all his hearers were drawn after him in a state almost like that of hypnosis. When he revealed his philosophic concern with the good life—at once sober and beguiling—a whole community was won over to sympathy. People ceased to think of the university as something far away and formidable. The phrase "our university" came spontaneously to everyone's tongue. Vincent communicated to each man a sense of possession.

It is curious that, though Vincent performed so many services in person that radio was later to do, he himself could never accept the microphone. Like many an actor of the old school, he needed to feel a direct contact with an audience.

During all of his life at Minnesota he refused to go on the air.

Once the sponsors of a dinner thought to trap him. Without his consent, they arranged to broadcast the speeches of the evening. In the course of the meal Vincent was told what was expected of him. He still refused to go on the air.

"But you are on," the announcer said. "There's nothing you can do about it."

"Oh yes, there is," Vincent said. "I shall use the words *damn* and *syphilis* in the first line I speak."

He didn't go on.

The sixth unit on which Vincent left his signature as redesigner was that of education. It badly needed attention, Vincent decided, for though it had existed since 1905, it had "failed to achieve distinction." With characteristic determination he set out to change all that, sweeping out lassitude, concession and the dusty rubbish of routine.

Again, he operated through a delegate so sympathetic that his dean of education was destined to become his successor as president. Lotus Delta Coffman shared with Vincent the conviction that teaching must be made a profession of dignity, stability and security. More than that, it must become a career worthy of a man's complete loyalty not—as it so often had been in the past—a temporary expedient, a steppingstone by which an ambitious man climbed to a higher goal.

His Christian names were borrowed (in an offhand moment by a mother who seems to have had absolutely no other sins upon her conscience) from a character in an obscure novel. None could have suited him less well. In all his strenuous life no one ever caught him pausing to eat a lotus of forgetfulness. But, though his friends resorted to the subterfuge of calling him "Jack," Coffman insisted upon acknowledging the names given him in baptism. He never hid behind the semi-anonymity of initials but continued to be Lotus Delta before all the world.

It was his mother, Coffman liked to say whimsically, who had inadvertently chosen his lifework for him. When the time came for him to choose a college, he had wavered between Indiana University at Bloomington and the State Teachers College (then the Normal School) at Terra Haute. He was still uncertain as the moment of departure approached.

When his mother woke him on his last day at home, she said: "Lotus, have you decided? I must know now. If you are going to Bloomington you will not need to eat on the train. But if you are going to Terra Haute I must kill the chickens for your lunch."

In that instant a career was decided. Nothing in the world was better than Mrs. Coffman's chicken. "I'm going to Terra Haute," her son said.

But if he actually became a teacher in that accidental way, a sense of destiny soon possessed him. He began immediately to work at being a teacher as though he were under a crusader's banner reading: *God wills it*. He moved fast through all the stages of the profession—from village schoolmaster to principal to superintendent of schools—working all the while at earning advanced degrees. Columbia awarded his Ph.D. The subject of his dissertation was "The Social Composition of the Teaching Population." In it Coffman anticipated the preoccupations of his career. To understand the teaching population and to improve both its outlook and its performance became his lifework.

His thesis turned up several important facts about the world of teachers. First, a majority of public-school instructors were themselves virtually children, too young to vote. Second, though normal schools existed in every state of the union, these were poorly attended and they produced only a pitifully small percentage of practicing teachers. Third, it was so much the rule for young men to teach only long enough to equip themselves for other jobs that an unending line of them trooped in one of education's swinging doors and out the other. As a wit said: "Teaching is not a profession but a procession."

It became Coffman's first interest at Minnesota to create

a College of Education that would be a separate and distinct entity. It had been really nothing but a courteous fiction to call it a college before. Every other unit had a hand in its affairs and all of them used that hand chiefly to make patronizing gestures of indulgence toward it. Education, Coffman insisted, "like the other sciences has passed through its period of apprenticeship." It had earned a right to develop its own techniques of operation and its own standards, too. Gradually, he rounded up all the sheep of what he considered to be his fold—the ones that had grazed so long on the agricultural campus and in the Arts college. The realm in which teachers were taught to teach became his own and he put a stout fence around it.

But his unique contribution to Minnesota tradition, made while he was still dean of education, was the creation of the Bureau of Cooperative Research. This was a kind of laboratory in which teachers could examine the results of their efforts. Later called the Bureau of Institutional Research, this division, made up of members of the faculties of many colleges, is devoted to the study of teaching techniques, of admission requirements, of administrative practices and of the progress of students. At Minnesota, since Coffman's time, no tradition has been allowed to become sacred. As he himself once said: "Every practice is subject to review. We test it, check it, look for better ways of accomplishing the same purpose."

This habit of self-appraisal has become—again, the words are Coffman's—"a prominent, if not the most prominent characteristic of Minnesota in recent years."

So, the morning and the evening were the sixth day, as Vincent, with Coffman's sympathetic support, refounded his sixth college.

One department of the university remained which, though it was in no need of refounding, felt Vincent's benevolent influence.

To the Department of Agriculture there had come in 1909,

a year before Vincent's arrival, a fine scientist and administrator, Albert F. Woods. He was Vincent's own sort of man and he needed only the friendly support from the president's office to get on with the spirited job he had been doing.

With the aid of Minnesota's own United States Senator, Knute Nelson, Woods had succeeded in getting additional appropriations for the teaching of agricultural subjects. He interested himself in the plight of the midwestern farmer, not then a sharer in the general prosperity of the region. One of the department's surveys showed that the average farmer received a return of no more than 5 per cent on his capital investment and was actually edging, ever closer and closer, toward bankruptcy. The diagnosis: lack of knowledge of his business. The cure (promptly applied by Woods): short courses and institutes in management, together with more and better bulletins from the experiment station.

Woods' concern with research equaled Vincent's own. He did not permit himself to be overawed by the snobbery of the main campus with its preference for pure, over applied, science. Said Woods: "Pasteur whose great work was done with domestic animals and industrial agriculture in the broad sense failed to sensitize the blind spot in the minds of the pure scientists."

If anything were ever to let light into "the dark caves of everyday living," it would be research in agricultural botany, agricultural physics, agricultural chemistry.

It may be said, without fear of extravagance, that it was the influence of Woods that laid the groundwork for the highly important contributions which the department and its men were to make during the next few years.

To the college Woods brought many gifted men. Edward Freeman was one. A Minnesota graduate himself, he had returned to teach botany. Later, he contributed an item to Minnesota's list of "firsts" by creating the first department of plant pathology ever to be established in an American university. And this was important not merely to Minnesota but to the whole world of American education.

113

Freeman and Woods were so completely in sympathy that the professor was later to say of the dean: "He and I worked together as parts of one man." Freeman's own benignity was such that for years all of the family life of the St. Paul campus revolved about him. Like an indulgent father, he invented traditions, poured out tides of good will toward undergraduates and, in his famous *Letter from Home*, communicated directly and intimately with alumni. In the midst of his genuinely significant adventures in agricultural research, he never lost the homely touch. Every interest was treated, first of all, as a family affair. He once gave, for example, this engaging glimpse of two of his distinguished students:

"I remember Stakman and Alden Potter counting smut heads in oats and barley, arguing endlessly and so vehemently that they seemed oblivious to the fact that they were sitting on barbs of *Cenchrus tribuloides*."

He worked quite as harmoniously with big, benign, booming Roscoe Thatcher who came to the experiment station in Vincent's time to push forward its research program. One of his many contributions to the state tradition was appropriately acknowledged when his name was given to a new kind of rust-resistant wheat developed under his direction.

Thatcher and Freeman balanced one another conveniently in temperament. The first was impetuous and enthusiastic; the other no less imaginative but more restrained. Thatcher used to say: "When I make a snap judgment, I'm wrong thirty-five per cent of the time and when I make a soberly considered judgment I'm wrong thirty-five per cent of the time. So why not save myself all that energy?" He and Freeman seem seldom to have been wrong the same 35 per cent of the time, and they made a good team.

The department brought in other good men. Frederick Alway (Ph.D., Heidelberg) was in a position, as Vincent might have said, to talk back as an equal to any pure scientist. As professor of soil chemistry he demonstrated his quality in many ways. As he once said to a student who had asked him why science was important: "Someday, if you stick at it

114

long enough, you will be able to do something no one ever did before."

One grim reminder of the past, when extinction had constantly threatened the College of Agriculture, disturbed this present serenity. In April, 1917, the United States declared war on Germany and suddenly the college all but disappeared. Its enrollment had been four hundred when the month began; at its end, thirty students were left. All the rest had gone into the "army of food producers on the farms."

This crisis once more roused the old enmities. There is a type of zealous alumnus who is always sure that the interests of alma mater are being neglected. Graduates of the School of Agriculture numbered some of this kind. Again the cry went up that the School was carrying the rest of the department on its aching back and that it should be separated completely from the university.

But the strength of Vincent became clear in this moment of revolt. He had only to speak out vigorously in defense of unity, and resistance melted away.

Indeed, the chief thing that Vincent had done for agriculture was to insist on its close integration with the rest of the university. In the cooperative mood that exists today this advantage, from a strictly academic viewpoint, is deeply valued.

Vincent and his wife helped to make that integration close and firm by establishing social, as well as academic links. The president loved the St. Paul campus. He and Mrs. Vincent together instituted a policy which they called "intermigration." No longer was it virtually true that a visa was required to cross from one campus to the other. The life of the two groups became one.

But an outward and visible sign of this unity was needed. Too long students who had classes on both campuses had suffered physical hardship in their laborious ploddings back and forth, often through blizzards and always through exhausting inconveniences. One home economics student was never able, in later years, to repress an ironic smile when she remembered that her schedule had required her to miss her lunch in order to get from St. Paul to Minneapolis in time to hear an instructor in dietetics go on about the absolute necessity of being regular in eating one's meals.

The intercampus streetcar service changed all that. Vincent had persuaded the Twin City Rapid Transit Company to put in a branch line between the two campuses.

One vehicle ran back and forth many times daily. The car itself was commodious to the point of luxury and the fact that it represented escape from the cold made the atmosphere within it warm to the point of joviality. And, as though he had been attracted to this service by some natural affinity of good will, one of Minnesota's finest eccentrics came to preside over the car as conductor.

No one now remembers the original name of this genius. Because he was devoted to learning and to original thought, he had had his name changed legally to Spencer in honor of Herbert Spencer, whom he considered to be his spiritual father. And as a follower of Emerson he had rechristened himself Ralph Waldo.

Skipper Spencer held his own lively and informal seminars in the intercampus special. Somewhat discursively they covered the whole range of the life of the mind. Like Folwell, the skipper was interested in everything from economics to literature. He took it hard when fares on his line went, as he thought, too high. Out of his own pocket he refunded pennies to needy students. When Oscar Firkins published a book on Emerson, the skipper bought the first copy. As he operated his car that day he held his captive audience in a fascinated state of horror while he pulled the work apart and pronounced it "the most delightful of all possible misinterpretations."

In the spring of 1917 Vincent resigned. He had intended to stay at Minnesota no more than ten years. "In that time," he once said, "any executive should be able to put his ideas into execution. If he has been successful his task will be accomplished; if he has not been successful, he should certainly retire anyway."

Actually he had been at Minnesota only six years. But the task of refounding the university had been largely accomplished. And the Rockefeller Foundation wanted him as its president. He felt that it was a "summons" and he went.

He left, as monument to his administrative efforts, the university as it exists today. His successors, Coffman and Ford, each in turn announced as his policy that of keeping Vincent's ideas alive and of pushing his purposes to the fullest development.

He left also the memory of an individuality that, while it glittered with wit, also glowed with charm. The combination produced a rare kind of attraction. In the opinion of one of his faculty at Minnesota it sprang spontaneously and refreshingly from "the deepest gentility."

Typical of Vincent's readiness was a flash of wit that endeared him to one of the last of his audiences in Minnesota. He and a committee from the board of regents had traveled all over St. Louis County looking for a new experimental farm. The day was hot and a light wind had persistently blown dust over the uncomfortable persons of the committee members. When Vincent was asked, after luncheon, to "say a few words" he got to his feet with something less than his usual alacrity.

"Gentlemen," he said, "your committee has, this day, covered the whole of St. Louis County—and vice versa."

Vincent did not forget the university which he had refounded, when he ceased to be its president. As head of the Rockefeller Foundation he had much to do with the further development not merely of the medical school but of many other divisions. Perfectionist that he was, he delighted in its progress under men who had been his appointees, friends and sharers of his convictions. The best feature of the fine memory that he has left at Minnesota may be indicated by saying that he made the way of the perfectionist seem easy, delightful and rewarding.

CHAPTER FIVE

UNEASY INTERREGNUM

Marion leroy burton, fourth president of the university, stood six feet, two inches tall; he had the shoulders of a fullback and the red hair of a matinee idol. Next to Cyrus Northrop he had greater personal popularity in the community beyond the campus than the university had produced until that time.

Burton tended to identify himself with Northrop and with Northrop's pattern of attitudes just as Vincent had identified himself with Folwell and with Folwell's habits of mind. So, once more, a kind of rhythmic alternation of beats was clearly marked in the long-range development of the institution.

During his short stay at Minnesota (three years) Burton accomplished a major step forward with his Comprehensive Building Program. This he was able to finance, partly at least, because he had so many friends in the legislature. As one observer said: "That man will cost the state of Minnesota millions of dollars. Every time he asks for anything the members will tumble over each other to give it to him."

It helped that, like Northrop, Burton "seemed like a western man." In his boyhood he had lived with a widowed mother in Minneapolis and had helped to support the family by selling newspapers. Later, he had taken his Bachelor's degree at Carleton College, Northfield, Minnesota and then gone on to Yale for his D.D. He had taught theology at Yale, and been pastor of a large church in Boston before accepting the presidency of Smith College. There all the susceptible young women had added grace notes to the theme of education by falling in love with him.

To Minnesota he came, still brisk, boyish and enthusiastic. "I have red hair and sand in my gullet and I'm going to talk to you with the brutal frankness of a blood relative," he would say to the student body. And the students, male and female, loved him for his casual high spirit.

But he came in a troubled hour. The whole academic world had collapsed under the impact of World War I. Since the spring of 1917 men had been entering the army en masse. Enrollment for the academic year 1917–18 was reduced by 40 per cent in the law school and by 6 per cent in the Arts college where gains among women partly offset the losses of men. Faculty ranks had been decimated, too. Three deans—Coffman, Ford and Vance—had gone to Washington to do war work. Fifty-seven professors of medicine were in uniform. So were teachers of chemistry, teachers of astronomy and teachers of history, for all of whom the government had found tasks associated with the war effort.

Burton's campus at Minnesota in the fall of 1917 resembled the slightly matriarchal world from which he had come. The fraternity houses along University Avenue had been turned over to matrons who rented "rooms for girls." Young women of resolution and enterprise had assumed the editorships of publications. They dominated what social life the campus still had.

This out-of-joint world produced chiefly disasters. Burton had three major ordeals to endure.

The first of these had to do with war hysteria and resulted in a bitter attack on academic freedom. The United States, unused to living in the arena of international contest, felt itself to be encompassed by enemies. Even at Minnesota the inland security of the pre-atomic age seemed not to be secure enough. A group of zealots, set up as a Commission of Public Safety, began to hunt down "pro-Germans." The university, because its faculty included many of foreign birth, offered a shining mark to "trigger-happy" investigators. Burton, almost on his first day in the presidency, was met with the report that every member of his German department, except one, was thought to be disloyal.

One by one these blameless men cleared themselves, but the investigators only moved on to other departments. Because of his German name Frederick Klaeber was suspect. Angry but far from frightened, Klaeber flung back two sharp challenges. It was an outrage, he said, for a man with his record of uninterrupted service to American youth to be accused of wishing to betray its interests. Second, he said: "The high spirit of scientific and technical research fostered in the German laboratories must be adopted by America if she is to win the war."

Even after these stalwart responses, the Commission still insisted that there were enemies within the gates whom the regents should investigate. On a hot September afternoon, which was to make university history, they did so.

The list of defendants had narrowed down to three. The first to be interviewed was Dean Owre. He came, mild-mannered and earnest, to explain that he was a pacifist, had always been one and did not expect to change his outlook. However, he was devoting some of his private time to raising foxglove from which he would make digitalis and turn it over to the government. More, he insisted politely, a man of his philosophy should not be expected to do. He was dismissed, free of the charges that had been made against him, to go back to his foxglove.

The second was an overworked woman from the farm campus who had been denounced for failure to join a Red Cross group. Weeping, she explained that she was responsible for the care of an elderly invalid mother. She, too, was exonerated.

And then came Professor William Schaper of Political Science. Electric with opinions as he had always been (many good ones which the university had been pleased to follow), he shocked the board with a shower of candid admissions and countercharges. With relatives in the German, as well as in the American army, he could only wish that the declaration of war had not been made. He considered himself to be a loyal American and would obey all the country's laws. But these did not require him to feel enthusiasm for war as a means of settling international problems. Further, he believed it to be "unwise policy," counter to President Wilson's declared objectives, to try to destroy the German government.

His hostility awakened hostility. "You are the Kaiser's man," one regent is remembered to have said excitedly. "You want the Kaiser and the Crown Prince to dominate the world, don't you?"

"That is an accusation, not a question," Schaper answered. "It is absurd."

In the midst of the heat engendered by this clash Schaper was asked to leave the room. Called back, half an hour later, he was told that "his attitude" made him "unfit to discharge the duties of his position." His "relations to the university" were "terminated."

Stunned, Schaper asked that charges against him be put into writing and that he be given a chance to answer them. But the board stood firm.

This was not the end of the matter. President Wilson interested himself in the case and asked his commission on labor conciliation, when it visited Minneapolis on other affairs, to consider the possibility of reopening discussion. Felix Frankfurter told his associates on the commission that, in his opinion, the action of the regents constituted "a plain case of czarism, the very thing America is fighting." But still the judgment against Schaper was not withdrawn.

Twenty years later the action was rescinded in dramatic circumstances. The courage displayed by the board in reversing itself helped to establish a high standard of academic freedom at Minnesota.

Burton was, of course, helpless in the face of honest opinion which hurtled so recklessly across his authority. He could only endure and wait for the next crisis. It came promptly.

During the summer of 1918 the schools of the country,

expecting their enrollments to be cut drastically, had cut back their whole operation correspondingly and were preparing to fight the battle for survival on the most modest terms possible. At that moment their heads were summoned to Fort Sheridan and told by the War Department that they must expand rather than contract. For, they too were in the army now.

The draft, calling for the enrollment of all able-bodied men between the ages of eighteen and forty-five, was to go into effect on August 30. Since it was obviously impossible to put so huge a segment of the population immediately into active training, a group of younger men were to be organized into a kind of reserve. The universities and colleges of the country were to offer themselves as containers of this manpower pool. Burton, as an important general of this campaign, had to hurry home and make ready to receive six thousand young men enrolled in the Students Army Training Corps. And all must be done within a month.

Actually a few weeks grace were added (though grace is scarcely the word with which to refer to the influenza epidemic which caused the delay). The university was not able to open under the new dispensation until the second week of October.

Meanwhile a new faculty and a new curriculum had to be improvised. Some unsung heroes of the war made valiant contributions. Professor A. B. White created a course, overnight, called War Aims. Professor William Stearns Davis, with the help of William Anderson and Morris Tyler, produced a textbook, *Roots of the War*.

And then the young soldiers came. Three thousand, assigned to the "collegiate section," were housed in a long-unused commercial building which stood high above the Falls of St. Anthony near the site of the university's first "preparatory" school. The other three thousand, assigned to special programs for blacksmiths, mechanics, radio technicians and carpenters, lived in another old building on the border between the cities. Suddenly, in a moment of misguided zeal, all the old ambiguities and wanderings-in-a-haze of inappropriate effort seemed to have been loosed once more out of the box of a most perverse Pandora.

The experiment was foredoomed, as one of Dean Johnston's studies later showed, because at least one-third of the young men of the SATC were not "college material" to begin with. In no other circumstances would they have been enrolled in a university. Even those who might have done well under normal conditions were in a state of chronic exhaustion because of the completely unrealistic demands made upon them. They were roused for reveille at six-thirty and then, before breakfast, were marched through the city streets of Minneapolis. This farcical burlesque of military drill continued for two hours. After breakfast the students were marched to classes, marched from class to class, marched into mess halls at night for "supervised study." Guard duty and duty on K.P. offered the only relief from a routine which proved so thoroughly insupportable that those who succumbed to "flu" counted themselves lucky. They were given the comparatively desirable surroundings of overcrowded hospital wards.

The rest of the members of the SATC merely slept. They slept as though under enchantment straight through their classes, in the library and over their books at night. Occasionally they would be roused in a lecture hall to hear strange snatches of the utterly unintelligible. "The style of Spenser," Oscar Firkins might be telling a class in English survey, "is willowy; it is billowy; it might almost be called pillowy." The members of the SATC looked at each other in complete consternation and went back to sleep without even reaching for a Spenserian pillow.

The disaster of World War I ended in November, 1918; the disaster of the SATC lasted a little longer but was brought to an end at Christmas time. It had been, in Dean Johnston's opinion, "an unequivocal failure" and it "left a deleterious effect on student morale" that was felt throughout the year.

But there was one indirect result that proved to be good.

It quickened Dean Johnston's determination to make sure that aptitude for college training would be tested in advance so that the hopelessly inadequate would never again clutter classrooms en masse.

One of Burton's messages to the SATC members contained a reference to the fact that they would be given "bayonet training to develop the offensive spirit." Nothing so lively ever actually happened. But an offensive spirit of a kind survived the war, nonetheless, and plagued Burton even in the last year of his administration.

The academic year 1919–20 began under a cloud of perplexities. Enrollment had leaped from the largest prewar number of approximately 6300 to nearly 8000. Servicemen were returning en bloc, and free tuition for veterans had encouraged a new group of students to experiment with higher education. Classrooms were overcrowded, teachers were overworked, supplies of all kinds were insufficient. "Our financial difficulties," Burton confessed, "have been perplexing. Our aim has been to meet the situation, day by day, as best we could."

It is not surprising that when the University of Michigan invited Burton to become its president, he was glad to accept. Michigan had been the beau ideal of state universities in the minds of many leaders ever since Folwell's time. It had, in particular, been Burton's. His Minnesota speeches are full of wistful references to its leadership. In December he announced that he must go.

But one trial still awaited him. His administration began with a struggle over academic freedom; it ended in a second.

This was the moment when the United States Attorney General, A. Palmer Mitchell, was extremely busy looking for subversives, or "Reds" as they were called in the vernacular of the time. It was feared throughout the academic world that this inhibiting influence might tend to curtail the free expression of ideas in the classroom. Burton rose quickly to say that it had not done so at Minnesota. The right of free speech was being jealously guarded.

An undergraduate publication, *Foolscap,* dared to challenge him. At Minnesota, as well as in other schools, the editors insisted, deans had "been known to applaud policies in which they did not believe because they had to." Professors had been known to say things they did not mean. An institution suffered "undeniable disgrace" when its policy "necessitates such conduct on the part of the faculty simply because their opinions were at variance with orthodox belief."

Foolscap was a bright publication, bright in the usual way of being audacious enough to make the dean of student affairs grieve, but bright also in the unusual way of being able to persuade faculty members and distinguished visitors to give its editors material. Mary Ellen Chase, Joseph Beach and Carl Sandburg were among its contributors.

The result of the undergraduate attack was that the university senate decided to investigate. Professor David Swenson became chairman of a committee empowered to "hear testimony and sense the feeling of the individual members of the faculty" on the question of whether or not there had been any inclination at Minnesota to curtail freedom of speech.

In June, 1920, the senate heard this committee's report. The essence of its finding was that in the postwar atmosphere of "intolerance and fear" there had become evident, in academic officials, "a certain readiness to receive criticism of faculty members whose long service should act as a presumption in their favor." This attitude tended to leave able men "unjustifiably on the defensive." The university community itself had tended to succumb to the idea that "the university, instead of having for its chief function the orientation of the student within the world of thought, is an institution for the indoctrination of opinion."

The report offered this statement of general principle:

"An institution of learning endowed by the state cannot make itself the champion of any narrowly conceived particularity of spirit; it cannot, therefore, make itself responsible for the private actions of its teachers and consequently cannot afford to lay down for these activities any special rules either written or established by tradition other than those which the law of the land and social decorum require."

It recommended also that the senate go on record vigorously as being determined to maintain academic freedom and that it ask the regents to accept as guiding principle that of dismissing no member of the faculty for his opinions, public or private, without getting the advice of a committee of teachers from the department of the man on trial. Obviously the shadow of Schaper loomed large over the committee's deliberations.

Not everyone liked the report. The senate wrangled over it and threats were made to force the committee to name its witnesses. Stanchly the committee protected the confidences that had been offered in private and assumed full responsibility for the interpretation of them. In the end excitement subsided with the suggestion that the matter be reconsidered at a full meeting of the faculty. No such session ever took place. Before it could be arranged Burton had ceased to be president and Swenson was on leave at another university.

But the incident left Minnesota committed, nonetheless, to a liberal position. It had the effect also of prompting the university to take vigorous action in later fights over academic freedom and tenure. The committee's admirable statement wrote into the history of the institution a strong plea for the rights and the dignity of the teacher.

Ironically, *Foolscap* was sacrificed in the process. The report of the dean of student affairs said, without other comment: "*Foolscap* will not be printed next year." But it had served a useful purpose as sacrificial goat. With that thought, at least, its editors—now all graduated anyway—might console themselves.

At Michigan, Burton was to become known as "the builder." In retrospect it is clear that he was a builder at Minnesota as well. Working in circumstances that were completely abnormal and nearly intolerable, he made Minnesota aware of the need for a modern plant. Wisely, he revived an old plan—that of architect Cass Gilbert—which called for structures of harmonious simplicity to be built around a central mall. Though he was at Minnesota too short a time to give the project much more than its initial impetus, he did inspire the building of an auditorium which, as he had urged, was named for his mentor, Cyrus Northrop.

CHAPTER SIX

CRUSADING SCHOOLMASTER

T HE PRESIDENTS of the University of Minnesota might be characterized, each in his distinctive way, by a dramatization of his relationship to the job. Only Northrop can be said to have "occupied" the presidency. Folwell marched through the presidency, obsessed with his vision, trampling out the vintage where the grapes of learning were stored. Vincent enveloped the presidency. Having made a lucid analysis of the function of a university, he used his authority to surround the scattered parts of the operation and draw all into one.

In retrospect, one sees Folwell as the soldier, the crusader of education, and Vincent as its statesman.

For Coffman that leaves the role which he would certainly have been proud to call his own—that of the scientist of education.

For eighteen years, from 1920 to 1938, he explored the techniques of his job in the dedicated conviction that they could, and must, be made suitable to the present needs of the state. He created with the right hand and adapted with the left and, out of his indefatigable experimentation, there emerged an institution as different from Burton's as Vincent's had been from Northrop's.

The effort to reconstruct Coffman's character reveals, in the very handling of his qualities, that the positive ones were large and solid; the negative ones, unimportant but often appealing. He was less attractive to the student body than

Northrop had been, but it is difficult to understand why. He shared quite spontaneously in many of the interests of the young. At a wrestling match he strained his muscles with every movement in the ring; at a football game he labored unconsciously to impart his personal drive to the open field runner.

He had much less personal brilliance than Vincent, but he taught himself to be a brisk and effective speaker and he always had something arresting and awakening to say.

It is clear from an early speech, made as president, that he wished to identify himself with Folwell whom he called a "seer" and with Vincent whom he described as "unifier of the university." He realized many of the purposes of the one, such as that of making a clear line of demarcation between junior and senior colleges; he built on all the principles of the second, particularly that of helping to make the teacher's job a vital one. His opportunities were far greater than those of Folwell; he devoted himself to the tasks of the presidency three times longer than did Vincent. Inevitably his influence was, in the end, greater than that of either of the men whom he took as guides.

If he had difficulties with regents and with students (in fact, he did) these rose out of the fact that he was the essential schoolmaster. He could not bring himself to make over to anyone else the responsibilities of the job. As one member of the board of regents said when he had been in office only a few weeks: "Mr. Coffman leaves no doubt in anyone's mind who is to be president of the university."

He had not sought the appointment though there were men among the regents who would have been glad to vote for him as Vincent's immediate successor in preference to Burton. He was not thinking of the presidency for himself in March, 1920, when the regents again began to consider him. His mind was on what seemed to be the much more tangible offers that had come to him, all at once, from five other schools. With characteristic conscientiousness and much pacing of the floor at night, he had been considering his opportunities in the light of his duty. In the end he told the regents that he would like to stay at Minnesota if he could have an increase in salary as dean. The regents answered with the surprising suggestion that he accept a large increase in salary and the presidency along with it.

Burton had taken office in a troubled hour; Coffman came in the midst of a storm. It helped him to endure his perplexities that he had expected to face nothing else. A society that was still in the process of designing its destiny must accept change—and a certain amount of concomitant violence—as its fate. Coffman liked to quote the witticism of a colleague who had once suggested that, as Adam led Eve out of the Garden of Eden, he had said to her: "My dear, you must understand that we are living through a period of transition."

The transition through which Coffman felt himself to be moving was that of the economic crises following World War I. For industry this was a period of exhilarating expansion but, for the agricultural world of the Midwest, it was a time of disaster. The bottom fell out of the whole enterprise. Farms were foreclosed; workers drifted into the cities; unemployment gnawed at the nerves and hunger at the vitals of thousands.

One effect on the university was to bring to its doors another great influx of students. Unable to find jobs, these young people turned desperately back to the schools, hoping that education might help them to find new patterns for their lives. During the academic year 1920–21, the university was seriously handicapped by having to spread its resources over the needs of many more matriculants.

But worse was to come.

In preparing the budget for the biennium of 1921–23, Coffman and the regents had pared their requests to what they considered the minimum and then, in an access of conscientiousness, trimmed the budget still more. To their utter consternation they found that the chairman of the legislature's appropriations committee expected them to make do with $3,000,000 less than their lowest estimate of what would be required simply for survival.

The response to this crisis was spectacular. Many groups on and off the campus denounced the legislature. *The Alumni Weekly* and the *Minnesota Daily* became prophets of doom, publicly rending their already tattered garments. Public leaders, men and women, rose everywhere to demand reconsideration, though they acknowledged that "the crying need of the state in everything is economy."

Only Coffman, the schoolmaster, kept his head. There must be no demonstration, he told the *Daily*, "to promote sentiment in favor of appropriations for the university."

But one huge demonstration took place in spite of him. Volunteers among the students worked all night to print handbills. A "legion of minutemen" placed themselves at the entrances to the campus to distribute this literature calling for a great mass meeting. Placards appeared everywhere. After the second-hour class a bugle sounded, firm and clear. Within minutes four thousand students were milling about, in happy expectancy of drama, across the length and breadth of the old drill field. The enthusiasm was highly gratifying to the organizers of the demonstration; the confusion was even more gratifying to drivers of trucks on University Avenue who, without knowing what the excitement was about, lent the voices of their horns to add to the pleasure of this inexpensive diversion.

Coffman hurried to the scene. He was unable, speaking from the steps of Folwell Hall, to make himself heard above the clamor. Climbing out on a second-floor balcony, he shouted through a megaphone urging that "nothing must be done to discredit the institution and put us in a poor light before the legislature."

The mass meeting did not, in fact, put the university in any but a good light. Divested of its features of hysteria and exhibitionism, it was seen correctly to be a public show of faith in "our university" and in its history of conscientious effort. The sense of an identity of interest between the university and the state, so carefully cultivated in Vincent's time, had never been so emphatically stated; never again was it necessary to affirm this identity with defiance. It became, quite simply, an accepted principal.

The legislature gave in. The budget of the university as it had been first presented, with only a few thousand dollars lopped off, was passed and everyone went quietly back to work.

A few weeks later, in an atmosphere of general reconciliation, the president gave his inaugural address. Diplomatically he sweetened the flavor of the occasion—and, at the same time, salted away the recent experience—by reminding his audience of the university's early history. It had been, he said, that of a free people struggling to establish a system of popular education. "The constant extension of education to lower economic levels epitomizes the struggle of the race for human freedom. Everyone knows that such education is expensive but the expense is insignificant compared to the enormous gain society receives from it."

He dedicated his administration to three major purposes: first, to training the largest possible number of applicants for work in the professions (numbers were important "since the best abilities may be found in the least promising places"); second, to reorganizing the materials of education to offset the tendency toward fragmentation inherent in specialized training; third, to preserve individuality within the huge institution by bringing together a "high-minded, right-minded faculty."

In short, the university must make a virtue of its bigness, by extending its advantages to as many citizens as possible, and yet not allow that bigness to degenerate into characterless giantism. As "pioneer on the frontier of knowledge," the university must "acquire a new breadth of interest and sym-

132

pathies in harmony with the age in which it lives and to which it owes its being."

The student demonstration, held in defiance of the president's request, was symptomatic of an assertive restlessness on the part of students during the 1920s. This continued to give the schoolmaster trouble. Undergraduates felt the irritating pressures of a society grown suddenly too sophisticated to endure the restrictions of its parochial inheritance and tradition. The revolt of elder brothers (and fathers and cousins and even a few scattered aunts) against Prohibition took the form on the campus of a revolt against all rigidities of discipline. Many students had been to war and they had come home feeling that they had seen the world. Or if they had not seen quite all of it, at least they had had tantalizing glimpses of something more stimulating than a Boy Scout rally.

Actually, the rebellion was mild, generally good-tempered—even humorous—and thoroughly democratic in temper. There was, for example, an attempt to "democratize" the fraternity system so that no one should be excluded from a Greek-letter society if he wished to join one. Nothing came of the effort, partly, perhaps, because the impulse to spread benignity by law always attracts only a few worthily perspiring adherents.

The effort served, however, to show that the influence of the Greek-letter fraternities in the midwestern universities was dwindling. A few years earlier it had seemed to be a virulent disease and was so represented in a campus novel by William McNally, called *The Barb*. Greek-letteritis, McNally thought, was marking the face of campus life with a juvenile irritation and might even be undermining the permanent health of university men and women.

It had been true, in the teens of the century, that the "Greeks," because they were organized for concerted action, tended to capture coveted editorships, to elect class presidents and select campus "queens." But within a few years, the life

133

of the fraternities and sororities was to become merely a peripheral adornment to campus life, one into which a student might enter gladly but without unbecoming glee or which he could forgo without chagrin. The vital energy of the student body found its social expression in activities open to everyone and in places where the doors stood open to Greeks and non-Greeks alike. (The very word *barb* became obsolescent in the language of undergraduates.) So the rebellion was not insignificant, after all.

Other rebellions were of a more particular kind which seemed to some observers to be likely to undermine intellectual stability. A group, called the Seekers, tried to place the name of Eugene Debs in nomination at a mock convention. This set one of the regents to worrying and clucking in a series of letters to the president. His comments seemed, just a little feverishly, to equate a preference for the Socialist platform to an endorsement of free love and a readiness to preach atheism. The same regent thought it highly dangerous for students to be allowed to hear Carl Sandburg read his poems in the Little Theater.

The instance of revolt that gave Coffman the worst anxiety of his first year in office was that of a law student who was reported to have visited a fraternity house with the smell of liquor on his breath. The young man had had a fine war record (he had enlisted as a private and earned a lieutenancy). His participation in student affairs had shown a high sense of responsibility and a marked degree of competence. But he had infringed on the letter of the university law and the dean of student affairs suspended him.

Immediately this became a *cause célèbre* on and off the campus. Student pamphleteers produced a publication, called *The Rubber Gun*, ridiculing the action. In the privacy of faculty consultations, deans spoke vigorously in the young man's defense. The governor of the state intervened. At last the suspension order was rescinded. After making proper apologies the student was permitted to return to classes.

But Coffman, who had supported the dean of student

affairs, was not pleased. He felt that his authority had been circumvented and said so bluntly to the board of regents. What good the year had accomplished, he said, would be "all lost." It had been unwise for the board to interfere as, in the end, it had done. Discipline would be harder to maintain. The "radical students" would be sure to catch up more "rubber guns" with which to bait and humiliate him.

He goaded himself with unnecessary fears, however. As the philosophic Adam of his own favorite story might have told him, this was a period of transition. The student body of the midwestern university was growing up rapidly. It was inevitable that there should be some shows of resentment at being kept in swaddling clothes, but there was little bitterness and only ripening intellectual curiosity in these attacks on tradition.

Happily the tendency to indulge in nagging personalities soon perished among the insurgent students. An "Angels' Revolt" of another period had in it so little vitality—a supercilious aptitude for boredom seemed to be the only begetter of this attack on the Arts college faculty—that the movement died a-borning. Later, there were to be important issues between Coffman and the undergraduates, but these were fought out with sobriety and dignity. The student body had begun to show those symptoms of maturity which Folwell had always hopefully valued in it.

Meanwhile student high spirit showed its most constructive aspects in two "drives" of the 1920s, to collect money for a new stadium and a new auditorium. Two million dollars was set as the goal of these campaigns, and it did not abash the young and enterprising to know that most of it must be collected in nickels and dimes left in depression pockets. The fact that they succeeded stands as a monument to the memory of such young men as Roman Bohnen. In the role of "rooter king," Bohnen displayed arts of wit and cajolery which broke down the resistance of alumni at every kind of public function—football games, student entertainments, "Dads' dinners." He very nearly lost his voice in the process—and a severe

135

loss to the theater this would have been. But the enthusiasm of the moment was so great that it would have been recorded merely as a "mete and proper" sacrifice.

One of the major problems of Coffman's administration during the 1920s was to find room, not merely for the stadium and the auditorium, but for all the other buildings of which the university, with its enormous new enrollment, had acute need.

Northrop, in his time, had faced a similar crisis, and his response to it had added an uncharacteristic, but giddily pleasing moment to the record. At a faculty meeting he had asked for suggestions about what new buildings should be added, first, to the campus. A woman member had answered that the university was in the situation of a newborn infant needing everything in the way of clothing. "Then," said Northrop, yielding to a rare impulse toward raffishness, "if you will tell me what building represents the pants, I shall know where to begin."

Now the university was in the situation of needing a whole wardrobe. The chief difficulty was that there was no place to put it.

A serious mistake, made long ago by the economy-minded board, had been that of selling a right of way straight through the campus to one of the railroads that served the milling district across the river. Freight cars, vying vehemently with the trucks on University Avenue, completed the dismal work of enclosing the campus in an atmosphere of noise, cinders and confusion. Vibrations ruined the instruments of physicists; smoke poured into chemical laboratories. From 1908 on, the plaints had grown louder and louder. The University, everyone said, had approximately as much academic seclusion as a boiler factory. But negotiations with the railroad's attorneys for some kind of compromise arrangement dragged on and on. For more than a decade nothing was accomplished.

But Coffman had a powerful ally in Fred Snyder, son-in-law of Pillsbury, prominent Minneapolis citizen and a mem-

136

ber of the board of regents. Together they succeeded, at last, in persuading the Great Nothern Railroad to allow the Northern Pacific trains to be rerouted over its tracks. This at least relieved the situation, freed a certain amount of land and gave the university a modest amount of *lebensraum*.

During the 1920s the new campus emerged. It was as different from the old campus as a modern gallery is different from a museum of oddities. The charm of the old quarter, with its buildings grouped around a knoll, was that of a world that had grown old, slowly and whimsically, offering no apology for the curious architectural tastes of the past. The old library, now Burton Hall, is perhaps the strangest of them all. Behind the façade of a Greek temple it becomes embroiled in a warfare of corridors and wings. Tradition says that it represents the ideas of two architects who never met. One working on the outside, one on the inside, seem to have engaged in a futile dispute over form and function. Folwell Hall, base of the Arts college, is an equally puzzling structure mixing in its massive bulk elements of many styles. Its congress of chimneys is so odd that many legends have sprung up to explain its inspiration. Such is the quite untrue one that each chimney once had its own gargoyle.

The new campus, blocked off from the old by the huge shape of Cyrus Northrop Auditorium, is made of rather severely functional structures lining the sides and end of a long rectangular mall. This much-modified version of Cass Gilbert's design represents a succession of compromises with cost. But the total effect (even allowing for a regrettable bow to tradition which has permitted the red brick façades to be marred by nonfunctional pillars) is one of pleasant serviceability.

This physical refounding of the university completed the tasks begun by Vincent in refounding the institution intellectually and of Burton in starting its brick and mortar re-establishment. Folwell's "University of the Twentieth Century" was ready, at last, for its major work.

*   *   *

But there were still many contests to be fought out doggedly and stubbornly before a philosophy of what Coffman called "education for democracy" could be enunciated unequivocally. The president paced the floor at night and struggled conscientiously with these problems of theory. He struggled also with his lieutenants and, out of each contest, a positive value emerged.

What is curious about Coffman's career is that he had many battles with men who were largely in sympathy with his attitudes. One of these was Dean Johnston who, like the president, worked all his life toward one goal, that of making modern methods serve the needs of twentieth-century students. Yet these men managed so often to edge each other to the periphery of an argument where they could bitterly disagree that their conferences often seemed to end in stalemate. The dean would leave the president's office, his mild blue eyes arctic with hostility, while, beyond the door, the president's voice was heard sputtering with frustration.

The difficulty was that, when Johnston spoke of the differential treatment of students, his mind was chiefly concerned with the special rights of an intellectual elite. He was not indifferent to the interests of a second group of students, those in the middle range of ability. For these, courses of less than four years should be provided, ones of "general information" which would train "self-reliant citizens" and give them a better understanding of "the social implications and values of their everyday work." But below this group there was a third which Johnston considered to have no place in a university. As he said: "Somewhat less than one third of our present matriculants could be denied admission without doing injustice to any considerable number of individuals."

This was the attitude that disturbed Coffman to the depth of his nature as a democrat. He believed, first of all, that a state university owed an opportunity to everyone. He believed, second, that, in addition to an intellectual elite trained for leadership, democracy needed an "intelligent followership." A democracy would be shortsighted indeed if it failed

138

to train as many individuals as possible to take a disciplined and well-directed interest in its own affairs. Death by inanition awaited a society based on the principal of self-government, if it became indifferent to the selfhood of the many.

Another of Coffman's tenaciously held principles was that, when an educational system produced much waste material, the system was at fault, not the material. His surveys showed an appalling mortality among members of the freshman class. Many did not return after the first year so that the university was forever renewing itself with beginners. (Sixty per cent of all enrollment was in the freshman class.) This failure to continue did not mean that the individual student's work had been poor. Each year more students at Minnesota made good records. Further, the record of those who did not return was only a little less good than that of those who continued. The real troubles were money, poor health, and lack of a sense of direction. The cures: (1) make education as inexpensive as possible; (2) provide the student with wise counseling in all his problems; (3) "reorganize the materials of education" so that a student might no longer wander in a haze of promises but find a pattern suited to his needs.

It was fortunate for Minnesota that it had two men like Coffman and Johnston who battled together so strenuously over ideas. For out of their debates came the many new experiments through which Coffman marched toward his objectives. What he wanted primarily to do was to "salvage abilities" and, in doing so, to broaden to the widest possible extent the influence of the university in providing "education for democracy."

He had, almost daily, the advice of his neighbor, Folwell. The former president, now in retirement but working steadily at his history of Minnesota, lived just across the street. The two men were in complete sympathy, for Coffman was engaged in doing what Folwell had once hoped to do: give the state a closely integrated system of education of which the university would be the "roof and crown."

When Coffman had accepted the presidency, Folwell had

congratulated him with the particular warmth of a fellow thinker. But he had added: "Sometimes you will feel as though you were riding five circus horses simultaneously." Coffman rode them with the firmness of a professional trainer.

As always, the medical school proved to be one of the most spirited, careening and head-tossing of all his chargers. In December, 1921, the publication *Journal-Lancet* offered an account of a session held by the Minnesota State Medical Association in which it was made evident that Coffman would soon have to risk an encounter with what Vincent had called "that buzz saw."

"It was a joy and a treat," wrote the reporter with the satisfaction of an old warrior whose sword had rusted too long in its sheath, "to hear the great acrimony and bitterness as the lie was passed back and forth."

The subject of the debate was the old one: "the medical situation at the university." In the estimation of the doctors very nearly everything was wrong with that situation. Too much attention was paid to graduate work. The autonomy of the school had been destroyed. There was no leadership in the development of educational policies. Fundamentals were being taught as pure science; the practical point of view was being neglected. The clinical facilities of the Twin City hospitals were not being utilized. The dean was not an M.D. Graduate instruction should be taken away from the graduate school and returned to the medical school. The advice of the medical profession should be sought in the development of programs.

This tabulation of faults sounds today oddly like praise spoken in reverse English. Being translated, it meant that the old enemies of Vincent still thirsted after the blood of his allies, particularly after the blood of the brothers Mayo.

At the university the targets of this wildly dispersed fire stood uninjured. Dean Lyon quietly defended his administration by saying that he believed in himself as a medical educator. He listed his accomplishments: liberalization of the curriculum; improvement of the dispensary; better library facilities; tighter organization of student internship. The medical school had been drawn into the pattern of the university as a whole. The graduate school was, as all modern educators held, the proper place for graduate study in medicine.

His calm provoked new attacks. The university, said the doctors, was poaching on the preserves of private practitioners. Nonsense, Regent Mayo retorted, in effect—and rather sinister nonsense, too. "I have never been able to accept the idea that God created sickness for the benefit of the doctor." Such "trade-unionism," he added, served the medical profession ill.

But the fights went on. The state government itself became involved as the doctors launched a distressing campaign to replace a faithful and extraordinarily useful regent for one who was known to be favorable to the position of the Medical Association.

The circus horse was now careening quite dangerously. But Coffman once more kept his head. He persuaded the regents to appoint a committee of disinterested observers to make a survey. This group consisted of Dr. Frank Billings of Rush Medical College in Chicago; Dr. J. M. T. Finney of Johns Hopkins; and Dr. V. C. Vaughan of the University of Michigan.

The result was complete vindication for the university. An eloquently eulogistic report declared that the faculty of the medical school had made important contributions to knowledge and that graduates demonstrated the excellence of their training in the many important posts to which they had gone. Dean Lyon received a gratifying vote of confidence as an "able, honest and conscientious" administrator; in national councils he was "prominent" and his opinion had "great weight."

Whether or not the doctors were won over by this endorsement, the public was. Gifts for the expansion of Elliot Hospital began to pour in. Friends of Dr. Frank C. Todd, who before his death during World War I had been head of ophthalmology and otolaryngology, raised money for creation

141

of a branch to bear his name. In 1922 Mrs. George Chase Christian gave, as a memorial to her husband, a quarter of a million dollars with which to build and equip a hospital for the study of cancer. During the 1920s, William Henry Eustis, a dramatic figure in Minneapolis public life (crippled in boyhood he had educated himself, become wealthy in real estate transactions, served as mayor and been the jolly patron saint of many of its enterprises, both civic and social), gradually gave his fortune to the university. First, a million dollars; then half a million more; then, at the rate of $10,000 worth each month, his securities, his office buildings, his parcels of land; finally, at his death, most of the rest of his estate.

Still the darts flew fitfully at the medical school. These attacks were quite impotent now, but conscientiously ill-tempered. Standards were too high, the critics said. Students were being driven away from Minnesota into less exacting institutions. They were being discouraged from taking up medicine as a profession.

Dean Lyon continued to maintain his patience. "The medical faculty," he explained, was "willing and anxious" to admit all students who could be properly trained. To accept applicants, knowing that they would have to be turned away eventually, would be "detrimental to the student" as well as a waste of money and effort. By admitting only high-grade men the university created a virtually ideal situation in which almost none failed.

Lyon's answers were always so reasonable that in the end complaints grew faint and died on a failing breeze of dissent.

But the dissenters made one last stand and achieved a sad little victory. In 1926, the suggestion was made to the city of Minneapolis that a new general hospital be built near the campus where the medical faculty of the university and private practitioners could work together for the benefit of patients and, at the same time, for the benefit of students. (The latter would profit, of course, by being exposed to a wide range of cases.) The General Education Board of the Rockefeller Foundation was willing to contribute $1,250,000 if the city council would raise the rest of the money needed to build. But the president of the Rockefeller Foundation was George Edgar Vincent. A gift, even one that came only indirectly from his hand, was unwelcome to his old enemies in the medical profession. Negotiations in the matter dragged on for two years. Then, at last, the board of regents was obliged to decline the offer. In the opinion of most observers this was a tragic mistake. The dissenting doctors had collaborated on a curious kind of surgical operation. They had removed a nose to spite a face.

The strenuous decade of the 1920s offered two examples of how Coffman embodied the spirit of the university in its struggle to protect integrity. One of these established, once for all, the right of the institution to control what went on in its classrooms without interference from any pressure group. The other episode established its right to independence in the control of its finances. Both set up important precedents in the fight for academic freedom. In Coffman's own words and those of one of his chief allies, the university as a "republic of free minds" was saved, in these crises, from "invasion" and from "oppressive tyranny."

In 1926, the Reverend William B. Riley of Minneapolis conceived it to be his duty to make Minnesota a battleground in the fight against the "teaching of evolution." This was a continuation of the struggle in which William Jennings Bryan had tragically involved himself, just the summer before, during the trial of the Scopes case in Tennessee. At a meeting of fundamentalists held in Fort Worth even earlier (1923) Riley had offered his audience this curious message of comfort: "Evolution is on its last legs and will shortly expire." Stanch anti-Darwinian that he was, Riley seemed to have fallen under the spell of the language of the doctrine. He hoped to make the "last" of those legs atrophy in a personally conducted mutation all his own.

Clearly, it was Mr. Riley's conviction that he represented some undefined authority which sanctioned his effort to super-

143

vise instruction in all the schools of the country, at least wherever his own field was involved. He had addressed audiences at many indulgent institutions and he demanded the same privilege at Minnesota. It was his suggestion that he be officially invited to appear before a convocation to speak on the question: "Should the Teaching of Evolution Be Longer Tolerated in This State University?"

To Coffman this sounded a little like asking a man to open his living room to a gathering of relatives before whom the question would be discussed: "When Are You Going To Stop Beating Your Wife?" Still, the dean of administration told Mr. Riley that he might visit the campus whenever he liked and speak to any group of students who wished to hear him. The University simply declined to sponsor such a session. This, Mr. Riley insisted, was like having the door closed in his face. Feeling that he was a surrogate of higher powers whose authority was being flouted, he complained that the university, alone among the schools that he had asked for invitations, had refused "to recognize" him "officially."

He held his meeting elsewhere. Its attendants voted to present a bill before the next legislature—meeting in March, 1927—which would forbid anyone in a tax-supported school of Minnesota "to teach that man either descended from or ascended from a lower order of animals."

Mr. Riley had often referred to an "evolution combine" at the university. For once he understated what he wished to say, which was that the faculty was united against him. There was, in fact, absolute unanimity of opinion that his attitude represented a threat to academic freedom. Dean after dean promptly made this clear. Lyon suggested that what Mr. Riley wanted was a "return to medievalism." Fraser showed shrewdly that a law against the teaching of evolution simply could not be enforced. A teacher could safely continue to discuss evolution if he merely took the trouble to point out that he quoted an accepted authority. Ford, with his usual neat turn of phrase, said that if Minnesota were to pass the

144

proposed law it would have to replace the gopher, as state mascot, with the blind mole.

Speaking for biologists, Professor Sigerfoos blew away a great fog of misrepresentation by speaking of the "unanimous acceptance" by science throughout the civilized world of the "doctrine of evolution."

Students—that is, the group that made themselves articulate—were united against this invasion of the university as a stronghold of free investigation. The *Daily* used its largest type to announce that the university faced an emergency, "the worst in its history."

On a day when the legislature was thought to be ready to consider Mr. Riley's bill, first-hour classes were showered with copies of a petition (written by the *Daily*'s able editor, Howard Haycraft) urging that the bill be dropped. A "flying squadron" covered the campus from Pillsbury Gate to Elliot Hospital to make sure that no undergraduate missed a chance to sign. At noon, five thousand students crowded the armory and stood throughout a rousing session. (There had been no time to bring in the "undertaker's chairs" and there would have been no room for them anyway.) An open letter, addressed to the men of the state house, was read aloud. It played cunningly on the lines: "You cannot legislate against thought . . . you cannot legislate against truth." Each time these words were repeated the crowd cheered as it had never cheered before for anything less than a Golden Gopher touchdown.

On the same day Coffman spoke in the capitol before a joint meeting of the committees on education for senate and house. If the proposed bill were passed, he said, the university's self-dependence would be destroyed. Its well-established reputation for freedom would be destroyed. Its prestige would be destroyed. A blight of ridicule would fall upon the campus. With a final flourish of boyish extravagance which marked his moments of eloquence, the president warned that scholars would "shun the university" as they would shun "a house with a smallpox sign on it."

The legislature accepted the warning. Only seven of the sixty-two votes in the senate were cast in favor of the bill. The house allowed it to die in committee.

It was, as a member of the faculty pointed out in the *Daily*, the complete unanimity of the educational community that had defeated the evolution bill. Presidents of other Minnesota universities—among them private institutions that were not affected by the proposed law—had spoken out vigorously on Coffman's side. More than 4500 students had signed the Haycraft petition. Still it was in a special way Coffman's victory. He had confronted the opposition with the unshakable firmness of his own conviction. On the merits of the case he had won positive re-endorsement for the charter of his "republic of free minds."

The students, acting on his example, behaved with admirable decorum. There were no bonfires to celebrate the victory; there was no shouting in the armory. As one young leader said: "The matter is dead. We are glad of it and that is enough."

It was during the same period (1926 to 1928) that Coffman had to deal with the other issue involving the university's integrity. This had to do with the question of whether the institution was to be regarded as a ward of the state or as a self-dependent unit of state government.

The problem was not a new one. In 1901, during Northrop's time, the legislature had created an agency called the Board of Control, the function of which was to supervise the finances of "the charitable, reformatory and penal institutions of the state." The board of regents had not supposed that this definition could possibly be thought to cover the university and had continued to operate its affairs. But, in 1903, the Board of Control had asserted, with considerable asperity, that, indeed, the university was a charitable institution subject to its supervision. A suit was won in the courts which ordered the university to submit.

The situation was as awkward as it was unjust. Teachers

146

could get laboratory supplies only by submitting requisitions to the Board of Control and often they had to wait three months for the satisfaction of needs that no longer existed when the materials arrived. Professor Conway McMillan was in the habit of supplying his students in botany with mosses that he collected on expeditions, for which he asked the university to pay only his actual expenses. The Board of Control chose to disallow this item and insisted that McMillan must order his supplies in the proper way through the purchasing agent. It delighted that sly man to present in his next requisition a long list of such items as archegonial turfs of *Marchantia* and sporophytic stages of *Polytrichum*. A baffled and angry purchasing agent told the board that he supposed Professor McMillan must be allowed to make his own field trips after all.

There had been other mighty crises, in Northrop's time, over eighteen cents' worth of cells needed for an electric clock in the library that had not run for a year while the Board deliberated and, on another occasion, over fifty cents' worth of paraffin for the lack of which a whole course would have had to be dropped.

Northrop had decided, at last, that he must act. Throughout his career he made a personal matter of every issue. When a professor offered his resignation, Northrop would say: "What's the matter? Don't you love me?" He said virtually the same thing to the legislature in asking for relief from the Board of Control. "I have put the best twenty years of my life into this university and I don't want to see the work of my life destroyed."

Dutifully, the legislature yielded. A bill was passed removing the university from the jurisdiction of the Board of Control.

But the issue had not been settled on its merits and it was bound to rise again.

In 1926 it did. The state was still feeling the pinch of the agricultural depression and Governor Theodore Christianson decided that the government needed to be redesigned in the

147

interest of economy. Straightway the university found itself back in the situation of 1903 with a state agency—called, this time, the Commission of Administration and Finance—telling it exactly what it could and could not do with its money.

Now, however, the members of the commission (the "Big Three" they were popularly—or unpopularly—called) had a different sort of president to deal with at the university. Coffman promptly sought out Dean Fraser of the law school, and they took a closer look than anyone had ever before troubled himself to take at the status of the university as it had been established by the founding fathers.

It was clear, Fraser discovered, that the territorial legislature had assigned to the board of regents the exclusive right to govern the university. The state constitution, adopted in 1858, had confirmed this right and perpetuated the university as an institution in no way dependent on the legislature. All the literature of state law, Fraser found, presented the university as a "public corporation, not subordinate to, but co-ordinate with the legislature."

Proceeding discreetly, Coffman and the board of regents agreed to submit the university's budget to the Big Three but with the express understanding that compliance did not constitute "a waiver of the constitutional rights and immunities" of the board. These, Coffman realized, would be hard to establish. For sixty years the regents had not asserted their authority "against legislative action." Northrop had virtually acknowledged the parental authority of the legislature when he had asked for relief as a personal favor to him.

The moment had come, Coffman and Fraser agreed, to make an issue of the matter and to show that the university's self-dependence was rooted in law, not in the shifting sands of sentimental indulgence. While they were speculating about when and how to proceed, the Big Three, all unknowingly, presented them with both a cause and an occasion.

The university had decided that it must have an insurance program to shore up the precarious economic situation of the teacher. Dr. Richard Scammon pointed out in a committee report asking for such a plan: "A professional man's capital is in his head. When a teacher becomes ill his capital is endangered. When he dies it is destroyed. We must protect against debility and death."

The Big Three took a less generous view. Presented with a budget which included an item of forty-five thousand dollars for insurance, they were outraged. The cost was bad enough in their opinion but, worse than that, if the university created an insurance program others in the state government would probably set up a clamor to get the same protection. A most unfortunate precedent would be established.

"If this item or any part of it appears in any estimate, we shall be obliged to disprove it," they said succinctly.

The assumption of the Big Three was that the university occupied the position of a helpless ward of the state. This was, in no sense, true. Even in the matter of revenue it had four sources over which the legislature had no authority: funds from the original land grants; funds derived from leases; student fees; federal aid. Reminded of this fact, the Big Three only stiffened their backs into complete rigidity. They answered, in effect, that if the university chose to act like a bad child and spend its own pocket money for indulgences and frills like an insurance program, the Big Three must play the role of stern guardian and cut out the bad child's allowance.

There was no longer any good in temporizing, both sides agreed. At Dean Fraser's suggestion a "friendly suit" was instituted over the fact that the state auditor had refused to issue a warrant for payment of an item of university expense—actually, a small debt incurred in preparing to establish the disputed insurance program. The courts were asked to settle the matter once for all.

Judge Hugo Hanft heard the case in the Second Judicial District Court of Ramsey County. A distinguished group of alumni made up the audience. These people listened with sober delight to the wittily phrased lucidity of Fraser's brief.

Its central point was that the law guaranteed the independence of the university as an institution coordinate with the legislature. Skillfully the limits of the philosophical discussion were pushed back to make room for every phase of the question of what constitutes academic freedom. It would be unwise, Fraser suggested, to take control of the university away from regents who could be counted upon to be disinterested and put it into the hands of a commission "whose outlook is necessarily political." Such an agency might yield to such another pressure group as had recently cast its shadow across the campus. A minority might wish to forbid the teaching of biology or to color the teaching of political science with its special views or even to interfere with instruction in medicine. A powerful zealot might someday feel so strongly about vivisection that he would destroy the university to keep it from destroying dogs. "The approach of tyranny may be scented in this tainted breeze."

But the breeze was quite blown away by Judge Hanft's decision. "The people speak in the constitution," he wrote. "They establish, by the constitution, agencies to serve them. The Board of Regents is such an agency for the university. It cannot waive or transfer its powers to the legislature."

An appeal to the Minnesota Supreme Court brought precisely the same result. Judge Royal Stone ruled: "The whole power to govern the university was put in the Regents by the people. No part of it can be put elsewhere but by the people."

A year had been spent in the courts to reach this decision. But, at last, it was authoritative and final. Coffman had made an important contribution to the history of the university. He had established it inpregnably as a university of the people.

At the end of the 1920s Coffman seemed to have put behind him both the great clamorous problem of academic freedom and the small daily one of housekeeping. He had reaffirmed the belief that a university is a "place of the spirit." He could turn, at last, to the day-by-day job of being an educator. These interests were summed up in two phrases that recur often in his speeches: "salvaging abilities" and "reorganizing the materials of education."

150

After a decade in the president's chair he had overcome the doubt in the minds of some who had been deans along with him that he would be the eternal schoolmaster to the end of his career. He had begun his administration with the suggestion: "Nothing would pay larger dividends than for faculties to become students of the art of teaching." Many had feared that he might use his authority as president to submit them to classroom disciplines. But the kind of battles he had fought and the way in which he had won them enlisted the sympathy of his colleagues and they were glad to work with him at the tasks that he now undertook.

In 1930 Coffman created a committee on Administrative Reorganization made up of six deans and his own special assistant, James Lawrence. The deans were Coffey (Agriculture), Ford (Graduate School), Fraser (Law), Haggerty (Education), Johnston (Arts), and Lyon (Medicine). Because their number suggested a mystical authority, above and beyond the academic, they were called the Committee of Seven. And indeed they did show a bold creative capacity.

They gave their attention, first, to the problems of the gifted undergraduate. This had always been Johnston's great concern. He had been a pioneer in the movement toward setting up interdisciplinary studies. Courses in Business Agriculture and Business Engineering had been designed under his guidance to fit the needs of special groups better than any prescribed courses of study in one college could do.

"University College," created by the regents in June, 1930, was a further development of this impulse to give the gifted student what he needed. The Committee of Seven agreed that such young men and women deserved more latitude than could be allowed to the average undergraduate. "Modifications and substitutions" were what the literature of the new unit officially permitted. Actually, selections of students to be given the privileges of University College were made so carefully that it was found possible to give its matriculants wide range through the fields of knowledge. Over the years students have generally justified this faith by showing fine records and graduating with honors.

The committee next turned its attention to students at the other end of the academic scale. These young people had baffled educators all through the years. Many complaints were made against them. They burdened teachers, said some, wearily; they lowered standards, said others angrily; they benefited themselves hardly at all, everyone agreed.

Just at that moment Robert Hutchins, the young president of the University of Chicago had, with jaunty vigor, tossed a bomb into academic circles with his radical plan for junking all the antiquated machinery of university administration. This called for the reorganization of his university into a group of professional schools together with divisions of the arts. His new units were: the humanities, the biological sciences, the social sciences, the physical sciences and the College. Hutchins hoped to end the era of routine education, with its almost inevitable concomitant of boredom for the many, by adjusting the institution to the individual. Throwing down the artificial barriers between academic disciples would, he was convinced, help to promote "cooperation in research" and produce a better kind of education for a better student.

His lively report did not neglect the student of no better than average ability and intelligence. His plan called for "an honorable exit"—that is, graduation without distinction—for "the man who wishes only a general education."

A state university, because of its obligation to receive all holders of high-school diplomas, needed just such an honorable exit for many of its students. As the Committee of Seven clearly saw, a new unit must be created to fit their needs.

These needs had never been satisfied by prescribed courses in languages, in sciences, and in the "tool" studies of various kinds. Unrelated, unabsorbed fragments of such instruction merely cluttered the minds of great numbers of men and women when they returned, as ordinary citizens or as housewives, to the tasks of everyday life. For all the good their edu-

152

cations had done them they might quite as well have spent their time exploring Outer Mongolia.

Let such students, the Committee of Seven decided, be given something in the way of instruction that might be expected to broaden their horizons without expecting those horizons to stretch very far in the direction of abstract thought.

In February, 1932, the regents authorized the creation of a new unit in which to experiment with respectable entrances into and honorable exits from a general education.

There were many different kinds of attitudes toward this experiment. The committee was anxious that it should not seem to be what Coffman had said explicitly he did not want, "a dumbbell college." They thought for a moment of naming it the "Institute of Social Intelligence," but when everyone else in the university said "No!" with the greatest possible emphasis, they compromised on General College. The president himself described it as "an adventure in higher education" and he hoped that "the most gifted students" might "elect membership in it." Johnston frankly welcomed it as a means of providing for students whose entrance tests showed no great promise. The Committee of Seven itself saw it as a place where students who did not expect to finish a four-year course and also those who "lacked ability to pursue prevailing curricula" might stay long enough to mature a little before becoming breadwinners and housewives.

Coffman persisted in the high intention of making the General College a true experiment in reorganizing the materials of education. He persuaded many of the best minds in the university to work on the development of special courses. The purpose was to reveal that core of significance in each of the fields of learning which may help a nonspecialist to understand, and to command, the experiences of everyday life. One of these "overview courses," as they came to be called, turned a particular light on physics and chemistry to show their importance to the man or the woman who must know something about materials and about household remedies. Mathematics became the study of how much interest a thoughtful budget maker could afford to pay for a loan. "Development psychology" undertook to say something meaningful about family relations—that is, about "life with father" or "how to live with your nerves." Other studies like "The Formation of Public Opinion" unwrapped the mysteries of propaganda or, like "Background of the Modern World," exposed the powerful hidden links between the past world of Peter the Great and the present-day world of party rule in Soviet Russia.

Many educators who later became presidents of other schools were co-designers of Minnesota's General College; among them, Malcolm McLean, later of Hampton, Frederick Hovde, later of Purdue, and Alvin Eurich, later of the State University of New York. These and others developed the techniques of visual education; created a group of "core" courses intended to reveal the student to himself; and established a pattern for a kind of instruction with which a young man could make an honorable exit from the academic world after two years. For successful completion of this course Minnesota offers the degree: Associate in Arts.

Much of the *exalté* tone of high expectation has been snuffed out of talk about the General College. So has much of the snobbish disparagement once expressed by the bright ones in such nicknames as "All Fools College." It is tacitly acknowledged that this unit exists to serve the university, in the way that Dean Johnston hoped it would, by relieving the traffic in the regular courses of slow-paced students.

The members of General College themselves do not blink the point. A hitchhiker once was asked by a faculty member who had picked him up on the way to the university how he was getting on. "Oh pretty good," the boy said. "You mean pretty *well*, don't you?" said the incurably corrective teacher. The boy looked up slyly. "Oh no, not *that* good, Professor. I'm in the General College."

Coffman's fundamental purpose had been fulfilled. With the enthusiastic support of the General Education Board of the Rockefeller Foundation, he had, at last, made a professional approach to an old and baffling problem of mass education. His disciples had set up many of the guideposts and written many of the guidebooks with which educators in many schools throughout the country were to make their way through similar adventures.

The only major job of refounding that Vincent had left unfinished was that of coping with the problems of engineering. Coffman inherited this unfinished business and carried it through to completion.

An astonishing fault of education, as it stands revealed today under fire from theorists, is that it has allowed students to elude the discipline—and miss the fascination—of science. Even after World War I when the United States spurted forward to leadership in many fields, no enthusiasm seemed to be lighted in young minds for this kind of intellectual enterprise. Industry must share the blame; it did little in those years to stimulate specialization. Though it absorbed university graduates into its plants, it offered them only routine jobs. Discouraged by lack of opportunity, fewer and fewer students elected to take chemistry courses and physics courses in the secondary schools. In many places such instruction simply ceased to exist.

The vicious circle spiraled upward through all levels of education. Industry brought no pressure upon the universities to do research. As a result few and inadequate facilities for doing research were provided.

At Minnesota leaders like Frankfurter in chemistry, Tate in physics, Appleby in mining engineering, Frederick Mann and Roy Jones in architecture had worked with brilliant effectiveness against the tendency. And still the College of Engineering, like colleges of engineering everywhere in America, had lagged behind other units in development.

The frustrations of the time were reflected in the history of technology on the Minnesota campus. Affiliations between related fields were made and unmade; deans came and went almost as though through a revolving door; bitter battles of faculty against faculty provided the only relief from boredom. One professor who was offered the deanship of the college declined without hesitation. "Those fellows," he said, meaning his colleagues, "will fight each other until there's a new dean and then they'll fight *him*. I don't want to be a dean."

It remained for Coffman to bring stability to the area. He had ambitious ideas about developing an institute of technology which would bring together under one head all the diverse interests of the field. These plans, however, had to wait for several retirements, after which, it might be hoped, old jealousies and rivalries would have lost their spur to intramural competition. Meanwhile Appleby continued to rule popularly and successfully in his separate school. Charles Mann revealed a combination of personal talent and enthusiasm for research which recommended him to a large following in the realm of chemical engineering. His course became so great an attraction that a separate division had to be created for him with a building to house it. The tendency was still toward fragmentation rather than unification.

Another separate unit, the School of Chemistry, received a tremendous impetus toward high achievement when Samuel Colville Lind came, in 1926, to be its head. Lind had studied under Madame Curie in Paris, and the announcement of his appointment took on the aspect of an important event in local history when it became known that he brought with him to Minnesota, as a loan from the National Research Council, one hundred thousand dollars' worth of radium. His career at Minnesota was to last for more than two decades. When it ended with his retirement in 1947, Lind, looking as indestructible as only a wiry academic can, began a new career as director of atomic research at Oak Ridge.

Lind's fine reputation attracted many important men to Minnesota. The determination to build up a faculty that could direct graduate work of truly creative character put him in the vanguard of leadership. Stimulated further by the fact that the National Research Council, using funds from the Rockefeller Foundation, was then establishing postgraduate fellowships in the natural sciences and in medicine, Lind first gathered up many of these prizes and then gathered the men to receive them. He brought to his faculty such men as Isaak Kolthoff (Ph.D., University of Utrecht) in analytical chemistry; Lloyd Reyerson (Ph.D., Johns Hopkins) in colloid chemistry; and Lee Irwin Smith (Ph.D., Harvard) in organic chemistry.

In 1935 the retirement of Appleby gave Coffman his opportunity to reorganize. He announced promptly that the time had come "when the various technological fields should be more concerned with interdepartmental relations and intercollege cooperation." The regents at his request created an Institute of Technology and the president appointed a committee to establish its pattern.

One of the tasks of the committee was to find a dean. Lind was the chairman and he canvassed the possibilities in and out of the state. But there were no candidates. The battles of the past had left no one feeling quite whole. To be dean in this field at Minnesota was thought, throughout the academic world, to be only a little less dangerous than walking a tightrope in a high wind over a pool of boiling oil. Everyone said: No, and said it with great emphasis.

When Lind reported the failure of his mission, Coffman answered briskly that the matter had been settled by default. Lind himself would have to be the dean of the new Institute.

Realizing that he could not escape his destiny, Lind accepted. He had only a few years of comparative serenity before World War II added its complications to the problems of building a school. But the dean had already demonstrated his gift as a fisher of men. What he had done for chemistry, he proceeded to do for the other branches of engineering. At the end of the war he had created an important school to pass on to his successor. In a few giant steps, taken under the most difficult of circumstances, he had covered much of the ground that had seemed to be unattainable during the laggard years.

*   *   *

157

Coffman's crusading spirit could never be at peace. For him there was always a new goal, and the attainment of it was a pressing personal duty. Having undertaken to help the least promising students by creating the General College and the most promising by inviting them into University College, he began to pace the floor at night, thinking of others to whom the facilities of education should still be opened. He regarded the process of becoming mature as a lifework and he wished to be of use to any others who might think of their own development in the same way.

The idea of creating "a graduate school of adult education" had been with him always but it reached a peak of urgency in his mind after an occasion when he had had a dramatic encounter with need. Coffman had been asked to address a group of ministers on the question of what they could do to fulfill their responsibilities more adequately. The year was 1933 and the depression had just settled like a moral blizzard on the Midwest. The church should be useful in such an emergency, the ministers believed. What they wanted was a plan.

Coffman, always the provocative schoolmaster, threw out a challenge. If the influence of the church had declined, perhaps, he suggested, it was because the clergy tended to live in the past, giving too much attention to dogma and to formal religious observance, too little to the immediate needs of people.

He was delighted, as any schoolmaster would have been, when the challenge was thrown back directly to him. "What have the colleges and universities done to help us?" one of the ministers asked.

What, indeed, Coffman began to wonder, had the colleges and universities done for *all* their graduates who had gone out into the professions, into business, into all the tasks of everyday life, perhaps to become becalmed in routine, never experiencing a fresh breath of enthusiasm for the job. It was an intolerable idea to Coffman that, in a world where values changed daily and new cargoes of knowledge were constantly being set afloat on the current of thought, many conscientious men and women profited little by all that effort. Doctors, lawyers and engineers, to be sure, had their professional journals and their meetings of learned societies. These tried to keep the fraternity abreast of the times. But at best only tantalizing glimpses were offered of a new world. There existed no kind of organized plan for the mental rejuvenation such as the ministers had asked of Coffman.

There was nothing new, of course, about the idea of adult education. Folwell had tried to launch such a movement in his early efforts at extension work; Vincent had been deeply and completely committed to it. There had always been at Minnesota short courses for farmers, teachers and housewives; there had been correspondence courses, summer school courses, courses in the regular academic divisions, scheduled for late afternoon, to catch willing adults. But still it was all too scattered to be much more than a harmless pastime for the curious. What was needed, in order to give adult education its proper status, was a place in which graduates of colleges and universities could come together for periods of concentrated and systematic effort. Only in that way could they really renew intelligence.

The opportunity to create such an institution within the university's pattern presently came almost with the ease of a miracle. Washington, at the moment, was deep in the business of working daily miracles to fight off the depression. The Works Progress Administration had asked Coffman, among others, for suggestions about possible projects with which to give its program permanent value. Coffman presented a dozen ideas. Among them was that of building an adult education center. To Coffman's surprise it caught the attention of the administration, and funds were made available for an immediate start. A new unit of university instruction had to be created to occupy the new building.

For this prodigy, born mature out of a crusading schoolmaster's mind, some prodigious names were suggested. Institute of Sustained Learning and Study was, perhaps, the most high-flown; Institute of Neo-Study, the most severely academic. Dean Malcolm Willey more realistically suggested Center for Postgraduate Study. Harold Benjamin, assistant dean of education, offered "continuation study" as perhaps more accurate. So the Center of Continuation Study it was christened by the regents on June 15, 1936.

Appropriately, it was Benjamin who became tutor to this new member of the university family. (Actually, his title was director.) The preliminary announcement made it clear that the university meant to have a real school, no mere refuge for people who had been frightened by the depression into vague yearning after self-improvement. Professional groups were invited to consult with the director about their needs; the university guaranteed to organize courses in many different kinds of fields and to supply the faculty.

The new building was completed. So skillfully had it been designed to fit into the landscape of both the old campus and the new that, as soon as the last red brick had been put into place, it managed to look as though it had always been there. Dormitory, social center, classroom building, all in one, the unit is self-contained and self-sufficient. As many as seventy-eight students may live under its roof, attend classes, use its library, patronize its dining room without any distraction from the outside world.

The Center offered its first institute in November, 1936. Within the first four months of its existence four hundred men and women had passed through its doors to attend discussions of problems in social welfare administration, hospital supervision, treatment of various diseases and new methods in surgery. The original schedule of one institute a week had to be expanded to meet demand. In the second year there were often three or four courses running simultaneously with groups numbering from fifteen to one hundred.

The public invented its own courses just as it had been invited to do. On one occasion an alumnus from Duluth, visiting the campus for a football game, was asked by a friend to meet him in the lounge of the Center. The visitor had not

160

known the purpose of the building but, when it was explained, he was suddenly alerted with enthusiasm. "We could use this place in my business," he said. "Too many of us are going, each in his own way, about the job of removing the over-burden in an open pit mine. We need a postgraduate course for mining engineers." Before the year was over they had it.

Doctors have used the Center more frequently than any one group. The university's director of postgraduate instruction in medicine, Dr. William O'Brien, was for many strenuous years the begetter of scores of courses. He believed with Julius Nolte (director of the Center after Benjamin resigned) that:

"It is as tragic for a physician to be shoved into mediocrity by advances in the technique of his profession as it is for a mechanic to be robbed of his job by technological advances. Society having invested large sums in the training of the professional man cannot afford to scrap him prematurely."

Dr. O'Brien, who was as jovial as Falstaff and as dedicated as Savonarola, seized on the imagination of undergraduates and postgraduates alike. He flung them all into the main stream of medical knowledge and kept them there by prodding, persuasion, and the sheer brilliance of his own example. Two courses for which he became famous were in medical terminology and orientation for freshmen and sophomore students. Everyone emerged from his presence touched by his ardor, the inheritors of his high spirit.

The center has taught everything from kindergarten method to diagnostic radiology, from office management to clinical medicine, from creative writing to heart surgery. It might well claim as its patron saint the first president of the university, who felt it to be the obligation of the civilized, responsible man to interest himself in everything from Plato to hog cholera.

But it is to Coffman that the Center stands as enduring monument. He imagined something bold and new and brought it into reality. As Richard Price once said:

"Not to every man is it given to conceive a unique educational project, to organize the plan, work out the details, to pass on the blueprints, to win the necessary support, to perfect the essentials of organization and then launch the enterprise on its destined course."

This is, indeed, what Coffman did.

One of Coffman's many lifelong battles was with those who contended that the university was too big. Nothing stiffened his back to quite such rigidity as the attitude, sometimes expressed by the solicitous parent of a timid son or daughter, that the mere size of the institution was necessarily crushing to tender sensibilities. Size, Coffman insisted, had nothing to do with the problem. If a school had a hundred students and an inadequate staff it was too large; if it had twenty thousand students and yet managed to provide a well-trained faculty and good facilities, it was not too large. A large university, with a large faculty, was more likely to have teachers of high grade than a small school with a limited staff. The student whose mind had been alerted to the possibilities of his world could have as much personal contact with his teachers as he wished; the conscientious professional in a big university could be counted on to *make* time for the eager member of a class. Only a hopelessly sluggish student could fail to catch the excitement of the "learning situation." And a boy with a talent for boredom can exercise it quite as luxuriously in a small school as in a big.

This was the theory, and Coffman took it as a major responsibility to make it all quite true. He realized, of course, that the day was gone when a president could speak to each student by name as Folwell had done. ("Good morning, John J. Jones," he would say with the soldierly briskness of a salute.) Gone, too, was the margin of time that had made it possible for Northrop to spend hours at a stretch advising his young men about personal problems. (Back and forth they would pace in the president's office, man and boy, side by side, a parental arm thrown across a dutifully receptive shoulder.) Yet the same concern could be expressed in a new way.

A scientific approach must be made to discover new techniques of guidance.

From the moment when Dean Johnston had begun his indefatigable testing, Minnesota had been preoccupied with the problem of knowing its students as individuals. Professor Donald Paterson, of the department of psychology, had created a succession of college aptitude examinations that were designed to predict performance, and these ratings had proved to be strikingly accurate. Coffman brought into the faculty a small army of educational psychologists who campaigned, during the 1920s, throughout the realm of the "learning situation" in a determined effort to control all its hazards.

In 1923 the Committee on Educational Guidance issued what has been called the Magna Carta of students' rights. Education, it said in effect, must not be content to say over and over: Know thyself; rather, it must provide the student with the keys to self-knowledge. Each entrant must be told in detail what the university could do for him. There must be orientation courses which would open all the doors on the various realms of learning. Each student must have a faculty adviser capable of interpreting individual needs on the basis of a careful study of that particular young man's "personality profile." Women students, too, because they had had less incentive in the past to work on the professional level, must be given special vocational guidance. The importance of psychiatric help was emphasized. (Now for the first time a university document had acknowledged that particular responsibility.) A "quality credit" rule was established the purpose of which was to stimulate the brilliant student to move at his own fast pace. He could actually reduce his time in residence by earning one such credit for every five honor points received in excess of the number required for graduation. . . . To teachers, this Magna Carta offered the warning that they must learn, not merely to be better members of their profession, but to be better human beings if they hoped to be adequate counselors.

To give reality to these hopes, many innovations were

163

adopted. During Freshman Week newcomers had the campus to themselves. They were given guided tours to acquaint them with the university's facilities and also with its atmosphere. Coffman, who had always believed that poor health was the cause of many a failure, insisted on the creation of a Student Health Service to which all matriculants were encouraged to take their colds and their fevers—and their psychological fluctuations as well. If a young woman could not be asked to recite in class without bursting into tears, the university must be able to tell her why she did so and how she could overcome the inclination.

Forever appraising itself, as well as the individual members of its population, the university brought all of its testing operations together, at last, in one unit. The Testing Bureau, established in 1932, was put under the direction of Edmund G. Williamson (Ph.D., Minnesota). This firm-minded young man believed, with Coffman, that, in the past, educators had been inclined to dismiss as hopeless students for whose failure they themselves were largely responsible.

Williamson said: "The smug retort, 'We cannot be expected to coddle our students,' sounds suspiciously like a defense mechanism; certainly it violates the basic psychology of incentives to learning. Students will learn if they attempt what they are capable of learning and if they are properly motivated to learn."

There was reason to be concerned about the average student. During the 1930s, depression conditions had sent many to college to whom the "learning situation" was totally unfamiliar. They were in school chiefly because they had, at the moment, no other place to go. To Williamson, however, this crisis represented not a nuisance but an opportunity. The university was being given a better chance than ever before to throw out a dragnet for talent and to salvage abilities. Testing must become more sensitively accurate so that this new type of student might be guided into his proper place within the university's pattern. Professor Richard Elliott created new examinations to discover mechanical abilities; Professor

164

William Brooke, one for aptitude in mathematics. No door must be left closed upon a student; self-understanding must lead him over the threshold into his own realm.

That Minnesota had taken leadership in this field other colleges and universities tacitly acknowledged by borrowing its tests. Dean Johnston's office became a clearinghouse of ideas. When the American Council of Education established its Advisory Committee on Testing, Johnston became its chairman.

It is, perhaps, the measure of Dean Johnston's conscientiousness as educator that, when he retired in 1937, he thought of the work to which he had given his life as barely begun. He was still unpersuaded that the university could be expected to cope successfully with the numbers sent to it and he passed out of the academic world still carrying the precious burden of his uncompromising idealism.

His example, if not his exact philosophy, still stimulated his successors. In 1941 other retirements left gaps in the university's counseling departments and the Committee of Seven advised a complete reorganization of its efforts. There must be, they urged, "some official or officials to whom students may turn with their human problems, for discussion, aid and advice." They offered innovative suggestions and out of the discussions that followed there grew a service which, at the time of its creation, was unique in the land-grant colleges.

In a new pattern of organization, the Dean of Students became the presiding official in charge of welfare activities. He has under his eye supervision of loans, scholarships, counseling, housing, student social life (including that of the Greek-letter fraternities), coordination of religious interests; in fact, every concern of the individual in a complex society. The Students' Counseling Bureau (descendant of the old Testing Bureau, renamed in acknowledgment of its broadened responsibility) is the agency through which he supervises the student's progress in the classroom. It first anticipates and later supports a full program of faculty counseling on academic matters.

Each college of the university has its own student personnel service. Members of the freshman and sophomore classes in the Arts college are assigned to advisers appointed by the Junior Counseling office. This member of the faculty reviews the student's test scores and assists in planning his program. After registration the student is assigned to a permanent adviser to whom he may go with any scholastic problem. In the third quarter of the sophomore year, an undergraduate may ask the Senior College office for further guidance. At last when he actually enters the junior year he is assigned to a major adviser who helps to plan his work for the remainder of his career, either in the Senior division of the Arts college or in one of the professional schools. In addition to all this, a Student Work Committee of the Arts college assumes responsibility for the interpretation to the student of all academic regulations.

None of these agencies is intended to take an aggressively disciplinary interest in the student. They exist to make him aware of how well or how inadequately he is progressing toward a goal. Indeed the philosophy of the dean of students, as expressed by Williamson, is that he and the students are fellow participants in an "experiment in understanding." While his office appraises the student, it also appraises itself in a constant effort to improve the university's service to the student as a human being with psychological adjustments to make.

It is no accident that Minnesota's name has become attached permanently to a testing device that is thought to have exercised a profound influence on practices of psychiatric diagnosis throughout the country. The Minnesota Multiphasic Personality Inventory—created by Dr. J. Charney McKinley and Dr. Starke Hathaway—explores the hidden recesses of the student mind, not to expose weaknesses, but to coordinate strengths. The university has assumed the responsibility toward the individual student of helping him to keep a sane mind in a healthy body so that he may move forward steadily toward fulfillment of his intellectual capacity.

Whatever may be the flaws of so gigantic an effort (however sad may be an individual failure to respond to its purpose) it cannot be said that Minnesota has failed to deal with the problem of bigness. The old resounding phrases of reproach—soulless machine, pulverizing human material blindly; jungle of data in which innocents wander lost—sound hollow, indeed, in an atmosphere where freedom and discipline have been made to conspire so wholesomely together.

This is the temper in which Minnesota has developed its particular kind of "student-centered" philosophy. Its intent has never been to encourage him in mediocrity. Rather it has insisted on finding the top level of his abilities. As Williamson once said, it would be "a terrible indictment" of an educational system if fine intelligences were to be degraded into commonplaceness simply because no one knew what to do with them. The "Minnesota point of view" has been that excellence is not "undemocratic." The traditional snobbism that "C is the gentleman's grade" has long been dead there. An elite has not only survived but has thrived under Coffman's philosophy.

Yet during his administration there was scarcely a moment of the serenity that Northrop had once claimed for his period. The last years of the Coffman regime, 1930–1938, were darkened by depression conditions just as its first years had been. Once more the legislature sharpened its pencil to cut the budget.

Floyd B. Olson, commanding spirit of one of Minnesota's periodically recurring third-party movements, became the Farmer-Labor governor of Minnesota in a moment of drastic emergency. But he refused to allow the university to become its victim. It would be "false economy," he said, to cut appropriations. It would be far better to leave the university unhandicapped so that it might "assist the people in our unemployment situation."

It is interesting that Olson should have felt so sympathetic toward the university, for in his youth the institution had dealt

167

harshly with him. Hard-pressed by poverty, Olson had found himself dropped from the law school in 1911 for nonpayment of fees. But his philosophy was high-spirited to the point of recklessness and in it personal spite had no place.

Coffman's own view of the university was similar to that of Olson. He saw it as a "public service corporation" created by the people and in duty bound to serve the people's needs. He and Olson, the one as conservative in his personal politics as the other was radical, made common cause to insure the university's stability. In Coffman's words, it must be allowed to continue its usefulness as an institution that could "utilize scientific resources to the utmost to create better living conditions and to create new wealth."

By 1933 when the foundations of the midwestern economy had finally cracked under the successive shocks following the collapse of the New York stock market, it was evident that the student community would dwindle disastrously if help were not provided. Coffman presented the problem to Olson who, remembering what it was like to be a penniless young man, agreed to back any promising plan. Within a month the president of the university, as chairman of a committee appointed by the governor, had outlined a proposal for student aid. The Federal Emergency Relief Administration adopted it immediately—the first effort of the kind to be made in the United States.

Once more the crusading schoolmaster had taken the initiative in devising a program which offered a model for the entire country. Only six months after Coffman's first plea to Olson that a critical need existed, his plan had been put into operation, not merely at Minnesota, but in all nonprofit-making collegiate institutions in the country.

Malcolm Willey, university dean and assistant to the president (later vice-president of the university) assumed active charge. His special committee took on the job of selecting students to receive aid. Remembering the nightmare of the SATC, these experts screened carefully. This time there came together no army of displaced persons, lacking proper credentials. The first men and women to be considered were students already in residence. After their needs had been met, new students with superior records were invited to apply for federal aid. Among these, sons and daughters of families on relief received first attention. Even the balance between men and women students was maintained at the normal ratio of 60 per cent to 40 per cent.

Coffman might well have looked upon his work and seen that it was good. In this emergency the university was doing on a large scale what he had always insisted it must do. It received all promising students no matter how little they might be able to pay for instruction.

Allowances were far from princely: fifteen dollars a month. To this the governor added ten dollars more out of state funds. Coddling was scarcely the word for such attention, yet it made the enormous difference, for many young people, between frustration and hope.

The "federal students" worked hard for a living between classes. They served as examination-readers, cafeteria assistants, typists, laborers on the grounds, even as art models. Prophets of disaster had warned that the group would constitute a special class of untouchables whose consciousness of inferiority would taint campus life. They need not have worried. The federal students were delighted with their status, and enjoyed their nonacademic tasks (as questionnaires revealed again and again). While they participated in all normal undergraduate activities, they clung to their specialness at least enough to organize their own parties to which the president of the university and the governor of the state were ceremoniously invited. They were really *special* only in the sense that, as a group, they were well above the average in scholarship.

There were many names for the agency of which these students were wards. It became, at last, the National Youth Administration. As such its guardianship was further expanded to include graduates of universities who had been beached by the contrary winds of the depression and were unable to practice their professions. Harry Hopkins, as head of the

NYA, was particularly concerned for their welfare. Why not, he asked, send them back to the universities to put their special aptitudes back to work?

And so there began what has been called "the golden age of research in the universities." Time has always been of the essence of the contract in research, as every laboratory man knows. A Minnesota scientist once pointed out that many a man of ideas has hesitated to institute a research project because he knew in advance "how indifferently he must go about it." As washer of his own glassware, feeder of his own animals and keeper of his own records he had little time left for experimentation itself. Now, suddenly, the depression which had destroyed so much had managed to create time—a great reservoir of man-hours. All that was needed was to bring men and projects together.

They were brought together at many universities to the enduring benefit of science. Men and women from the relief rolls of the Work Projects Administration, many of them highly trained, entered the laboratories of the St. Paul campus and the Minneapolis campus to give support of inestimable importance to projects of many kinds. A scrupulously accurate witness, Dr. Maurice Visscher, has testified with regard to this golden age that many of Minnesota's cancer studies "could not have been carried on without this assistance."

Frivolous and uninformed satirists of the "leaf-sweeping movement" should be invited to take notice of the fact that the "made work" of the depression period has left many monuments to the spirit of man. America's touching faith in the magic of education was never before so fully justified as in this moment. For the universities were able to bring triumph out of tragedy and an increased store of knowledge out of the collapse of the false values that had shaken the economic world.

It was under the sobering conditions of the depression that Minnesota's student body seemed to reach maturity. The prevailing tone of its leadership became subdued, thoughtful,

170

concerned with the important issues of the day. Stimulated by a set of surcharged young intelligences, belonging to members of the "Jacobin Club," students crowded into a succession of mock political conventions, mass meetings and forums, to hear sometimes earnest, sometimes feverish appraisals of fascism, communism, the movement to outlaw war. One of these student leaders was Eric Sevareid (known to his contemporaries on the campus by his other name, Arnold). In the pages of the *Daily* he tugged and prodded the student mind into attention. His now world-famous earnestness urged upon tomorrow's electorate a rededication to democratic values.

One of his objectives was to rid the student body of the burden of compulsory military drill. As he later wrote in his autobiographical study *Not So Wild a Dream*, there seemed to be "something revoltingly ignoble about the process of jerking arms and legs this way and that to the shouted orders of a beetle-browed sergeant."

For sixty years it had been considered to be an inescapable duty of the land-grant college to require students to take drill. The Morrill Act provided that schools receiving its endowment were to teach agriculture and mechanic arts "without excluding other studies and including military tactics." After World War I had made the United States conscious that it lived in a potentially explosive world, the War Department had organized the Reserve Officers Training Corps. Beginning in 1920, all students had been compelled to enroll in it.

Now, however, protests against war-mindedness began to be heard in colleges everywhere. The most dramatic version of rebellion was that of the young men of Oxford who offered the world of youth its famous oath not to "bear arms for flag or country." The impulse of imitation flashed across the United States touching off revolts at California, Maryland and Ohio. Wisconsin made drill optional. De Pauw abolished it entirely. The learned journals were full of discussions as to whether or not the program should be maintained. Minnesota's Dean Johnston offered the suggestion that, under a new interpretation of the law, students might be trained for the emergency of war, not by going through the largely ineffective preparation for the battlefield, but by special instruction in their own fields—chemistry, physics, navigation, electronics. Their task would be to "support the military arm." Dean Freeman explored the idea further with the proposal that, since defense of the nation was what everyone wanted, students of law, government, public health, dentistry and every other academic subject could make their contribution toward preparedness by studying courses that would show how law, government, public health and the rest could serve in any war situation. "So, the irritating problem of military drill would," he thought, "vanish into thin air."

Meanwhile a former Minnesotan, William Mitchell, then Attorney General of the United States, gave down the opinion that "an agricultural college which offers a proper and substantial course in military tactics complies sufficiently with the requirements even though students are not compelled to take the course."

Now the issue was in the open and the peace-lovers began to shoot off their glitteringly innocent fireworks. Passive resistance developed its own kind of force, and the tone of the pacifists became curiously belligerent. The regents were bombarded with demands that drill be dropped or that it be made optional. A brilliant philosophy student offered himself as a martyr by refusing to report for military training. At a student forum young men rose and recited the Oxford oath in unison.

Coffman, though his personal convictions were strong and though he was more than ordinarily well supplied with male assertiveness, behaved with fine reserve, even with indulgence. Once more he was in direct opposition to the prevailing sentiment among students. He believed in the necessity of military training. His travels, as educational adviser to other countries, had taken him far. He had been in New Zealand and Australia on one excursion and, in 1928, before the iron door clanged shut, he had visited Russia. His observations made

172

him sure that economic conflicts would grow greater as distances between neighbors shrank. He was sure, too, that the Soviet government had not foresworn its enmity toward the West. Europe could not fail once more to become a battlefield.

Nor did he believe that the United States was in a position to take the lead in disarmament. Though he "deplored all forms of excessive emotion and super-patriotism that lead to war," he saw that his own country had made "little progress in developing sentiment favoring peace." The United States was not even a member of the League of Nations. Its resistance to proposals for international cooperation did not promise much in the way of peaceful negotiation. This, surely, was no mood in which to renounce the idea of military preparedness.

But, despite all these firm convictions, Coffman did not permit himself to play the role of intransigent schoolmaster. He refused to expel the rebellious philosophy student. He did nothing to discourage mass meetings as he had done earlier in his career. Even when a "peace strike" was organized against his administration and its policies, he made no attempt to exercise discipline. Even the request to use Northrop Auditorium in which to stage a great protest gathering brought no rebuke. Permission was not granted, of course. It would have been a strange irony to have required Northrop, the conciliator, to preside in spirit over an outburst of open revolt. ("Prexy" certainly wouldn't have liked it.) It would have been an even greater irony to have forced Coffman, who had protected the university so often against outside interference, to abdicate his independence to the dictatorship of students.

However, the meeting took place on the steps of the Auditorium with Governor Olson as its chief speaker. The president watched it from the window of his office in the administration building across the mall. It must have seemed to him an altogether fantastic occasion. At its climax a student orator shouted, in full release of his feverish emotion: "Next time when they come and tell us we must invade the land of some other misguided people we will not listen to the scream for slaughter."

Yet even this utterance, though it was not notable for restraint, may have pleased Coffman a little. The session which took place on the steps of Northrop Auditorium demonstrated two things simultaneously: first, that the university still knew how to protect its own integrity; and, second, that it was determined to protect freedom of speech even for those with whom it disagreed.

He was, however, to lose the fight. In 1933 the board of regents was a different body from the one which had long stood firm on the issue of military drill. Three men and one woman of Governor Olson's political party had become members. One of the first acts of the group was to make drill optional by a vote of six to five.

During the military drill struggle, Coffman had been constantly under fire from the political left. On one occasion a young member of the legislature's university committee gave himself the privilege of a democrat, untrammeled by niceties of feeling, to ask: "Mr. Coffman, what is your salary?"

The same challenge had once been tossed at Vincent, coupled in more provocative tone with a second demand: "Do you think you earn it?" He is said to have remembered the moment, not bitterly but unhopefully, when, a few weeks later, he had to ask himself the question of whether or not he would resign to go to the Rockefeller Foundation.

Coffman's response was characteristic of the self-disciplined schoolmaster he had become. He took off his glasses and passed a hand slowly over his head. Associates who knew him well recognized these as gestures of soothing his own ruffled feelings.

"Young man," he answered, speaking with more than his usual crispness, "I am glad to tell you what my salary is." (He named the figure.) "I'm sure you would like to know also about other earnings. Inside Minnesota I accept no fees for speechs. Outside the state I do. When my expenses have been paid, I turn over what is left to a scholarship which my old

174

college, Education, has done me the honor to create in my name.

"I think you should know, young man, that I could double my earnings tomorrow by accepting a standing offer that I have elsewhere. One reason why I don't accept it is that I received this university from my predecessor unburdened and unhandicapped by political influence. I shall never resign until I can hand it over to my successor the same way. And that I could not do today. Young man, have I made myself clear?"

He had at least made himself clear to those who were capable of understanding overtones and of appreciating integrity.

Faithful democrat that he was, Coffman was able to accept defeat in the matter of military drill without suffering any bitterness. Still unpersuaded that wisdom had prevailed, he allowed himself to say only that there was, at the moment, "no public sanction for this social need."

It would have interested him to have watched the epilogue to the drama. When America entered World War II—Coffman had been sure that it must share in another global crisis— Lee Loevinger, the young man who had said that he would not listen to the "scream for slaughter," went on the first naval mission to England. And it was the voice of Eric Sevareid—Coffman's most articulate opponent among the student rebels—that brought from every theater of action news of the "war for survival." Curiously unreconciled to Coffman as a man, Sevareid nonetheless made an amende honorable to him as theorist and thinker. In his autobiography, he asks the question: "Why did we help however minutely to disarm our country?" And he comments in rueful apology: "We, along with college men and women all over America, were involved in an astonishing paradox."

Coffman's tenacity of purpose is touchingly dramatized in the fact that he is the only one of Minnesota's presidents to have died in office. He suffered so severe a heart attack during the summer of 1937 that he was obliged to take a year's leave. But, still unable to acknowledge a limitation of any kind, he was preparing in September, 1938, to take up his tasks once more. He had worked all evening at an address to be given before the opening convocation when he had another heart attack and died.

But he had accomplished what he meant to do for the university. The crusading schoolmaster had followed his own exacting rule by learning, each year, more and more about the techniques of the job. He had broadened his philosophic outlook so conspicuously that even the deans who had feared that he might be only a narrow pedagogue had ended by calling him an educational statesman.

Building on the organization refounded by Vincent, he had expanded university opportunity both horizontally and vertically. New units, like the General College and the Center for Continuation Study, broadened the base on which the institution stood. New facilities for higher learning and for research strengthened its upward reach. With perennially youthful enthusiasm he had protected the self-dependence of the university against all comers. He had defended it, from without, against partisan politics and, from within, against regents who would have limited his right to protect academic freedom. Conservative in his own outlook, he had given no aid or comfort to those who would have invaded the university "to clean out the nests of radicals," as extremists of the right were fond of saying that they wished to do. No less vigorously, he refused to allow the university to become "a sounding board of propaganda" tossed off by extremists of the left. His own stanch occupancy of the middle ground strengthened the university's position as a stronghold of the liberal mind. Coffman kept it "open and tolerant, ready to face new situations and to interpret them in terms of social welfare."

On high ground above the Mississippi River at the end of the mall stands the Coffman Memorial Union. It was added to the campus after the president's death. The building commands a sweeping view of the university world and of the city across the river. Its rooms are always full of students, grouped around the piano in the great hall, sharing meals in the many dining rooms, holding conferences, playing games. It is the handsome, comfortable, much-used center of student life.

It is appropriate that this place should be presented to the newcomer as the outward and visible sign of Coffman's concern with students. He instigated the writing of their Magna Carta; he devoted his life to salvaging their abilities; his only ambition was to promote their finest ambitions.

But the university itself—the big university with flexible sinews, responsive nerves, and unlimited intellectual sympathies—this is his real monument. He helped the institution to grow by giving it unreservedly of his own inexhaustible creative drive. Men who were close to his administration came to feel that it was impossible to distinguish between the university and Coffman because they were one. The president influenced every decision, guided every movement, virtually put his initials to every document. And as he made ready to end his career he signed, sealed and delivered to his successors an institution that was as much of his making as Vincent's university had been in his time.

CHAPTER SEVEN

DEFINER OF A FAITH

M EN WHO HAD BEEN LONG at Minnesota found themselves fearing the effect of Coffman's death as much as they had, long ago, feared the effect of his elevation to the presidency. In the course of his long administration he had so completely justified his purposes that a continuation of them was what was most to be desired. Another period of disruptive uncertainty could scarcely have been endured by faculties that were now accustomed to a strong directive influence.

Happily, the key to continuity lay close to a highly experienced hand—that of Guy Stanton Ford—and he was persuaded to use it.

Close to Vincent, as delegate in the task of refounding the Graduate School, Ford had also been close to Coffman as virtual collaborator in the great enterprise of supervising the university's growth. The late president himself had said that the "contributions to general administration" made by his senior dean had been "invaluable." On two occasions Ford had temporarily supplanted the president and acted in his place during long absences from the campus.

The first of these occurred in 1931 when Coffman was invited to visit New Zealand, Australia and the Philippines as a consultant on educational problems. (He had traveled also as representative of the Carnegie Endowment for International Peace.) The president had been reluctant to go, but Ford had insisted that so fine an opportunity must not be missed. Again in 1937, when Coffman's heart attack had

178

forced him to take a leave, Ford had become acting president.

In the course of his long career in the Graduate School, the dean himself had been called upon many times for temporary service to national organizations. During World War I, Washington had drafted him to become head of the division for educational publications of the Committee on Public Information. In 1924 the Laura Spelman Fund had sent him to Germany to advise the conquered country on rehabilitation of its libraries. He had served frequently on committees to name Rhodes scholars and Guggenheim fellows. Besides all this, he was a tireless traveler from session to session of the American Historical Society and of the Association of American Universities.

Ford once said of Vincent that he had the incomparable gift of imparting enthusiasm to intellectual pursuits. So complete was the sympathy between the two men that one may borrow the words to describe Ford himself. He loved the academic round: lecturing to classes in history which became so popular that they had to be scheduled for halls that would seat six hundred; presiding over endless committee meetings and pulling their sentiments together into neat, epigrammatic statements; directing the administrative work of the Graduate School; participating in every aspect of university work, from wording a top-level decision on policy to interviewing candidates for fellowships.

This was all part of his major passion which was for collecting men. His various assignments had given him as wide an acquaintance with scholarly manpower as anyone in the academic world could then claim. It had been his policy to lure as many such men as possible into the graduate faculty at Minnesota. It must, he insisted ever more emphatically, be a distinguished group—one that was capable of justifying its existence by contributing to basic knowledge.

"I have no sympathy," he once wrote, "with a college president who through a series of years neglects the opportunity to build up a faculty that can turn out alumni who will establish their institution's credit before the educational world.

Let your faculty have freedom. It pays to gamble on getting worth-while men."

Nor did he look only in the obvious places for outstanding leaders. Quality might show itself anywhere to the discerning eye. Indeed, a special value might reveal itself in a man who had managed to "survive residence in a monohippic institution called a college."

Ford was fond of this word that he had coined to mean "one-horse." Latin, he obviously felt, belonged to him more particularly than to most men, for he had wrestled with the language in his youth and won a unique victory over it. When he decided to take his Ph.D. at Columbia, he learned that a knowledge of Latin was required of all candidates. Having eluded it earlier, he cheerfully undertook to teach it to himself during one busy summer. On long walks at night he chanted conjugations, disciplining the irregularities of verbs with the same confident authority he had used in disciplining all the days and nights of his life.

One other cardinal principle had guided his activity in the Graduate School. It was to indulge in no snobbish notions about "purity" in research. He wanted no interference from "stiff-necked arts faculties" with "narrow" interpretations of their jobs as investigators. The world was Ford's laboratory and everything in it his material. "Let us concern ourselves," he said, "more with the spirit and qualifications of teachers who undertake research, less with subject matter. One of the best young geneticists I know is concerned with hens and roosters. If you exclude such men you would exclude Pasteur."

The result of Ford's broad acquaintance with men capable of doing significant research, and also of his broad sympathy with all their purposes, was that the Graduate School grew from a student enrollment, in his first year as dean, of 175 candidates to 3300 in the year before he moved into the president's office.

Under his influence many top-ranking scholars thrived at Minnesota. To physics he brought John Tate (Ph.D., University of Berlin), who managed in the course of his career to combine the task of directing research in his own field with editorship of the *Physical Review,* chairmanship of the committee for University College and, finally, deanship of the Arts college itself.

To political science came a distinguished group of men each of whom seemed to have heard Folwell speaking to him directly. With him they shared the belief that the "University of the Twentieth Century" must train all men to be intelligent inheritors of the privilege of self-government and that it must equip leaders to be creative interpreters of the highest functions of public office. William Anderson (A.B., University of Minnesota; Ph.D., Harvard) accepted the task of broadening the work of the Municipal Reference Bureau. As director he undertook to reduce problems of state planning, charter making, and interpretation of constitutions to the terms of an exact science. To mayors and legislators, potential and actual, he opened up all the insights of a genuine laboratory of government.

Morris Lambie (Ph.D., Harvard) while he was at Minnesota, before his return to Harvard, became obsessed with the idea that graduate studies in administrative problems should offer practical training for public service. It was no longer possible, in his opinion, to leave the work of public officials to amateurs. The universities must assume the job of training a citizen army of experts. Lambie was influential in organizing a series of national conferences in the course of which the concept grew. At last, in 1936, the Public Administration Center was established at Minnesota with the support of funds from the Rockefeller Foundation. Once more the graduate faculty which Ford had done so much to build up was able to make a genuinely creative contribution to the techniques of education.

Other recruits of the dean's time were Harold Quigley and Harold C. Deutsch, who were to share the task of developing Minnesota's plan of courses in International Relations and Area Studies. The lead that Coffman and Ford had taken together in "reorganizing the materials of education" showed the liveliest kind of results in this field. The idea, which has spread through American education today in response to the challenge of the one-world concept, is to awaken the student mind to the interesting complexity of the unfamiliar corners of the globe by turning upon them, all at once, the search-lights of anthropology, language study, economics, sociology and political science. The old routines which kept each academic subject in its tight compartment are being freed to reveal the unity of knowledge in its application to human affairs. Ford's vigorous graduate faculty may be credited with an important share in the movement to make education really liberal in its concern with international relations. Minnesota students have been offered fine opportunities to train themselves for service in world affairs.

To sociology there came in the same period the man who was to build up Minnesota's influential School of Social Work. F. Stuart Chapin, its chief creator, came to the state at a moment when farm foreclosures were daily occurrences in the lives of hundreds in the agricultural community. The drift of idle men and women into the cities produced a critical situation with which the university, as service agency, felt obliged to deal. Seizing upon the emergency, Stuart Chapin transformed it into a kind of opportunity. Greatly expanding its activities, the department of sociology received, at the graduate level, a great army of students to take intensive and immediately practical instruction for the task of offsetting this social breakdown. Six settlement houses of the Twin Cities were served, under a kind of internship program, by young men and women from the university. They coached sports, gave medical care, offered psychological guidance and directed the efforts of volunteer workers.

The undertaking had a distinguished success. As its cool-headed guide, Chapin worked on the principle that "a sort of tough and sinewy elasticity" in the American social body "facilitates adaptation to sudden change." All that it needed was a certain disciplined steering "through the swirling eddies

182

of innovation." The unhysterical adaptability trained into Chapin's students made his course famous. In the early 1940s its advanced students constituted one of the largest groups in the Graduate School. In 1942 the School of Social Work was made a separate unit within the Arts college.

Even before he had been made president of the university, Ford was called upon to preside over the solution of major problems. One of these was the easing of the institution's conscience in the *cause célèbre* known as the Schaper case.

The memory of that injustice deeply troubled those who wished to see the university's brave words about academic freedom justified by deeds. In 1937, while Ford was acting president, the circumstances of that dismissal were thoroughly re-examined. Removed by twenty years from the dusty arena of discussion where fear had troubled all other consideration, the case was studied in an atmosphere much more like that of a laboratory, sterilized of all prejudice.

This time no hysteria was evident. Even those who played principle parts in this drama of penance entered the case without exhibitionistic enthusiasm. Chiefly involved were two close personal friends, fellow historians, who wanted only to see that justice was done and a new precedent set for the protection of academic freedom.

Charles Beard, veteran champion of causes, had been asked to make a public issue of the Schaper case. To his intimate associate, Ford, he wrote: "It seems that when there is any trouble I am chosen to be the goat." Ford answered sympathetically, yet with a word of caution, suggesting that "discriminating friends of Schaper" must regret seeing the matter reopened. Schaper had, indeed, been a difficult colleague, thorny with apprehensions for his own prestige. "If you knew him," Ford added, "you could easily see how the whole German people had become obsessed with the encirclement idea."

Nonetheless Beard persevered. In the *New Republic* he presented the matter as one that offered an opportunity to strike a blow for abstract justice. Professor Schaper, he pointed out, had long since found another academic assignment (at the University of Oklahoma); he needed no personal relief. But, Beard insisted, "the university by confessing that it charged Schaper falsely in 1917 will give encouragement to all who labor for the maintenance of liberty in inquiry and teaching and will, through forgetting the pique of pride, lift itself into immortality."

At the same moment Elmer Benson, successor to Floyd Olson in the governor's chair, was also urging immediate action. "The integrity of the classroom and of the teaching profession must be preserved," he wrote, echoing what Coffman had said to the state government in the evolution fight.

University officials, clearly aware that they owed a duty, not merely to academic freedom but to their own religion of self-appraisal as well, began a thorough review. At Ford's request, his administrative assistant, Malcolm Willey, prepared a report. It ended with the recommendation that the university make "a gesture that will indicate that we now in 1938 are aware that war hysteria does produce actions that in our more balanced moments we regret."

Finally, and once more at the request of the acting president, Willey drafted a resolution to be presented to the regents. Its central idea was that "the classroom must be regarded as the teacher's castle." The university should impose no limitation on a teacher's exposition of his subject in the classroom and should put no restriction on his choice of research problems. Correspondingly, the teacher must not abuse his rights by introducing "controversial subjects not pertinent to the course of study being pursued." In speaking or writing outside the university "on subjects beyond the scope of his own field he is entitled to the same freedom and subject to the same responsibilities as attach to any citizen but in added measure." Willey's statement declared the university to be free of responsibility for the private views of faculty members. It concluded with the important commitment to principle that, should a question of a teacher's fitness arise, this must be submitted, first, to a committee of the faculty. Any decision would be subject to review before the board of regents, but "only upon sufficient notice."

Willey's resolution was based, in part, on principles enunciated earlier by the American Association of University Professors. Its adoption by the regents offered public endorsement of the general theory of education and enabled one important institution to go on record, in a test case, as being willing to take a stand even under difficult circumstances. The resolution of the Schaper case accomplished what Charles Beard had hoped that it might. For here was a voluntary commitment to principle that might offer an example to other universities in other moments of doubt. Its importance was far greater than that of a mere local incident.

The drama ended on a note as quiet as that of its opening scene had been shrill. Schaper was "rehabilitated" as professor emeritus. A sum of money equal to the salary lost for the academic year 1917–18 was voted by an entirely tranquil board.

It is true that one member of the board of regents abstained from voting. The veteran Fred Snyder had been a member of the group that had dismissed Schaper and he felt he "could not let the old board down." He spoke as a lawyer in saying publicly that he could not vote on a review into which "no new evidence had been introduced." But this display of loyalty, accomplished with no rancor, did not undermine the spirit of the occasion. There was universal satifaction with the day's work, and the solution of the Schaper case strengthened—as it dramatized—the devotion of the community to "our university," now renewed and replenished in self-respect.

Ford wrote the event into the record of his administration with fine sobriety. But he wrote it off, with attractive jauntiness, in a private letter to Beard. "After yesterday's session of the Board of Regents," he told his old friend, "I just want to say to you that it is a damn sight easier to sit in New Milford and write letters to the *New Republic* than it is to

185

get something done and done right. I hope you will agree that that is what the Board has done."

Quick to build on this achievement, Professor Benjamin Lippincott spurred the appointment of a committee of the senate to establish fixed principles for tenure. The work progressed slowly and was interrupted when Lippincott, along with many of his colleagues, went to World War II. Effort was revived in 1945 and was brought to successful conclusion in an enlightened and eminently workable program.

In September, 1938, Ford was preparing to return to his job in the Graduate School when suddenly he was called to the president's house to receive the news of Coffman's death. In this not unexpected, yet unprepared-for, crisis, a kind of paralysis seemed to settle on the minds of the members of the board of regents. There were sharp differences of personal opinion among them on many questions. The one thing on which they seemed to agree was that this was an awkward moment in which to have to choose a new president.

The chief difficulty was that the conservative element feared the influence of those members who had affiliations with the Farmer-Labor party. It would be the effort of the "radical group" to name, as president, a social experimenter of leftist tendency. At least so the others feared. Each group within the board was uncertain of its ability to control the choice and each hesitated to risk a decision.

Actually, political pressure had never been brought upon any member of the board—conservative or liberal—to act against his own convictions. One member named to the board by Governor Olson had good reason to know that he was not expected to deliver his vote into the keeping of the Farmer-Labor party. As secretary of the Minnesota Federation of Labor, George Lawson occupied a conspicuous post. But its interests were locked up securely in his St. Paul office when he traveled to the campus to serve as regent. And that, Governor Olson had said by implication, was as it must be.

Lawson himself has told the story of his appointment. It

came quite unexpectedly as he and the governor were discussing other matters. Olson asked suddenly: "George, what do you know about the university?" Very little, Lawson admitted. "Then," said Olson, "you'd better begin learning because I'm going to make you a regent."

(There was at the time a certain vagueness about the appointment of regents and governors of the state had been filling vacancies on their own authority. Practices have become clarified since that time, and members of the board are elected by the legislature on the recommendation of the governor.)

At the time of their first conversation Lawson was by no means eager to accept Olson's offer. Just as Pillsbury had once done, he protested that he could not become a regent because he was not a college man. This argument Olson brushed aside as having no relevance. "But," Lawson still objected, "I may not be able to do the things that you want me to do there."

Olson laughed. "There's just one promise I want you to make me," he said, "that you'll attend all the meetings."

And that, Lawson said much later, "was the beginning and the end of Olson's effort to influence my vote on the board of regents."

Fred Snyder was also aware that the Farmer-Labor members had shown no tendency to constitute themselves a special bloc within the board. As he wrote in a private letter to a former colleague among the regents: "The governor has appointed four so-called radicals. Strangely enough, they have been assimilated by the Board and no radical action has appeared as a result of their appointment save and excepting the abolishment of compulsory military drill. I have found in my long service that the responsibility of serving on the Board mellows the judgements and views of those who become Regents."

And still he feared that the choice of a president might prove to be another exception. So the stalemate continued.

Everyone would have been pleased with the arrangement of having Ford continue indefinitely as acting president.

Everyone, that is, with the exception of Ford himself. If he were to be president now, he decided, he must be so in name as well as in fact. During his twenty-five years at Minnesota he had had many offers to go elsewhere. The Spelman Fund (before it was merged with the Rockefeller Foundation) had wanted him as its head. The University of Texas had looked hopefully toward him when it had a presidency to offer. Other universities had come rapping at his door with similar suggestions, but he had said No firmly in all preliminary discussions. He could not bring himself to leave Minnesota because he had so strong a sense of identification with the place he had helped enormously to build.

Still the talk of whether or not to make him president dragged on and on. Several of the regents approached him privately to say how deeply they admired him. But these votes of confidence were still not votes for the office. Ford was asked solemnly to remember that at sixty-five only three years of his academic career remained. Would it not be better, they urged, to spend them still as acting president? Among these was George Lawson who salted his faith in Ford with doubt of fate itself. Was it not tempting fate to commit the university to another administration as short as Burton's had been?

But Ford stood firm. No title, no Ford. And presently the academic world came to his support. Many members of his graduate faculty urged his election. His old president, George Vincent, sent a wire urgently recommending the appointment.

As the day approached when the matter must be decided it was still clear to Fred Snyder that the board was evenly divided. And in the end it was George Lawson who made the decision. Summoned home from a Federation of Labor meeting in New Orleans, he broke the deadlock by casting his vote for Ford.

It was a triumph of the democratic process and of the benevolent, if erratic, influence that its temper works on human affairs. Ford himself was the author of a brilliant anatomization of that spirit. Its strength, he wrote, arises from that fact that it is "born in dissent and preserved by doubt."

Ford greeted the board for the first time in his role as president with a briskly ironic challenge. "I am young and impetuous," he said. It would be for the board to check his boyish ardors.

But, in a sense, George Lawson had been prophetic. The period of Ford's presidency proved to be no time for innovation. Fate indeed had intervened.

The administration began in 1938 just at the moment when Germany had become obsessed once more with the "encirclement idea." With the *Anschluss*, Hitler made the first of his extravagant bids for the ownership of the world. And Pearl Harbor lay only a few months ahead in history when the Ford administration ended. In that three-year pause, before the United States joined in the struggle for the survival of civilization, the best thing that a university could do was to manage to survive. As Ford once said, speaking of ways in which democracy could fight Fascism: "The edge and very substance of inimical doctrine is nowhere more quickly worn away than in a university."

It was Ford also who worded Minnesota's credo, carved over the entrance to Northrop Auditorium:

Founded in the faith that men are ennobled by understanding
Dedicated to the advancement of learning and the search for truth
Devoted to the instruction of youth and the welfare of the state

For nearly thirty years, as dean, acting president and president—a period of influence longer even than that of Northrop and five times as long as that of Vincent—he put that philosophy into daily operation. More than any one man of Minnesota Ford deserves to be called the definer of its faith.

CHAPTER EIGHT

MASTER OF CRISES

THE SEVENTH PRESIDENT of the university, Walter Castella Coffey, was one of the most popular figures of all the state's history. As broad of shoulder as he was of outlook, as cool and disciplined in the conduct of affairs as he was warm and convivial in human relations, he recommended himself to fellow teachers, to the legislature, to the agricultural community, to the citizens of cities and towns—large and small. And he did so without the sacrifice of the smallest fragment of the solid self-esteem that made him, before all else, a man of principle.

When he first arrived in Minnesota as dean of the Department of Agriculture, a group of farm leaders, who were familiar with the fine work he had done previously at the University of Illinois, gave a dinner in his honor. The hosts belonged to the company of overzealous enthusiasts who held that the teaching of agricultural studies was the only significant responsibility of a land-grant school.

"We want you to know," said one, when the fraternal temper of the occasion had been comfortably established, "that we don't give a damn for the rest of the university. But you can have anything you want."

Coffey thanked them and then added firmly: "However, I have to say that I could never accept anything for my department that might hurt the university as a whole."

His successor in the presidency was to phrase in three words the philosophy that animated Coffey's performance as administrator. "Education is indivisible," James Lewis Morrill liked to say. To Coffey this meant that the strength of the university sprang out of the health of its whole body, the vigorous and effective coordination of all its parts. He would no more listen to nonsense about the superior claims of agriculture than he would have listened to patronizing talk about the superiority of the colleges that were concerned with "pure" scientific investigation. All must work together with one purpose: "to weave the fabric of life" for the protection and comfort of all men everywhere.

As Coffey said in his valedictory to his life's work:

"Were the University to disappear as with the wave of a magician's wand everyone would recognize how completely and fundamentally its activities have become interwoven with the fabric of life in Minnesota. There is scarcely a family with whom it has not had instructional contact; the results of its research have made life better and more secure in rural and metropolitan areas alike; its services, whether in providing medical care for the sick, in helping the farmer with his problems, or in aiding industry and the professions, ramify through the entire population."

So it was "our university" as an indestructible unit that Coffey wished always to advance through his own contributions in the field of agriculture.

Despite the flourish of promises made by his first Minnesota friends, Coffey found that the things he wanted for his department were not to be come by easily. The moment of his arrival in Minnesota, July, 1920, was not a propitious one for agriculture. But the new dean was the son of a man who had combined the interests of teaching and farming, back in Indiana, during the harsh days of post Civil War adjustment. Walter Coffey himself had combined these tasks all through his own youth. No one could have been better equipped to face another such crisis in the harsh days of adjustment after World War I.

From old friends of the academic world he received a warm welcome on the Minnesota campus. Both Coffman and Ford had known him at the University of Illinois and valued him as an enterprising colleague. But "time and fate" had arranged a much less cordial reception. In August, 1920, farm prices collapsed and the argricultural community had to begin tightening its belt over shrinking markets. A succession of disasters: loss of credit, foreclosures on farm properties, mass unemployment, migration from rural to urban areas—all these followed in dismal course, reducing the agricultural community of the Midwest to one of its lowest points of recent years.

The effect on the university was immediate. Enrollment on the St. Paul campus fell again and again; 19 per cent in the first year of Coffey's administration as dean, 5 per cent more in the second. The troubles of the 1920s bore a tragic resemblance to those of the first bleak years of the department's history when it was constantly in danger of complete obliteration.

While Congress bickered unrewardingly and rejected every practical suggestion for farm relief, the university could only follow the advice of Voltaire and cultivate its garden by helping what farmers remained on the land to cultivate theirs.

Agents of the extension division took as their project number one the relief of the people's distress. The increase of farm income by better methods of operation became their whole concern. Veterans of World War I, still enrolled in the department's educational program, were put on farms to combine theory and practice as "hands" to hard-pressed wheat growers and dairy operators. There were constant consultations between the laboratory experts of the college and dirt farmers in the fields. By actual record, one million such interviews took place between 1920 and 1927.

Faculty members of the department met frequently with government officials and collaborated with them on measures to alleviate the crisis. They analyzed markets for the benefit of the Federal Tariff Commission and cooperated with the Federal Farm Board on scores of projects.

Meanwhile, the industrial community looked on indul-
192

gently from a distance, imagining that these were merely agriculture's perennial problems and no great concern of anyone else. The stock market crashes of 1929 rudely corrected that impression. But agriculture found no comfort in the universal misery. Tax delinquencies multiplied until it seemed possible that an unintended de-settlement program might return all land to public keeping and the wilderness close in around civilization once more. Even the brash humorists who suggested "giving it back to the Indians" appeared almost to have a point.

But the university continued to cope with basic problems. The "land-use" studies, made by Professor O. B. Jesness in collaboration with the United States Department of Agriculture, looked toward a long-range legislature program designed "to make the best use of available land resources." Jesness emphasized the tragic waste of effort that allowed men to struggle with submarginal lands. He advocated a vigorous plan for reforestation to repair the damage done by the greedy lumbermen of the pioneer period. He offered a proposal for rural zoning. A dramatic sense of the emergency, combined with unintimidated candor in the statement of his point of view, enabled Jesness to draw from his charts and statistics an alarming picture of neglect. Certain whole communities were becalmed in despair, their farms abandoned, their men without work, their women without medical care, their children without schools. Only by taking effective thought for the future *now*, Jesness observed, could the process be reversed. It was a public duty to restore to each community the standard of living which the good soil of Minnesota should be able to maintain.

Using these land-use studies as their guides, the department of agriculture faculties worked with federal agencies—the Agricultural Adjustment Administration and the Production and Marketing Administration—to help the farming economy zigzag back to normal. Their practical success in reversing a deteriorative tendency was so great that, within a decade, the agricultural community of Minnesota was ready to enjoy a period of unequaled prosperity.

Yet the St. Paul campus, like other campuses of the land-grant schools which had been similarly occupied in other parts of the country, received small recognition for its efforts. Many thinkers of the moment continued to regard agricultural education as a dispensable frill. Through its Washington correspondent, Arthur Sears Henning, the *Chicago Tribune* launched a policy of incredible shortsightedness. Its editorials urged the President of the United States to strike from the national budget "all standing appropriations for agricultural education."

Dean Coffey and Dean Freeman were alarmed. "Things are popping fast in this section of the country," Freeman wrote in a private letter, "and the gloom steadily thickens." He and Coffey, he said, were "scurrying around to see if we can stop the cut." In company with like-minded men from other institutions, they scurried to good effect. The cut was not made.

Freeman, like Coffey, was a stanch believer in maintaining the health of the whole university. He saw that, in the evil hour of the depression, agricultural research was more important than ever before. Its successes never failed to contribute to the well-being of the people.

But applied research had always to fight for its rights. In an article for the magazine *Science,* Freeman wrote:

"It has become popular to make a new distinction. *Fundamental* science is claimed as the peculiar field of those not engaged in applied science."

But an absurd and dangerous kind of snobbery betrayed itself in that appropriation of the word fundamental. Mendel, Freeman pointed out, had discovered "a real research gem of very great biological value." Yet he never thought of himself as a "pure scientist." He was a farmer, "moved by the same spirit as is a good experimental station worker of today."

"Is there anything grotesque," he demanded, "in the idea of a state agricultural station functioning as an institute for

194

fundamental science? I cannot see that there is. More than that, I cannot conceive of an agricultural experiment station which is living up to its duties and responsibilities which is not engaged in at least some problems of fundamental science."

Men like Freeman managed, even in the depths of the depression, to keep agricultural research alive by their unceasing demands for support. Even in 1925, when funds were hardest to come by, Congress passed the Purnell Act by which the Minnesota experiment station profited to the extent of $20,-000 a year for research.

It may be claimed for the agricultural colleges of the country that their dedication to research managed, in a bad hour, to preserve the principle of government support for such efforts. The nation has just wakened to the realization that other branches of science would have done well to be equally strenuous in offering their claims. Agriculture showed the way to many laggards.

A team of brilliant men used the federal appropriations to pursue studies that made brilliant contributions to the outlook for agriculture. Dean Freeman himself had been a pioneer in the study of plant diseases. It was inevitable that he should have gathered about him investigators like Elvin K. Stakman, Herbert K. Hayes and Clyde Bailey whose work in the development of disease-resistant grains brought international distinction to the university.

Hayes by crossing and recrossing grain and corn varieties discovered the strains that were most likely to survive under exacting conditions. He and fellow geneticists became so familiar with the characteristics of many strains that they could predict, with the greatest accuracy, the behavior of all types.

Stakman studied the problem of why crops fail. He subjected new strains to every known disease and his investigations clearly identified the feeble or doomed varieties so that agronomists need bother with them no further.

Bailey completed the process by analyzing the composition

of the new grain varieties, testing wheat for its baking quality, barley for its malting aptitude, and flax for its oil content.

Together, they have produced many sturdy and reliable grains, all of which help to lighten the labors of the farmer and to brighten his prospects: Thatcher spring wheat, Mindum durum wheat, excellent for making macaroni; stiff-strawed varieties of oats and barley that do well even in the unsympathetic environment of heavy soil; Vetvet and Glabron barley; Gopher, Anthony and Minrus oats; Chippewa, Winona and Redwing flax; the Minhybrids of the corn family. Fundamental and applied research collaborated on these creations. Their steadily excellent behavior has reflected great credit on the genius of their creators.

An important part of the work of the agricultural scientist is to gather full family histories of grains and to study their processes of growth. A full understanding of the pattern followed by a disease in working its damage often leads to a cure of the disease itself. Since 1920 Stakman has charted the trails of wheat rusts from Minnesota to Mexico. Science knows, as a result of his studies, how these destructive fungi are propagated and how, in many circumstances, they can be controlled.

Stakman's leadership brought him many distinguished honors during his career at Minnesota. Among them is the Emil Christian Hansen prize offered by the Danish government. To Clyde Bailey have gone such awards as the Thomas Burr Osborne Medal and the Nicholas Appert Medal.

Many others of Coffey's carefully chosen faculty have brought recognition to the university. Willis B. Combs put the nation in his debt by creating the famous "blue cheese," developed in the laboratories of the St. Paul campus and ripened in the sandstone caves along the Mississippi River. William Alderman gave the *coup de grâce* to the die-hard theory that Minnesota's climate is too harsh for the successful growing of fruits and berries. He developed some fifty varieties of apples, grapes, plums, pears and raspberries that thrive on northern soil. Laurence Winters has become one of the conspicuous benefactors of animal husbandmen by developing the Minnesota Number One hog—a creature so aristocratic that the Worshipful Company of Butchers of London has led the world in doing him honor.

Prodded into attention by such achievements as these, Congress did not turn its back on the land-grant colleges, urgently as it was asked to do so. The depression was in its deepest dip (1933) when the Agricultural Adjustment Administration was created and in that period the government depended more than ever on the counsel of the universities. Washington gratefully received their help in controlling the production of wheat, corn, hogs. Minnesota's experts went into the drought-stricken areas to participate in relief work. An indirect result of this collaboration was that Congress passed the Bankhead-Jones Act giving additional funds to extension divisions. The purpose: to carry the word of government policies to the people and to recommend its policies of agricultural reform.

By the mid-1930s the agricultural campus looked nearly normal once more. Registration leaped upward, by more than 60 per cent in a single year. Coffey had brought the department through the doldrums and every division was more active than ever before. The laboratories, in addition to promoting their own creative projects, were concerned with helping to implement the government's erosion and rural electrification programs. The classrooms were full. Curricula were expanded. The full college course now covered a five-year period. The College of Agriculture collaborated with the newly created Institute of Technology, with the School of Business and with the School of Journalism on interdisciplinary studies. New courses for agricultural engineers, agricultural administrators and agricultural journalists appeared in the catalogue.

The year 1941 ushered in another period of crisis for the

Department of Agriculture, as it did for the university as a whole, the country as a whole and the world as a whole. Before its end the deafening sounds of Pearl Harbor had reverberated around the world and more than half of the nineteen hundred students on the St. Paul campus had gone to war.

This did not leave the department without a function. In wartime, as Coffey was quick to point out, the job of the university became "greater than ever before and more essential."

The events of the year proved to be only momentarily unsettling. Even when Coffey moved out of his office as dean and into that of the president of the university there was no need to mark time. The extraordinarily able Clyde Bailey simply moved over into the dean's chair.

Coffey had not expected or wanted to be president. His willingness to accept the responsibility testified once more to his gifts of loyalty, adaptability and calm in the face of an emergency.

A curious contretemps brought about his election by the board of regents. Preparing for the retirement of Guy Stanton Ford, Snyder and his fellow members had once more canvassed the field of candidates. A successor had been selected and public announcement made of his appointment. Then, quite without warning, this young educator from a small college in the East succumbed to an impulse that he was never able to make clear. Whether he was overwhelmed by the thought of directing an institution so large or whether the blandishments of a board of regents at home proved to be irresistible can only be guessed. But he announced that he could not, after all, accept the invitation to become president of the University of Minnesota.

It was far too late to choose a new unknown and Coffey was persuaded to fill the gap. With only a few years of his own academic career before him, he moved once more into the familiar atmosphere of a critical situation and, uncomplainingly, took up difficult tasks.

"My whole life has been spent in the atmosphere of agriculture," he said as he prepared to go. "My greatest inspiration has come from men who love the soil. My deepest friendships are among those who have labored in the belief that the advancement of rural civilization is worth the best that anyone can give in thought and deed."

But the university as a whole still stood higher in his loyalty than the part to which he gave his personal devotion.

It was as though he, too, had been drafted to go to war. For his administration almost exactly covered the period when the campus must once more become a camp with Coffey as its commander.

A calm master of crises, Coffey accomplished what the war years required of him. Against the blight of the abnormal he preserved the wholeness of the university, believing, as he had always believed, that "the future vitality of this country is bound up with the vitality of its educational system."

CHAPTER NINE

WE, CITIZEN RULERS

BY A CURIOUS AND DRAMATIC COINCIDENCE the surname of the eighth president of the University of Minnesota is the same as that of the United States congressman who originated the idea of the land-grant college. There is no kinship, by lineal descent, between President James Lewis Morrill and Congressman Justin Morrill, but in the fraternity of ideas their relationship is close. No more devoted and enthusiastic exponent of the idea implicit in the tradition of the land-grant school is alive today than President Morrill.

It is eminently appropriate—indeed, in retrospect, it seems almost inevitable—that Morrill should have come to Minnesota. The concept of universal education is the unique contribution made by experimenters in the United States to the theory of education, and the University of Minnesota is unique among American schools for the completeness and thoroughness with which circumstances have permitted it to develop the program of providing instruction for all the state's citizens.

President Morrill once said of the Land Grant Act of 1862 that it might be called the Emancipation Proclamation of higher education, "freeing it from the old-world concept and opening wide the door of educational opportunity at high levels." He believes it to be the "reciprocal responsibility of a state and its university to upgrade the welfare of their people. By endowing the many with the gifts of education, once reserved for the few, the state makes an investment in the future of society and receives in return rich values in the greater competence of its citizens." A university's research is "the catalyst of change," the always unfolding "potential of a large prosperity and a better way of life."

These are the principles that animate all the land-grant colleges. What makes the University of Minnesota a particularly interesting realization of the philosophy is that, unlike some of the others, it has large units for research into the problems of agriculture, of engineering—and broadening Congressman Morrill's idea—of medicine, all closely integrated with other schools and colleges of traditional pattern (arts, for example, and education) in an enormous university system. It has an advantage, as time has shown, in its metropolitan location, one that has helped to make its work familiar to a great majority of the members of the community and has earned, as a result, a remarkable loyalty from them. Within the university itself a long-standing tradition of cooperation eases the difficulties of crossing departmental lines. In fact no one seems to remember that such difficulties ever existed. Scientists in the field of medicine sit down at luncheon in the Campus Club with scientists of agriculture to discuss their projects in an atmosphere of perfect sympathy. Their joint investigations are numerous; their readiness to acknowledge interdependence is not merely unforced but spontaneously grateful. This sort of communication among educators—direct, constant and subtly stimulating—is what Congressman Morrill hoped to see established.

The years of President Morrill's administration have corresponded exactly with the period of a tremendous upsurge in research. As an intense believer in all the values that the land-grant idea came into existence to fulfill, the present head of the University of Minnesota has made it his job to invite every opportunity and to accept every responsibility for advancing investigation in all fields but particularly in agriculture, engineering and medicine. The emphasis upon research has been the identifying feature of his administration.

That the effort has been successful, during the past dozen

years, the ever-growing prestige of the institution in many fields demonstrates abundantly. Eager witnesses come forward in steady procession, from the federal agencies, from the great foundations, from groups of private citizens, to offer unmistakable proof of admiration. Donations for research have amounted in recent years to $2,500,000 annually for medicine, a like amount for engineering, and impressive sums for agricultural projects. In a moment when the United States has just become acutely aware of its dependence on basic and applied research the University of Minnesota, under Morrill, is able to give a good account of its stewardship.

In 1944, as the time approached when Walter Coffey must retire, the board of regents realized that he must be replaced by a young man who would be able to stay with his task for approximately as many years as Coffman had done. It was their assumption, as it has been with others who have had to make such appointments in recent years for other institutions, that the president of a big, expensive, modern university must be a specialist in administration. The personal history of James Lewis Morrill suggested to Fred Snyder and his fellow members of the board that he was precisely such a man.

At fifty-two he had held strategic posts in two universities. At Ohio State, from which he had been graduated in 1913, Morrill had progressed through many levels of responsibility to the position of vice-president. Though his youthful ambition had been to be a teacher of classical languages, the need of an immediate job had taken him, in his early twenties, into newspaper work. After one false start (a city editor failed to admire his account of a yacht race) he found a solid base and performed a kind of rocket ascension from the job of reporter to that of managing editor, all in a few years' time. Along the way, he had served the *Cleveland Press* as political and legislative correspondent, an experience which did much to help him cope with appropriations committees in later years. During World War I he was drafted by the United States government to serve as executive secretary of the Food Administration in Ohio and also to head the state's branch of the Council of National Defense.

When the war was over, Morrill returned to Ohio State University as alumni secretary and editor of the alumni magazine. This opportunity to combine his interests, as journalist, educator and administrator, gave final direction to his career. Once more eager for academic training, Morrill took graduate courses looking toward a degree in his special field. But his alma mater had other uses for him. After teaching courses in both education and journalism, he became junior dean of the College of Education. Later he was made vice-president charged particularly with responsibility for the university's public relations.

All the impulses of his temperament had now converged happily on a sympathetic assignment. The office of this friendly, socially gifted, always gracious man has been described by Ohio associates as a "shrine" to which "students, parents and teachers—even regents and legislators—came as supplicants seeking counsel." But Morrill's influence must have been rather more like that of a psychiatrist whose soothing gift it is to make nerves unknot and hackles descend. According to Ohio witnesses, it was his particular ability "to reflect back to supplicants both sides of their problems, letting them make their own decisions."

Many at Ohio expected Morrill finally to become the university's president. But when the post fell vacant, he failed of appointment because, in a local war, he had earned, at the hands of certain political leaders, wounds for which the just admired him. Still he stayed on at Ohio, serving loyally under the successful candidate, advising him, as he had advised three other presidents, on matters of policy.

In 1942 Morrill was elected president of the University of Wyoming. His administration was destined to last only three years, but, in that time, he was able to spur a comparatively underdeveloped land-grant college (Wyoming's enrollment reached 1000 only in 1925) into a greatly accelerated program which gave it increased appropriations, a new research foundation and broadened prestige.

When the Minnesota regents began to examine candidates in 1944 they were inevitably impressed by the qualifications of a man who had already had such wide experience. Some of them were acquainted with him personally for he had been under consideration in 1941 when the elusive eastern educator had been unwisely elected. Now the regents returned to Morrill with the conviction that they should have had him long ago.

His reputation everywhere was that of a deft coordinator of diversities, a center of patience in the midst of the clamor of large operations. He knew how to draw upon centripetal force to merge many interests into one. His individuality had not so much *seized* upon the imaginations of those with whom he was associated as *encompassed* their awareness of him with a kind of pervasive graciousness. At Ohio State it had been a widely accepted formula for wooing wisdom to say: "Let's see Lew Morrill."

So on July 1, 1945, he came to Minnesota.

The new president showed immediately that he had made a close study of the job he had undertaken and of the tradition of the institution he had come to head. His inaugural address reflected a close sympathy with all the significant figures of Minnesota's history. He echoed Folwell's belief that the "University of the Twentieth Century" is "morally committed" to the broadest possible expansion of three fields: instruction, research, and service to the community. He admired, with the insight of a fellow expert, the skill that had enabled Vincent to refound the university and to give it distinction. (Happily he resembled the perfectionist Vincent in the flexibility and fluency with which he used the English language.)

To these assets he added another; he was virtually a disciple of Coffman. The two men had once met at a session of the Association of Land Grant Colleges in 1935 and Morrill had written later, in a private letter, that, of all the spokesmen of the land-grant philosophy, Coffman was the most "compelling." As junior dean of the College of Education, Morrill had steeped his mind in the principles for which Coffman had stood so pertinaciously and done so much to advance. In a moment more exacting, actually, than any Coffman had ever had to face—a moment when the university had suddenly doubled in size—Morrill was well equipped to struggle as his predecessor had done, for the right of all citizens to a share in educational opportunity.

Morrill's first request, made to his board of regents, was entirely characteristic of his modesty. It was characteristic, also, of his devotion to the best academic tradition. If there must be a formal inauguration, he urged, let it be made the occasion for a "nationwide conference of real importance and benefit to the community and to the academic world with the actual inauguration ceremony as a very minor event in connection therewith."

On April 23, 24 and 25, 1946, such a conference was held. Its themes were "the crises of mankind . . . the urgencies of one world . . . the potentialities of human intelligence." Upon them a group of distinguished educators developed their ideas of the outlook for humanity. Among them were James Conant, then president of Harvard, Winfield Rieffler of the Institute for Advanced Study at Princeton, and such representative alumni of Minnesota as Frederick Hovde, president of Purdue, and Wayne Morse, United States Senator from Oregon.

Despite his modest rejection of prominence, Morrill remained the significant figure of this occasion and his expression of opinion—for the Minnesota community—the most important. In his inaugural address he offered his own proposal for dealing with the crisis of mankind.

"The best sense of direction for our state university will emerge from our ability to identify the problems of our people—problems which our resources for training, for research, for public service will be adapted or newly procured to help solve."

In other speeches, Morrill had used his unforced, persuasive skill in turning a phrase to identify the character, the rights and the responsibilities of the scholar. For him the "special genius of the educator" lies in his willingness to accept a "Spartan discipline" as he goes about the search for truth. A "passion for the dispassionate" enables him to ignore the hostility of those who would put walls of special protection around "the happy inertia of complacency, the vested interest of the status quo." If the discovery of truth is to be—as it should be—a fresh adventure for each new day, "then those who travel the road toward the unknown must be free."

However, this freedom will be exercised honestly, appropriately and sufficiently only if it spreads the awareness of truth as far and wide as possible. The modern guild of scholars must accept as its responsibility that of seeking out the educable, of drawing them into the fellowship of the instructed, of imparting "to each his own" out of the great fertile body of learning.

This is, for Morrill, a significant enlargement of the traditional responsibility of a school, which is to provide instruction for those who come to its doors. It becomes an important part of the adventure to look for the gifted student and provide him with the special program of instruction that will nourish his superiority. It is from this company of "citizen rulers" that the democratic world must draw leadership in the tasks of protecting and improving society.

"University City" (the fourth largest in the state of Minnesota, measured by its population) must be, Morrill has constantly insisted, the capital of its intellectual life. "Clearly our institutions of higher learning are challenged to make themselves more strongly felt for what they really are amid confused and competing pressures. Immediately useful today, their larger usefulness (as designers of the pattern for tomorrow's world) must be publicly perceived and protected."

In the opinion of those who have been closest to the Morrill administration, it is the steadfastness with which the leadership of "University City" has been preserved and advanced that gives the period significant character. In a time of rugged struggle, when the practical problems of sudden growth have been formidable, when pressures upon the university have been many, when demands for its services have been flattering but often oppressive, President Morrill has allowed his own poised and urbane presence to represent the temper of the university itself as it appears before the community.

He has never stood up before the world to bespeak the university's cause without improving that cause in the eyes of the great majority. No one, a close observer has said, ever faced a legislature so well. Answering each lawmaker by his name, showing a grave respect for the background and special interest of each in turn, Morrill has displayed the skills appropriate to high diplomacy in every visit to the statehouse. In the president of a university, which must have the support of many people, it is an incomparable advantage to be at once a human being and an ambassador well equipped to represent a special, highly prestigious world. Morrill has found it not always easy, but always possible to enlist the loyalty of legislators and regents, of faculty and students, of trade union officials, of philanthropists and heads of foundations, of vaudeville performers, of Masons, of business leaders—indeed of all the great, diverse company of citizens which nowadays has business with a modern university. It is to the credit of a university that it attracts so many different kinds of clients. But it takes a special kind of gift in a university's administrative head to make them all feel at home, wanted and needed.

Morrill came to the campus at a moment when an inexperienced eye might have perceived only chaos. Many troubles disturbed the surface of its activities. Though Coffey had kept the university's chief functions running smoothly, even while it masqueraded as a military camp, his approaching retirement, after a short administration, had left much unfinished business, particularly in matters of long-range policy.

One unhappy group on the periphery of university affairs

were the nonacademic workers. Strikes and threatened strikes among them had plagued the board of regents and the other officials who must wait, for final decisions, until the new president should be installed.

Another group of objectors were representatives of other state institutions who believed, or at least allowed their spokesmen publicly to suggest, that the university was the arrogant, self-centered, elder child in Minnesota's family of schools, stealing the rights and nullifying the usefulness of all the others.

The most persistent critic of the university and its between-terms administration was the student publication, the *Minnesota Daily*.

Chained to his desk in the first year of his administration, suffering many perturbations in private and in silence, the conscientious new president struggled, day and night, with issues left too long in abeyance. And his gifts of persuasion stood him in good stead, as he undertook to show that the mountains of disagreement were mere molehills of theoretical difference.

One by one the troubles of his administration were soothed away. From his first day in office there have been no work shortages among nonacademic employees though there have been many changes in civil service regulations. Today, the trade unions with which the university comes in contact sponsor scholarships instead of looking jealously for conflicts of interest.

Typical of the Morrill technique of assuagement was the entirely peaceful absorption—after many dubious battles, covering a decade—of the Duluth Teachers College. Northern Minnesota, where a large part of the state's natural wealth exists, had convinced itself that the legislature showed partiality to the university in its appropriations and neglected the interests of a hard-working and productive community. As long ago as the time of the Ford administration there had been tense, and even angry, protests about what was owed to

Duluth's educational institutions. Yet no workable solution of the family feud could be found.

In 1947 the legislature played the role of a Solomon, come to judgment, by authorizing the transfer of the Teachers College to the university as a branch. Under the pacifying influence of Morrill, old enmities faded away and the whole problem was resolved in an atmosphere of perfect harmony. The Duluth Branch of the University of Minnesota maintained its autonomy, held together its own staff and gained in prestige by association with the older institution. It has continued to specialize in teacher training, and the happy result has been to ease the load carried by the university itself in this field of instruction.

During the early years of the Morrill administration there were other problems that reflected the uneasy temper of the times. With the end of World War II, anxiety flared once more over the possible infiltration into academic institutions of teachers with leanings toward, or even covert loyalty to, the communist philosophy. Minnesota had its share of such difficulties and, in dealing with each of them, Morrill showed a firm determination to allow no mere suspicion of subversion to interfere with academic freedom.

Fortunately, the three cases in which the administration had to reach decisions were all quite clear. In the first, the temporary appointment of a Negro teacher was terminated not, as a few insisted on believing, because of his race or because of his private beliefs but because, in the estimation of a majority of his associates in the Arts college, he was inadequate to the academic task. (From a later appointment, in another institution, he was also dropped for the same reason.)

In the other two cases young teachers faced charges of disloyalty. Morrill protected their positions until it became clear that both had put themselves outside the shelter of the most liberal interpretation of academic freedom, one by refusing to cooperate with investigating authorities in Washington, the other by lying about his affiliations.

Minnesota, having been through the fires of hysteria in the

period of World War I, was determined not to repeat its unfortunate experience. The nature of the president—sensitive on the one side to the danger of injustice to the individual and on the other to the injustice that an individual may work on an institution, on society and on the state—suffered acutely in making these decisions. But, in the end, his cool, impersonal judgments served the theory of academic freedom well. Indeed, his decisions wrote a passage of sober, critical insight into the long discussion of civil liberties.

As Morrill justly and temperately pointed out, "a wave of international immorality" had, in that moment, swept the world. In this crisis, the teacher must seek high ground on which to keep his outlook clear. Political propaganda, inspired by a foreign power, would try to persuade him that he should "abandon to dogma and deceit the pursuit of truth." This would be done again and again on the theory that freedom of discussion demanded it. But the teacher must remember that "responsibility is the core not the curtailment of freedom." As a responsible person he must not allow the invasion of his ranks by those who had surrendered their own sense of responsibility into the keeping of others. The teacher, with a proper respect for his own integrity, could not be expected to live in the shadow of a philosophy that had publicly proclaimed the propaganda value of the "big lie." There must be a new ethical code for teachers which would enable them to "police their profession" and to exclude from it those who had no controlling integrity of their own. In a time when "clever dialectic" offered itself as a substitute for intelligence there was need of constant vigilance to protect the health of the academic body and to keep its mind "free and fertile."

A ruling principle of the Morrill administration has been to give the teacher not merely the responsibility of policing his own profession but the means of doing so. The president's speeches refer often to Minnesota's "policy of decentralization." The theory has been to make each school, college and institute autonomous as far as this is possible within the limits fixed by the tradition of close cooperation. In practice the idea has taken the form of a system of committees, each having a share in the formulation of university policy.

This desire for democratic control of university affairs has led also to the reorganization of the senate. What had been a mass forum, subject to the familiar fault of being addicted to talk and averse to action, became a representative body able, through its committees, to give effective voice to faculty opinion.

Nor are the committees limited in membership to teachers. Students are represented on many that are concerned with student affairs.

It is Morrill's particular point of pride that he has been able to develop this technique of sharing administrative responsibility with "my colleagues on the faculty" and with students, too. As a public figure, constantly in demand for service in such national organizations as the President's Committee on Problems of Higher Education, the American Council on Education, and the American Association of Land Grant Colleges and State Universities, the president has been often absent from the campus. The committee system has served effectively as a means of delegating authority, far down the hierarchy of administration, in a truly democratic way.

Indeed it may be said that the history of the University of Minnesota has traced, in its nearly one hundred years of continuous operation, beginning with Folwell's time, the whole record of institutional evolution. It survived precarious infancy under the limp paternalism of Northrop; achieved maturity under the directive, organizing genius of Vincent; grew prodigiously as Coffman's firm, disciplinary hand forced its expansion to parallel that of the American economy itself in the years following World War I; and now has achieved, under Morrill's supervision, an aptitude for self-study and self-discipline which makes it virtually self-sustaining and self-governing.

The progress toward the goal of self-sufficiency was shadowed by a formidable responsibility in the mid-1940s.

This was the sudden advance on the university of one of the most spectacular mass movements of educational history, the descent of ex-soldiers of World War II. Exercising their rights under Public Law 346 (the GI bill) a whole generation of American youth suddenly decided to embrace higher education. There were those in the academic world who remembered such impulses of the past and remembered them chiefly with a kind of horrified awe. Such people did not hesitate to say that the embrace was brusque and that its results might be disastrous for society and for the schools. But this could not very well be the point of view of the land-grant college, and the University of Minnesota made ready to receive its share.

The mass movement of the GIs was not the less overwhelming for the fact that it was peaceful and, for the most part, cheerful. Wearing their army haircuts, their T shirts and their sun-tan trousers, they came swarming across the campus in the fall of 1945, baffling those who were used to the blunt speech of the sovereign citizen of the Upper Midwest with their holdover habit (it proved to be a temporary manifestation) of addressing anyone in authority as "Sir." In October more than 1500 of these young men added their number to normal enrollment. By the winter quarter their ranks had reached the 6000 mark and in the spring they were 8700 strong. They needed counsel, sleeping quarters, places for wives and some provision for babies, either actual or imminent.

The university had prepared for their appearance by establishing the Bureau of Veterans Affairs in January, 1945, well before the rush began. But still there was not enough of anything—dormitories, classrooms, teachers, facilities. Unmarried men crowded into the limited quarters then in existence, and the floors shook under their mighty tread. First one, then a second village for married students appeared almost overnight between the Minneapolis and St. Paul campuses. Handball courts in the stadium were hastily converted into living quarters. The whole district assumed the appearance of a gigantic experiment in communal living such as might have intimidated even Brigham Young.

Provision for classroom instruction had to be improvised with equal imaginativeness. Ugly wooden structures needed no longer by government plants in the neighborhood were moved to the campus and identified by such names as Temporary (everyone hoped) South of Mines. Students soon found better names. The building near Murphy Hall (School of Journalism) became "Mrs. Murphy" and a certain special affection clung to her until her demise.

The university received these numbers with a cheerfulness which matched the GIs' own good will. A new orientation program, devised by the counseling bureau, undertook to "warm them up to this big institution." The great majority responded well to this sympathetic treatment. The GIs were found to be sober and far more mature in outlook than any previous generation of undergraduates at Minnesota had ever been. They were curiously appealing both in their desire for help and in their awareness that long service in the army had tended to diminish their capacity for independent thought or —as they often said—"slowed them down." The large compensations for this handicap of having traveled widely, of having been exposed to cultures other than their own and of having explored, at least a little, the European heritages of their forebears helped them conspicuously to gather speed once more and made them men and women of braver countenance than the "shining morning face" of studenthood had shown in the past. Folwell's faith in western undergraduates would have been further deepened and refreshed by an encounter with this not always happy, but basically earnest, breed. The excuse sometimes offered for a late paper that the baby had been sick the night before (as substitute for the traditional one having something to do with the demise of a grandmother) might have assured him that the student body had grown up completely and that his University of the Twentieth Century had become a reality.

By the fall of 1946 the veteran enrollment had leaped again

to a dazzling 16,000, raising the total number of students from a prewar peak of 15,000 to 28,000. This battle of the "veterans' bulge" would continue, as everyone realized, through many academic years. Even when it began to slack off with the graduation of the GIs, there would be only a temporary pause before it would begin to climb again. Birth rate figures indicated clearly that between 1953 and 1970 the numbers of young men and women in America of college age would increase some 70 per cent. Normal student enrollment must be expected to reach 30,000 by 1960. An estimate of 42,500 by 1970 seemed "not at all unreasonable."

The university drew a deep breath and prepared for expansion of every kind. The legislature before which Morrill had his debut as president was generous, making the largest appropriation in all the institution's history: $24,000,000 for current operation during the biennium and $7,000,000 more for buildings. By the next biennium eleven new structures had appeared on the several campuses. Some of these were dormitories and service units; the others were intended to house new facilities for investigation in the three scientific fields—medicine, engineering and agriculture—and to push forward at an accelerated rate the projects for which the university already was famous. As Morrill said:

"Who can believe that the intensification of research that has characterized the past decade will lessen in the decades ahead? One can only believe that there will be further intensification. The University and the state must prepare for this lest they both fail to maintain the advantages that present policies of support have made possible."

Through the ups and downs of legislative support (there have been disappointing periods, such as the biennium of 1950–52 when retrenchment was once more the word) the university has managed to maintain steadily its intensive programs of research. Long ago Minnesota committed itself to the belief that the well-being of democratic society—possibly its very hope for survival—depends upon the training of superior students in the fields of science and of training them to the

214

utmost limit of their abilities. In the conviction that upon the creative efforts of such people the future of a free society must depend, the colleges of medicine, technology and agriculture have spent the very large sums entrusted to their care in the training of a vast army of men and women many of whom have achieved high distinction.

Perhaps the most conspicuous of all Minnesota's individual colleges is that of Medical Sciences. The enormous prestige that it has earned in recent years may be explained most accurately by a trained observer from within its gates. Dr. E. T. Bell, exercising with restraint the prerogative of pride that belongs to a colleague in retirement, has offered this comment in a brief history of the college:

"During the past two decades the medical school has developed from a second-class training unit to one of the foremost research institutions of the country. How has this remarkable change come about? The strength of a medical school is proportionate to the number of recognized leaders of medical thought on its faculty. Good teaching is necessary and not incompatible with investigation; but only research men make a university famous. The primary purpose of a medical school is to train young men and women to be competent physicians; but it is also the obligation to advance medical knowledge. A department which does not encourage investigative work soon stagnates and even its teaching deteriorates. The medical school at Minnesota has made continuous progress due to the appointment and promotion of outstanding men."

Though there had been hints and promises of distinction from the very first moment when Vincent brought Dean Lyon and Dr. Jackson to Minnesota, it was in the 1930s that a culmination was reached in this creative enterprise. A highly infectious enthusiasm swept through the school until all its leading figures had become, by virtue of their contributions to science, men of importance not merely to the nation but to the world.

One of these was Owen Wangensteen, whose work in intestinal obstruction has brought him international recognition. Raised by Dean Lyon's own hand, prompted to early achievement by the many opportunities that Guy Stanton Ford, as dean of the Graduate School, was able to put in his path, Wangensteen became head of surgery at an age when most men are still laying shrewd long-range plans to escape from instructorships.

Brisk and authoritative, with a confidence as enormous as his stature is diminutive, Dr. Wangensteen virtually required everyone about him to become a superior investigator. He set an excellent example by writing an entirely new chapter into the history of surgery. His discovery that death from obstruction results, not so much from the loss of water by vomiting as from prolonged elevations of pressure resulted in his invention of the Wangensteen suction tube which draws off gas and fluid ahead of the point of pressure. This device has reduced mortality from postoperative effects to a fraction of what it was before. During World War II, abdominal wounds had priority on operating tables, and, because of the omnipresence of the suction tubes in field hospitals, nurses called the ward in which such cases were treated "Wangensteen's Alley." Sober witnesses, within the profession, testify that the tube has saved thousands of human lives.

A typical team of the 1930s was that of the doctors Winford Larson, Arthur Henrici and Robert Green who pooled their talents for investigation and worked so harmoniously together that they won the attention of the entire medical world with their announcement of a revolutionary theory concerning the fundamental nature of viruses. Having worked for twenty fruitful years as a team, it seemed to be impossible for any of them to accept the status of an individual operator. When one died the others soon followed; each, almost literally, in the laboratory which had become a sort of shrine to all.

In the field of pediatrics, Dr. Irvine McQuarrie helped to make Minnesota a place to which the nation looked for leadership in the conquest of children's diseases. His success and that of his fellow workers has been so great that, within half a century, mortality tables have been completely rewritten. A Minneapolis physician said late in the nineteenth century that "half the deaths that occur in daily practice are to children under five." Today, only 7 per cent of all deaths in Minnesota occur to children under twelve.

Dean Lyon's genius for identifying the superior student enabled him to put two more of his students at the head of departments in the college, posts which they hold today. One is Dr. Maurice Visscher, physiology; the other Dr. Cecil Watson, medicine.

Under Dr. Visscher's adroit and imaginative guidance a research unit of brilliant productivity has been created in his department, one that was constantly at work on cooperative projects with physiologists of the agricultural campus and physiologists of the Mayo Clinic. Their undertakings included cancer biology studies and investigations in support of the dramatic achievements of the team of heart specialists.

Visscher has a taste for drama which he was once able to put to lively advantage on the public platform. He engaged in a series of debates on the controversial subject of vivisection and his opponent was Irene Castle. After the close of her career as a dancer Mrs. Castle had made a second career of trying to outlaw this important technique of science. At a first meeting with Dr. Visscher she had been prompted by her sense of theater to score an advantage against him. Managing to be late, she made a great entrance after Visscher had started to speak and by each hand she led a magnificent dog. But Visscher did not accept defeat. At the next of their platform meetings he managed to be late and made an entrance after Mrs. Castle had opened the discussion. And he led by each hand an extraordinarily beautiful young child.

Dr. Watson, nationally and internationally regarded as a leading authority on internal medicine, wrote his name indelibly into the history of research during World War II when his knowledge of hepatitis helped to arrest the progress of that disease in western Europe and the Pacific theater of war.

It was over this company of talents that Dr. Harold Diehl, also one of Dean Lyon's young men, came to preside as dean in 1935. He was named after a distinguished man from the East had declined the appointment, saying succinctly: "There isn't any future here."

In a moment of doubt, such as must afflict any sensible man embarking on a new job, Dr. Diehl might have agreed. For, despite the presence of a brilliant staff, opportunities for research had been severely limited by the lack of money. In the first year of his deanship, the medical school of the university received from outside sources—that is, from donors other than the legislature itself—only some $20,000. In recent years it has been normal for the medical school to receive one hundred twenty-five times that amount from foundations and private individuals who have been eager to empty their pockets.

Annual gifts for research in the field of medicine, made to the University of Minnesota, equal those given to any research institution in the country. The sum is from four to ten times as much as is given to neighboring universities of the region. Deans of other schools are sometimes prompted to ask a little plaintively: "How do you fellows manage to attract so much more support than we do?" The answer would seem to be simple. All that is necessary is for a school to devote itself conscientiously for half a century to the task of assembling a company of distinguished scientists capable of inspiring original work on the part of their students. When the news of their discoveries has spread all the way from eastern Europe to Australia, nothing can stop the flow of money for the support of further projects. Even in the realm of research, where scrupulous devotion to basic truth precludes any temptation to exploit the immediate advantage of a startling discovery, the word of steady progress gets about. Nothing still succeeds like success.

The reputation of the medical school has brought many

brilliant men to its staff during the Morrill administration. In its laboratories, such investigators agree, the very atmosphere stimulates originality of effort and achievement. Shy of eulogists, not at all sure that the uses of publicity are sweet, the men of the College of Medical Sciences have been obliged, again and again, to open their doors to the press—especially during the last decade—because their revolutionary methods have made news.

Perhaps the most famous of all these revolutions has been in the field of heart surgery. An operation, developed by the team of Drs. C. Walton Lillehei, Richard Varco, Herbert E. Warden and Morley Cohen, has become world-famous.

All that these men asked of themselves was the working of a small miracle: that of finding "some simple method of working inside the heart." Their first experiments were made with laboratory dogs, and the result of them was the evolution of a technique whereby a simple mechanical pump was substituted for the heart while the operation was in progress. Meanwhile the animal's own lungs purified his blood.

Drawn on by the irresistible prompter that speaks within the creative mind and says, "Surely, there must be a better way," the team began to work with the idea that an operating room donor, of the same blood type as the patient, might lend his healthy lungs to the procedure in a more effective, a "simpler" way.

The final result, shown to the world for the first time in April, 1954, was an operation in which a great gaping hole in a child's heart was closed successfully, saving her from the possibility of premature death and from what had been before the certainty of chronic invalidism.

Surgery, performed with the aid of the new "controlled cross circulation" method, makes the circulatory system of the patient one with that of the blood donor who is anesthetized on an adjacent operating table. In the instance that first made medical history, daughter and father had their circulating systems connected by thin plastic tubes, passed through a mechanical pump. The patient's heart was tied off and the lungs were collapsed. The mechanical pump took over the job of conveying pure blood from the body of the donor and of carrying dark, venous blood from the patient back to his lungs for purification. It became possible for the father actually to breathe for the daughter while the surgeons were at their work of repair. Gone was the fear that the patient might bleed to death on the table; gone the fear of injury to the brain by impairment of circulation. The surgeons worked in a blood-free operating field under "direct vision"— unhurried, unhampered, unhandicapped while the patient's healthily nourished heart beat steadily away.

Combined with the effective practicability of this method, the symbolic appeal of this linking—so that one human being was enabled literally to give his life not *for* but *to* another— was deeply moving to observers. If more drama had been needed to make the event gleam in the parental mind as one of the great advances of all time, it was provided by the "before and after" pictures of the patient. The first of these showed a little wisp of utter pathos; the second showed her transformed into a sturdy alert little creature in full possession of all those attractions which once inspired a writer to suggest that "a woman reaches the peak of her charm at the age of five."

A later development of the constantly continuing heart research at Minnesota has enabled the same team to develop a method of controlling the very beat of the heart for surgical purposes—a conquest of the impossible that must stagger the imaginations even of poets who have had so much to say about the uncontrollability of the heart. The doctors, in our time, have beaten the poets at their own game of imagining wonders.

It is this sort of experience that has made Minnesota's own community come forward eagerly with support for "our university." Cooperation has been offered spontaneously by every sort of organization.

The clinical development of the cross circulation method was underwritten by the Variety Club of the Northwest. This organization of theater men, urged on, perhaps by their sense of drama, somehow conceived it to be the duty of the group to encourage the university in the study of diseases affecting children after attacks of rheumatic fever. They thought, at first, of buying a long-unused public school building in the neighborhood and of reconditioning it as a hospital for investigation and research. Dean Diehl met their suggestion with his usual prompt sympathy and also with his tactful talent for redirecting effort into the most rewarding course possible. A new hospital, he said, would cost hardly more and it would, in the end, represent a better contribution to the work of the university.

The Variety Club, its own heart splendidly unimpaired, went to work strenuously to raise money for a hospital to repair the hearts of the less fortunate. On September 23, 1946, it was ready to make a significant progress report. A dinner, held at the university, brought together town and gown, together with the Variety Club's motley, for a unique occasion. Sharing the head table, President Morrill and the late Fred Allen (who might be described as having been dean of a one-man school of satiric arts) matched their skills—one with his characteristic urbanity, the other with his inimitable wry wit modified into mellowness by the spirit of the meeting. The purpose was to turn over $250,000 to the university for creation of a heart hospital. The club promised also to give $25,000 a year toward maintenance of a hundred beds.

In the end, the Variety Club, intoxicated by its own success, gave much more than its first or second impulses had foreseen. The final cost of the Heart Hospital was $1,400,000, and of it the club raised $500,000. By the time the doors were opened in 1949, the institution had become so important to the entertainment men that they immediately expanded their plans to include further donations for research on a large scale. Support of the Heart Hospital had become something very like a second profession to them and they gave it the same sort of enthusiastic loyalty that, by tradition, they have always given to the first. "The show must go on."

Minnesota's projects in cancer research have attracted a similar kind of support from the public. To the first donation, made by Mrs. George Chase Christian of Minneapolis, many have been added since. In 1948 the Minnesota division of the American Cancer Society gave $300,000 toward the establishment of a detection center, now part of the new laboratory group named for Dean Lyon. The National Cancer Institute of the Public Health Service has contributed funds for expansion of the project. The Masons of Minnesota are planning to raise money for a hospital which will be devoted to the care of terminal cases; the American Legion has made large donations and the Minnesota branch of the Veterans of Foreign Wars proposes to help create a unit, to be added to existing hospital services on the campus, which will be concerned exclusively with cancer research. A touching faith in "our university" has swept, like a benign contagion, through the community and each gift, prompted by this faith, has added to the position of authority now held by Minnesota doctors in the field of cancer control.

A sign of recognition has lately come to the College of Medical Sciences in which the university takes a pride that is tinged with regret. The American Cancer Society has lured away the dean, Dr. Diehl, to become one of its executive vice-presidents. Capitalizing on the experience he has had at Minnesota, he will coordinate research in all the organizations of the country to avoid duplication of effort and to push investigation forward at an increased rate.

Dr. John Bittner, cancer biologist, has made important contributions to knowledge through his studies of some twenty generations of mice. The enormous amount of data which he has brought together has aided the studies of research men everywhere. His own discovery that mice born to mothers of highly cancerous strains often do not develop the disease when they are suckled by healthy foster mothers led to close investigation of the ingredients of milk and to the definite identification of one as a cancer inciter.

Dr. J. A. Myers made similarly significant contributions to the work of tuberculosis control.

Dr. Wesley Spink has been a pioneer student of the sulfa drugs. Building on early investigations of brucellosis, made at Minnesota, he has collaborated with research men on the agricultural campus whose interests are similar to his own. (Bang's disease which afflicts cattle results from the same kind of infection). When, in February, 1951, agencies of the United Nations set up twenty-two world centers for the study of brucellosis, Minnesota was chosen as the center for the United States. Dr. Spink became its head.

This Minnesota habit of cooperation in research had a typical manifestation in the creation of the Laboratory of Physiological Hygiene, the purpose of which is to fill in the strangely large gaps in science's understanding of the process of growing old. Under the direction of Dr. Ancel Keys, human biology has been examined from the standpoints of the physicist, the biochemist, the bacteriologist, nutritionist, pathologist, histologist and psychologist. All have sat down together and compared notes on the effects of disease, of diet, and of all the pressures of social life. At last the animal, man, is beginning to be known with something comparable to the intimacy of the husbandmen's knowledge of livestock. During World War II Dr. Keys and his associates had an extraordinary opportunity to study the effects of partial starvation when a group of conscientious objectors volunteered to become experimental specimens. Weighed, measured and probed in every possible way during the process, these gallant young men, through their momentary privations, were able to add much to the lore of science. These discoveries were given to the profession at a National Conference on the Biology of Human Starvation, held at the university in 1948, and in a two-volume report published under the same name by the University of Minnesota Press.

As it is seen today from the west bank of the Mississippi, the university crowns the crest of the river terrace with a cluster of red brick buildings. In the midst of these is one that rises fourteen stories high. It catches the attention of the most casual observer with its air of challenging the architectural interest and the commanding dignity of the structures that mark the milling district only a mile away. The scene dramatizes the close relationship of the modern university to modern industry. Even Folwell himself, who foresaw the inevitability of the growth of commercial enterprise at the Falls of St. Anthony, might have forgiven Pillsbury and his fellow regents for keeping the university in this tight corner of land if he could have foreseen the final outcome. By building vertically the university has overcome its handicap of space; by retaining its closeness to the metropolitan center it has achieved certain unique advantages.

The tall building that rises so noticeably above the promontory is the Mayo Memorial and it encloses within its walls the story of a determined effort, covering seventy years, to lift the medical unit of the university out of competent mediocrity into distinction. It dramatizes also the intimate relationship between the university and the Mayo Clinic. Its name honors the men who were the developers of that extraordinary monument to idealism and imagination. The two country doctors, who achieved in their lifetime the sufficiently startling triumph of unifying research on a large scale throughout the state of Minnesota, might have felt that they had received the satisfying reward for all their effort could they have known that in December, 1950, the Nobel prize would go to two men of the Mayo Foundation, the Drs. Kendall and Hench, for their discovery of cortisone.

The series of surprising events which long ago began bringing up the stricken from every corner of the globe to Rochester, Minnesota, as to a court of last resort in cases of difficult illness, needs no further recounting. It is too well known to the entire world. And yet observers still find it amazing that so much conspicuous effort in the conquest of disease should be concentrated in Minnesota. As a visiting journalist from

224

the East recently said: "It's hard to believe but I guess if I had to be sick, I'd want to be sick in Minnesota."

When "Dr. Will" and "Dr. Charlie" died in 1939 these men, held in awe-stricken affection by thousands of fellow citizens many of whom knew them only as figures in a legend, entered straightway into that special relationship to time and eternity that demands special recognition. Their own brisk habit of making the humanitarian ideal show itself forth in deeds demands that any monument to their memory be of a kind that serves human need.

Governor Harold Stassen started the movement to raise on the campus an appropriate memorial to the Mayo brothers. It was not, however, until 1943 that the legislature put its prestige behind the plan by appointing a committee of "Founders" to make the project assume reality in brick and mortar. They wanted, of course, a memorial hospital.

Working under the direction of Dr. Donald J. Cowling, the retired president of Carleton College, the Committee of Founders developed their plans carefully. In the first years of the Morrill administration the members, representing the House, the Senate and the public at large, put a complete proposal before the people of the state. This called for the erection of a skyscraper complete with everything that a great hospital needs, from beds to research laboratories. The legislature studied the estimated cost of $2,000,000 and voted $750,-000 toward it with the provision that the rest must be raised by popular subscription.

Then, for nine years, every kind of vicissitude associated with human effort rudely crowded the project as though some malevolent force wished to see it edged into oblivion. Though the original goal was reached quite readily, inflation in construction costs, following World War II, made all the carefully perfected plans look almost childishly illusory. Additional funds, amounting to half the original total, had to be raised. The Founders went stubbornly ahead, but, in the spring of 1948, before much could be accomplished, costs began to spiral dizzily upward once more. Estimates had to be revised a second time. The project now had assumed national importance and two medical research agencies came forward with offers to contribute if building plans could be revised to make room for a school of public health, a cancer research institute, and a medical library. The Committee of Founders, to which revision had become a kind of lifework, revised again.

Even before the actual building could be begun the bravely modest $2,000,000 project had become an operation involving the expenditure of six times that amount. The legislature had committed itself to $7,000,000 instead of the $750,000 it had first appropriated. The public had dug for much more than the $1,250,000 first asked of it, and the rest had come from the private and public agencies.

In the summer of 1950, President Morrill turned over the first spadeful of earth and the erection of what was planned as a twenty-two story building began.

Simultaneously, a very different kind of happening managed to throw its shadow halfway across the globe over the framework of the Mayo Memorial. The outbreak of the Korean War sent costs soaring again. Steel shortages brought construction to a standstill for many months. A strike of steelworkers delayed progress when work was just about to start once more. The building had shrunk, under these pressures, to a fourteen-story affair, with three six-story wings. These spread out to join the already existing hospitals and laboratories to form the large quadrangle of the medical center as it is today.

Dodging all the "arrows of outrageous fortune," the Committee of Founders brought their project through. On October 21, 1954, the Mayo Memorial was dedicated and Minnesota was able to assemble its medical interests in one central place where opportunities for research are as complete and as stimulating as those of any research institute in the world.

When the Mayo Memorial was opened, a majority of the old leaders of what had been called "America's first team of medical investigation" still answered to roll call: Bittner,

Diehl, Spink, Visscher, Wangensteen, Watson. Their long-established habit of crossing departmental lines to ask aid from colleagues flourished in a new atmosphere of complete satisfaction with the conditions of work. In that healthy atmosphere projects multiplied. As Dr. Wangensteen has said:

"Today active research is in progress in every major teaching division. Transmitting passively the lifeless body of knowledge of the past to succeeding generations of students is not enough. The leaders in medicine of the future must receive the nurture of stimulating instruction at the hands of teachers whose thinking is sharpened by active conflict with medical problems crying out for solution.

"Studies prosecuted in various departments include the nature of fatigue, the heart and circulation in health as well as in disease, disturbance of respiration, cancer biology, nutritional disorders, metabolism in its broader aspects, endocrine disorders, diseases of the nervous system, affections of the kidney, liver and bile passages as well as those of the eliminary tract.

"The luminescent flash of the firefly, the dimness of candle-light and the incandescence of the electric light reflect relative differences in the luminosity of our present understanding in many pressing problems. Persistent fact-finding through research is the only instrument which can dispel the veil of darkness which obscures our vision and defies our understanding. The faculty of the medical school mindful of its great trust is endeavoring to justify the faith of the people of Minnesota in their assurance that research brings better medicine to them and added luster to their medical school and university."

The greatly disturbing drama of 1957 which saw the Russians anticipate the efforts of the United States to put earth satellites into the sky, in celebration of the Internationl Geophysical Year, has served once more to remind the academic world that there is need to stimulate the study of fundamental science in our universities. It may be said without recourse to the wisdom of hindsight that, through its dean, the Institute of Technology at Minnesota has been preaching for years what is now everyone's gospel.

When Lind retired in 1947 the university found it impossible to make an immediate appointment of a successor. Men of high distinction had been drafted for various kinds of special service in the research units of the army and navy and they did not return immediately to academic life when the war was over. But at last in 1950 the Morrill administration made one of its most brilliant appointments by attracting Athelstan Spilhaus to Minnesota. Born in the Union of South Africa, Spilhaus had had his academic training, in part, at the Massachusetts Institute of Technology. Natural aptitudes had enabled him to travel fast through an assortment of elements—in the air and under the sea as well as on land. When he reached Minnesota at the age of thirty-eight to become dean of the Institute, he had already been a teacher, an inventor, a meteorologist, an oceanographer, creator of the bathythermograph, and an officer of the United States Army.

In his first half-dozen years at Minnesota, Spilhaus caught up so many honors and responsibilities that only a young and quite indestructible man could have borne their weight. He has "put a girdle round the earth" not once but many times in service as a member of the United States National Commission for Unesco, as technical adviser on many matters to the Assistant Secretary of Defense, in various assignments from the National Research Council.

Ruddy, positive, given to great decisiveness and picturesqueness of expression, he represents at its most vigorous a new kind of international temper among educators. Such men are concerned, simultaneously, with service to society in the widest stretch of all its economic and cultural needs and with service to science at its most fundamental and exacting. They are men of the world and, at the same time, men of the still unknown world of theoretical investigation. Superficially, there may seem to be a contradiction between the impulse of practical idealism that sends a man like Spilhaus on constant journeys to the Philippines, to Siam, all over Europe, to Uruguay, to New Zealand, taking the benefits of modern science to the farthest corners of the world, and the other impulse of his character which is to be deeply dedicated to the work of basic science independent of concern with immediate results. But, actually, the two aspects of this temperament are in natural sympathy with one another. The major interest of each is to find the unity that flows through all things: the unity that may make the social world one, the unity of principle which operates in many sciences making them all basically one.

It was inevitable that Spilhaus should become an ambassador of good will representing the intellectual world. Internationalism is in his blood. His mother was a Scottish woman; his father, a citizen of the Union of South Africa in whose origins Portuguese and German strains were blended. An incident dramatizing the fact that the globe has become one cozy family neighborhood for Spilhaus concerns an old friend of his parents, the late General Smuts. During World War II Spilhaus was sent to South Africa to establish a meteorological service. He went as a citizen of the United States, and it amused General Smuts enormously to discover that the young expert who came representing a great Western power was none other than the neighbor boy from across the street.

Spilhaus believes that such agreeable small ironies are characteristic of the world of science. In its councils personal relations of great intimacy and mutual trust are still the rule, with only Russia insisting upon a grim exception. Science offers a common ground on which men of different ideological outlooks can stand together and let their minds stretch across differences. In his experience even Soviet scientists have been known to indulge in moments of respect for Westerners when they prove themselves to be "real professors." Some oriental scholars know the art of bridging gaps with tolerant wit. A very important personage of the East once said to Spilhaus with a droll smile: "You know my Christian name is Mohammed." The scientist, Spilhaus believes, will always be reluctant to be drawn behind an iron curtain and the laboratory door will be the last to close.

One aspect of Spilhaus' travels that he considers to be of importance to the university is that it keeps him in intimate communication with the best brains of the world. In more than one instance he has used opportunities, offered by his travels for Unesco, to add distinguished men to his staff. In his philosophy it is the job of a dean to seed his faculty with "enough germinating members to bring the others along."

His exploits are sometimes criticized. When he introduced into his faculty a German scientist who happened to be one of the world's great authorities on heat transfer, some of his colleagues murmured among themselves about "men with Nazi backgrounds." "See here!" said Spilhaus with withering authority, "*that* war is over." When he brought in a Japanese mathematician with an unequaled record of originality in his field, it was pointed out by the same kind of doubter that the man did not speak English. With unbaffled confidence, Spilhaus said: "It will be far easier for ——— to learn English than it would be for anyone else in the world to learn mathematics of *his* level of genius."

This independence of spirit has let great gusts of fresh air into the councils of the Institute. Respect for tradition is what kills all the values of education, says Spilhaus briskly as he proceeds to renovate theories of engineering instruction from top to bottom.

In the short time that he has been at Minnesota Spilhaus has advanced the prestige of its Institute of Technology to the point where many of its departments challenge comparison with the oldest institutions in the country. He has achieved this success by liberalizing the engineer's training so that it may produce men who are at once civilized citizens of the world and investigators with a new awareness of the basic principles of science.

He points out that Minnesota is one of the few technical schools in the country that requires five years for training its graduates. This program was begun at the close of World War II by Dean Lind and it has his successor's enthusiastic support. The great advantage offered by the two years of preliminary instruction, now required at Minnesota, is that during this period the student may develop more fully before he is plunged into field specialization. His outlook remains flexible and he may postpone final decision about what branch he wishes to enter until he knows himself intellectually.

The dean is determined that these freshmen and sophomores shall be neither neglected nor patronized. Indeed, it is essential to his theory that, in the first years when students are being grounded in the fundamentals of physics, chemistry and mathematics, they must be exposed to the best men of the faculty—to those creative intelligences that take delight in nourishing young brains. Only an infusion of enthusiasm from high levels can maintain the steady stimulation needed to produce the great company of scientists necessary to satisfy the requirements of our present-day society.

In redesigning curricula for the upper three years, it is the dean's intent to turn back from a preoccupation with the immediately useful toward basic science. He points out that thirty, even only twenty, years ago much engineering was based on empiricism; engineering courses were concerned largely with practical instruction. Today, the enormous importance of engineering, not merely to the well-being of society but actually to its future existence, depends on a new approach, that of the analytical method. The vastly increased complexity of every branch of the field can be encompassed only by a broad understanding of fundamental phenomena.

A spirited talker, Spilhaus offers a graphic picture of the educational revolution in which he feels himself to be involved. The university laboratories of the old days were "synthetic factory buildings with miles of lathes." These must go. They must be replaced by small laboratories appropriate to the intimate study of such complexities as those of heat transfer, fluid mechanics, theoretical aerodynamics. "When you bolt down machinery," says Spilhaus, "you bolt down ideas." In a day when nuclear engineering must be made something more than a "mere letterhead" department no one can afford time for old-fashioned procedures.

The old historical categories of "military" and "civil" engineering must be finally and fully retired. What is needed is to build departments which cut across all the old artificial boundaries and divide engineering functionally.

Even a subject like mining engineering must take a long look forward. The students of the future must study the fundamental structure of rock. The molecular-sized vacancies within the formations may, in a sense, offer the holes for a break-through of a new technique in rock crushing. The final purpose of crushing more rock more cheaply will be served best by taking the new short cut offered by analytical insight into fundamental phenomena.

The dean is devoted to the principle that "a university is a place where university work is done." Other work, no matter how respectable and useful it may be, does not belong to its pattern. In following this belief faithfully he has often seemed audacious. On two conspicuous occasions he has boldly eliminated units that were too little concerned with engineering as basic science. Each time the traditionalists raised a roar of protest; each time, Spilhaus was firm.

One of these units of instruction was a two-year course for draftsmen. It attracted men who were "motivated toward engineering" but who lacked ability to earn engineering degrees. It was designed to turn out high-grade technicians of the field and it was so successful that students, enrolled in the course, had all found jobs even before they were graduated. When he saw how popular the course had become, Spilhaus abolished it. He wanted no such brisk little tail wagging his dog.

Dedicated as he is to fundamental subjects, Spilhaus has moved steadily with the future in their development. Wishing to stimulate the study of mathematics, he bought a $60,000 electronic computer. At first there was little knowledge of its working even among experts in electronics and, correspondingly, little interest in it. The dean allowed companies of the community to buy time in order to support the activity of the first year.

Enthusiasm among users proved to be highly contagious. Everyone in the neighborhood with a tricky problem began to seek out the help of the computer and presently it was so busy that more equipment had to be added. One Minneapolis concern, after this indoctrination in the new ways of science, bought six computers of its own. In the end, the University of Minnesota, with the aid of the National Science Foundation, found it profitable to buy a $200,000 computer for the services of which there is already so great a demand that it will probably have to be worked in three shifts.

Spilhaus's insistence on a close link between teaching and research has the enthusiastic endorsement of the engineering community. There is no need to explain his desire to "escape from the plumbing and hardware point of view." Funds for fundamental research flow steadily into his coffers from government agencies, from the great foundations, from private industry. Under the present regime the budget for research is equal to the total budget for the Institute of Technology as this is presented to the legislature, and 95 per cent of this support comes from non-university funds. The public, once so apathetic that in the 1880s one student a year was graduated from the engineering course at the University of Minnesota, knows its good fortune at last in having received the bounty of the Morrill Act.

An important event of the Spilhaus deanship was the absorption by the Institute of the department of physics. This administrative arrangement had been proposed when the Institute was first created in 1935. But, at the time, the dean of the College of Science, Literature and the Arts was John Tate, the very eminent physicist. His disinclination to injure the prestige of his own college by relinquishing his own subject had to be respected.

The department of physics at Minnesota had long been well supplied with original intelligences of the kind that Spilhaus coveted. Tate was particularly conspicuous among them. As a young scholar he had been made editor of the *Physical Review*, and the thorough knowledge of theoretical investigation brought to him by this assignment proved to be a kind of intellectual bonanza for his students. The Tate digests of these studies were so brilliant, as he presented them in his course called Modern Experimental Physics, that many students enrolled again and again. Greater love hath no student than this.

That he had the authentic genius of the teacher none of Tate's disciples doubted. His influence stimulated them to attempt original work of their own. They soon found it had to be work of the highest order or Tate would be majesterial in his rejection of it. Once a brilliant young physicist-in-the-making offered a suggestion for an experiment. It sounded, said Tate, like something General Electric might have studied years ago without bothering to publish the results. This rebuke so stung the young man that he returned to Tate's office the next day with a stunningly bold alternative suggestion. This time the teacher was so pleased that, when the work began, he haunted the young man's laboratory, watching progress.

In a world where only the best effort is considered good enough there is likely to be much first-rate accomplishment. Tate's success with his students may be estimated by the fact that, in the years when the reference volume *Men of Science* starred the names of scholars whose distinction seemed to be particularly glittering, there were nearly as many Minnesota graduates among this elite in the field of physics as there were graduates of the Massachusetts Institute of Technology. No other institution even came close to these leading rivals.

Tate had an important share in the development of two of America's major physicists of the atomic age. Alfred O. C.

234

Nier was his student at Minnesota and John G. Williams his close collaborator on projects that originated in the university's laboratories. He also affected the career of another young scientist upon whom Minnesota was to depend for the advancement of its work in engineering. It was Tate who first suggested Spilhaus as a possible successor to Lind. Nothing could be more appropriate than that Tate's three disciples should have come together at last as important figures in the Institute of Technology.

A history of the physics department, recorded in longhand by Henry Erikson who was for many years its head, contains this extraordinary statement:

"In March and April, 1940, Nier established U 235 as responsible for the slow fission in Uranium. This gave rise to a great interest."

The second of these sentences deserves to be added to the permanent literature of understatement. The "interest" to which Professor Erikson referred was destined to spread in ever-widening circles until it covered the whole world of thought and touched the world of action, too, at strikingly significant points. The work begun at Minnesota led on directly to the creation of the atomic bomb, to the development of atomic power and to the whole present-day drama of international politics.

It was Enrico Fermi who first urged Nier to work concentratedly on the job of separating uranium isotopes to determine which was responsible for fission. To that end he developed a mass spectrometer, one of the few in the entire world and, at the time, the only one capable of analyzing uranium.

A passage taken from an account of this investigation, written by Nier himself, says much by implication with regard to a certain fine disregard on the part of the true scientific for self-exploitation.

"In the summer of 1941 at the request of the Office of Scientific Research and Development, the writer attempted to separate larger quantities of the U 235 isotope. A new mass spectrometer for the purpose was constructed. Unfortunately the amount of money available for the work was so meagre that the apparatus simply was not adequate to do a really good job. When Professor E. O. Lawrence at the University of California became interested in the problem and placed the entire resources of his laboratory, including one of the cyclotrons, on the work, it was no longer possible to compete here at the University of Minnesota and the writer turned his attention to the problems of helping other laboratories then undertaking various methods of making separations."

It is reassuring to know that, in the mind of the unselfish investigator it is the work that matters, not the reputation of the individual worker. The subsequent history of the original mass spectrometer also reflects interestingly on the casual attitude of the research man toward the mere tools of his trade. They have no sacredness in themselves. As Nier has reported:

"After these separations were performed at Minnesota the mass spectrometer tube was removed from the large magnet between whose poles it was fitted and placed on a shelf. There it remained along with a lot of scrap glass until it was recovered shortly after the war."

John Williams, who took his Ph.D. at California when he was only twenty-three years old, came shortly afterward to work with Tate at Minnesota on experiments in nuclear physics. Before, during and after World War II he explored what he has called "the enormous little solar system of the atom," at first with an electrostatic generator put together out of parts belonging to an old X-ray machine and stepped up—one might almost say *dragged up* by sheer will power— to 200,000 volts. Later, he worked with a Van de Graaff atom smasher, provided by the Rockefeller Foundation, one that reached 4,000,000 volts.

The trio—Tate, Nier and Williams—was absorbed, during the war, into the work of producing the A-bomb. Nier, trudging patiently back and forth between New York and

Oak Ridge, made inventions to order so that things never done before might become parts of a daily routine. In 1943, Williams and a group of assistants whom he had trained at Minnesota moved en masse to Los Alamos.

Since their return to Minnesota Nier and Williams have continued to work on the development of atomic power. The former has extended earlier studies in the use of the mass spectrometer. Recognizing the importance of Williams's share in the progress of nuclear physics as a multibillion-dollar operation, the Atomic Energy Commission has supplied him with a linear accelerator (Linac, as it is popularly called for short) which reaches 66,000,000 volts.

This progress in voltage from 200,000 to 66,000,000 helps to measure the increase in public awareness of the importance of physics in the modern world. A still more significant change is reflected in the expenditures for investigation. The budget for the department reflected the fact clearly that the days of improvisation with old X-ray machines are over. The amount of money made available to the physics department from all the sources of support is exactly four times that of its budget as it appears in the request for appropriations from the legislature. That is to say, for every dollar spent on the day-by-day operation of the department, three are spent for research. Recent developments in the competition with Russia for scientific supremacy will undoubtedly send the figure for research soaring far higher.

Physics, now officially linked with the Institute of Technology in the administrative pattern, is ready to meet current demands for more physicists, new ideas, new methods and new tools. Its record of courageous pioneering in the days of its poverty promises well for a future of generous support.

Despite the shift of emphasis in the Institute from applied research back to basic research, one contribution of the former approach has written a fine passage into the history of the university and of the state. This is the development of taconite.

For forty years, a mild-mannered but very stubborn professor, E. W. Davis, kept reminding Minnesota that the rich deposits of iron ore in its north country—representing a third of the nation's supply—were rapidly diminishing. With its economic security pegged to steel, Minnesota had allowed World War I to wolf away a million tons a year with little thought for the future. Something must be done, Davis began to say ever more and more urgently, to find a practicable and economical way of utilizing low-grade ores.

Minnesota's iron range has been described by Davis as a gigantic plum pudding 110 miles long and two miles wide. The plums are the deposits of high-grade shipping ore, containing 50 per cent of iron; the rest is taconite. Spread in layers 175 to 300 feet deep, this mass of material contains 25 per cent of pure iron particles. The trick—a difficult one as Professor Davis knew well—was to retrieve it for use at a cost that would not be prohibitive.

There were many problems. One had to do with taxes. No buyer of these stores could be found under the laws then in existence. They would wipe out any possibility of profit even before the operation could be well begun. Davis crusaded vigorously to change these regulations. But at session after session the legislature proved to be quite indifferent to his arguments.

The major perplexity, however, was the technological one of separating the metal from the waste matter. During the teens of the century several approachs to a solution were made. One had the support of a Wall Street syndicate. All ended in failure. After World War I the price of steel dropped and projects with regard to taconite were dropped along with it.

Only Davis was zealous still. He knew that the Indians had used a method of flaking off taconite for their arrowheads by building fires over the rock. Under heat, chips separated by expansion. Using a liquid oxygen and kerosene torch, Davis managed to let this concentrated heat melt its way through

238

the rock. He also created a new crusher which cost only half as much as an earlier device had cost.

Other problems remained. In the process of recovering ore the iron particles were reduced to a fine powder which showed a disheartening inclination to blow out of the smelting furnaces. Undiscouraged, Davis, in another burst of inventiveness, achieved a method of reducing the ore to "tailor-made marbles," consisting of 64.5 per cent pure iron, 8.5 silica with no unwelcome impurities in the remainder of their composition.

Jubilant, Davis traveled east to report progress. "Go home and play with your marbles," said the operators brutally. Costs, under existing laws, were still prohibitive.

Now the issue became political, as well as scientific, in importance. The Junior Chambers of Commerce of Hibbing, Duluth and five other communities of northern Minnesota took up the cause, sponsoring a bill before the legislature which, in their opinion, took a more realistic approach to the problem than did the old laws. They were successful at last in getting their measure adopted.

This called for a tax to be paid on all taconite that had been processed but for none on holdings in the ground. It also excluded from taxation all capital invested in taconite production. Within three months of the bill's passage, two hundred prospectors had surged across the range country and all deposits of taconite had been claimed.

Three major companies—the Reserve Mining, the Erie Mining and the Oliver Mining Company, a subsidiary of United States Steel—promptly became active, each investing millions in the new process, building scores of miles of track from the taconite deposits to Lake Superior, creating three new towns with homes for a new army of workers.

In July, 1953, the board of directors of the Reserve Mining company announced that the processing plant at East Beaver Bay would be known as the E. W. Davis Works.

No more appropriate tribute could have been found for a man who combined devotion to science with the crusading vigor of a social benefactor. Vibrating with the greatest energy between the laboratory and the public forum, Davis had satisfied Folwell's idea of what a university man should be, a source of counsel and information to the entire state. But, more than that, he had restored tremendous wealth to Minnesota and the nation, brought new vitality to industry and created work for thousands of men. Taconite processing requires the labor of seven men for every one engaged in open pit mining and the operation goes on all year round instead of being, like ordinary mining, a seven-month occupation. In the opinion of economists "the outlook for Minnesota" never has been better, partly as a result of the fact that "taconite can now be exploited in large tonnages." A new billion-dollar business has made its debut thanks to the imagination, knowledge and inexhaustible patience of one man. Minnesota has made long-range plans to protect its development far into the future. A bill signed by Governor Orville Freeman in April, 1957, extended the original taconite leases for thirty or forty years to come.

But Professor Davis is by no means through with his projects. Now in retirement, he continues to guide the imaginations of others toward the future when "atomic power may blow the top off the iron range" to free some 250 million more tons of underground shipping ores.

The "plum pudding" still has richness in it. Research men have only to follow Professor Davis's example to find the means of pulling out the plums.

An example of how imagination constantly prods at the mind of the research man is offered by a dramatic moment in the career of another member of the Institute faculty. This professor went out one day shortly after the close of World War II to visit a government ordnance plant that was in the process of being dismantled. His modest errand was to buy surplus material for his department. But, in addition to his supplies, he brought back a dazzling idea that was to result in the creation of a research laboratory of gigantic size.

John Akerman had had previous experience with bold concepts. He joined the faculty at Minnesota as a teacher of aeronautical engineering at a moment when only a very small group of educators believed that there was any future in the field. Fortunately, Dean Lind had been one. Though the heads of other schools, visited in the course of a survey, had told him placidly that science had no responsibility toward the circus game of flying, Lind persisted in building up a vigorous division. Because of his superior brand of confidence in the importance of the field he had no difficulty in attracting to Minnesota scientists like Jean Picard, whose experiments with lighter-than-air carriers have been of enormous importance to stratospheric research.

With Akerman as his chief ally, Lind had created a branch of instruction which, in the first decade of its existence, had sent out graduates to fill top posts in forty of the leading aeronautical concerns of the United States.

And it was Akerman who indulged in the poet's "wild surmise" out of which the University of Minnesota created its most striking research unit.

The Gopher Ordnance Works, occupying twelve thousand acres of land fifteen miles south of the Twin Cities, had been set up during the war for the mass production of powder. Delays and crises of various kinds had kept it from getting into full production until the moment of the Battle of the Bulge. Reminded tragically that the war was not over yet, the government had suddenly speeded up activity. Then, after only a few months of gigantic effort, it had become useless once more, a sad monument to the wastefulness of war.

But, as Akerman realized with a creative man's start of delight, it need not remain useless. Waste could be transformed into a wealth of space for the university's laboratory men, all of whom were clamoring for facilities. He had no difficulty in communicating his enthusiasm to associates in the colleges of medicine and agriculture as well as in engineering. The government, acutely aware after World War II of the need for research in all fields, fell in with the proposal

241

of the university to take over some eight thousand acres of land and 182 of the old buildings.

Out of a scrap heap rose one of the most fabulous laboratories in the world, the Rosemount Center.

There, working side by side, crossing departmental lines as quickly as a man can cross a corridor, scientists contribute to each other's investigations in a field of study as wide as all human activity and need. Anything may be studied at Rosemount from soil enrichment to supersonic aerodynamics and everything that can be got under a microscope or into a wind tunnel has had its whims explored.

The preoccupation of all colleges, during the Morrill administration, with large-scale research problems is nowhere more evident than on the St. Paul campus over which Harold Macy now presides as dean. It is significant that the two recent heads of this division have been men whose own contributions to investigation have been distinguished. Macy's studies in the bacteriology of milk have advanced knowledge in ways no less important to the "bread and butter state" than Bailey's studies of grains.

In another dramatic way Dean Macy represents the international temper of the modern educator. For his service to France in the work of sanitation and public health, during World War II, he earned the privilege of wearing in his lapel the symbol of a chevalier of the Legion of Honor.

Nothing could be more dramatic than the contrast that exists between Dean Macy's position and that of his predecessors in the early days of the university's development. Professor Porter, who spent his strenuous days wooing the good will of the agricultural community and his nights praying for financial support, would have regarded as millennial the mood of today which brings all Minnesota to Macy's door asking for help. Even Dean Woods, who had to fight off the snobbish enmity of the main campus, looking down its Greek nose at applied research, would have envied Dean Macy's prestige among his colleagues.

At Minnesota, under the present dean of the St. Paul campus, a well-established technique exists for dealing with problems brought by the farmer or by his ally, the country banker. All the talent of the agricultural faculty is brought together to find the "right approach." Often men from "the other campus" are invited to share in these conferences. When the essential character of the problem has been determined, it is broken down into its elements and each of the consultants goes to his own laboratory to investigate a particular phase of it. Often there are many joint conferences in which findings are pooled and progress in new directions is charted.

Both federal and state governments support such long-range projects generously. The Research and Marketing Act of 1946 (Hope-Flanagan, as it is popularly called) increased the funds made available to the experiment stations of all land-grant colleges. The 1440 acres added to Minnesota's outdoor laboratory by the acquisition of Rosemount have multiplied several times over the space in which agricultural experiments can be conducted. Properly impressed by the university's independence in enterprise, the legislature voted large sums for the improvement of these facilities. It has later given the St. Paul campus many new buildings—dormitories, a student center, a forest products building, and a $1,000,000 dairy building for which the dean had not even asked.

An important addition to the pattern of construction was the creation of a School of Veterinary Medicine. A conspicuous gap in the training of experts to serve a bread and butter state had existed too long, the legislature decided. The unit, created shortly after World War II, is a separate school with a dean of its own. But it is only from an administrative point of view that this distinct individuality is preserved. Following the principle of integration, so closely cherished at Minnesota, the very active School of Veterinary Medicine cooperates with other units of investigation. The most dramatic example: its contributions to the university's work as a world brucellosis center.

On January 1, 1953, the history of agricultural instruction

at Minnesota had another small, but not insignificant, event written into its record. A new name was set up, figuratively, over the gates of the St. Paul campus and the *Institute* of Agriculture came into being. The early improvisations had allowed a certain mild confusion to creep into the terminology of organization. In most academic patterns departments are subordinate to colleges. On the St. Paul campus the monotony was varied, just a little whimsically, by making *colleges* and *schools* subordinate to a presiding authority labeled *Department*. Seeking to cut a tight Gordian knot of semantics, the board of regents authorized the new name. Whether or not all possible bewilderments have been dispelled (for *institutes* are sometimes merely intensive short courses of study designed for postgraduates in the Center for Continuation Study), the Institute of Agriculture now officially exists and, vis-à-vis the Institute of Technology, it occupies a place of solid prestige within the university pattern.

What Folwell called the "roof and crown" of a university system is its Graduate School. Laboratory for the evaluation of the findings of all our human past, center for the organization of data serviceable to human need in the present, factory for the ideas of the future—it justifies the effort of a whole program of instruction. Upon its creative vitality the life of the institution depends.

Minnesota has been peculiarly fortunate in the history of its Graduate School. From the moment when it was first put actively to work by Vincent it has been under the direction of two men, Guy Stanton Ford and after him, with only a short period of adjustment intervening, of Ford's student, disciple and intimate, Theodore Blegen.

The two deans have shown the same pattern of aptitudes for their task. First of these is a striking ability to identify talent. The second is a thorough liking for the responsibilities of nurture which has enabled each, at just the right moment, to provide a fellowship, a grant, support for research which has "nursed along" many a brilliant man and brought his work early to distinction. The third is an almost unequaled skill in finding money to further the projects they have launched.

As Blegen, still presiding as dean of Minnesota's Graduate School, has said, this wide-spreading branch of instruction has made our universities "real universities."

To an observer only vaguely familiar with the commerce of the academic world, it might be startling to discover how varied the activities of a graduate school's "merchants of light" have become. At Minnesota many units have been brought together under its guidance. There are, for example:

The Social Science Research Center, the purpose of which is to study the "problems and trends of the geographical area of the Upper Midwest." Annual public discussions turn light on every aspect of the future of the region. The series conducted in 1955 on *Social Science and Freedom* proved to be so valuable that, when the studies appeared in printed form, some twenty thousand copies were distributed by the Fund for the Republic.

The Minnesota Institute of Research, the funds of which are applied to examination of problems relating to the utilization of the industrial and natural resources of the state. Supported by special legislative appropriation, the effort of the institute is directed toward such projects as the one which has resulted in the enormous success of the taconite program.

The Forest History Foundation, which is destined to perform services for the future in the realm of lumbering such as have already been performed in the realm of mining.

The Cedar Creek Forest, which is a natural outdoor laboratory of 3200 acres in which biologists and zoologists have a rare opportunity to study the natural conditions of plant and animal life. The unusual combination of forest, swamp and grassland has preserved the environment of many species quite unaffected by the fact that civilization has turbulently happened all about it. Close to the university, easily accessible to its scholars, this natural laboratory to which indoor laboratories have lately been added "greatly enhances the facilities in this general region for productive studies in natural history."

Equipped as it is to work in many fields, the Graduate School has inevitably become the recipient of bounty from individuals and organizations with special problems on their collective minds and consciences. The Dight Institute and the Hormel Institute came into existence out of impulses to improve human stock and human well-being.

Dr. Charles Dight, in whose honor the Institute of Human Genetics is named, was a Minneapolis physician who became nobly obsessed with the idea that science must devote itself to the job of "developing human thoroughbreds." While he lived he crusaded so effectively for certain kinds of reform that, in 1925, a sterilization bill of his authorship was written into Minnesota law. At his death he left his entire estate to the university to support advanced courses in eugenics and to conduct research in problems of mental instability. Dr. Sheldon C. Reed, director of the institute, has made its work distinguished. Studies in the biology of breast cancer and others into the family histories of mentally retarded people have been conducted for many years. More recently the National Multiple Sclerosis Society has supported its investigations in that field. In 1956 Dr. Reed headed the American delegation to the First International Congress on Human Genetics, held in Copenhagen.

In the late 1930s, when the startling news had just begun to reach a startled people that one third of the world's richest nation was "ill-fed, ill-housed and ill-clothed," the late George Hormel, then head of a Minnesota meat-packing plant at Austin, Minnesota, conceived it to be his duty to do something about the crisis. He created at Minnesota postdoctorate fellowships for the search of better ways to utilize plant and animal foods. In characteristic Minnesota fashion its biochemists, experimental surgeons and bacteriologists came forward eagerly to help.

Early results were so successful that, in 1942, Jay Hormel, son of the originator of the plan for advanced study, decided to expand its program. The board of regents accepted his

246

offer to create, equip and maintain laboratories on his company's property at Austin, guaranteeing to the university absolute independence in research.

In the early years of the Hormel Institute, research concentrated, naturally enough, on diseases, nutrition and genetics in swine. Within the past two years it has shifted its balance and now deals with basic problems of nutrition in many species of animals. It has assumed a leading position in the field of lipid chemistry (the study of fats). In its exploration of the problem of atherosclerosis it has broadened its relationships to scholars of the field throughout the world.

Because it has been such a busy catalyst in the acceleration of intellectual change the Minnesota Graduate School has had a very large enrollment. In recent years the average number of individual students has been 5750.

In the academic year 1955–56 the University of Minnesota granted a total of 962 advanced degrees: 729 M.A.s and 233 Ph.D.s. Of these approximately a fifth were awarded in the fields of the agricultural and biological sciences, a fifth in medical sciences and a fifth in the physical sciences. A fifth were in education. The rest were divided chiefly among students of language and literature and the social sciences.

Critics of higher education could hardly dismiss as frivolous or fragmentary a graduate program offering the opportunity for long-range studies in one hundred twenty-four major fields of learning. The concern with basic science is obvious in a random catalogue of projects in progress which deal with mass spectroscopy, the mineral exchange between tissue and skeleton as determined by the radioactive isotope, the monosomic analysis of wheat, the metabolism of cholesterol, the relationship of the physical characteristics of middle age to the development of coronary disease, the search for white dwarf stars, and the relations between protein structure and enzymic function.

A few years from now when the present administration has had the last item added to its record, it will pass into history as the period when a quickened awareness of responsibility started a vast program of research.

It was President Morrill himself who proposed the principle which animated the work of the 1940s and the 1950s. He said:

"Today we citizen rulers must share the responsibility for decisions which may determine the destiny of the world. To deserve democracy requires that. We can't dodge the need of doing a better job for a better day. It is the job of making democracy work."

❧

KEEP THE DOOR OPEN

TURNING THE LAST PAGE on an account of the development of a huge university is a little like zipping up an over-stuffed plastic bag. The packer struggles to keep the container shapely while he realizes that it bulges in one corner and, just possibly, might have room for one or two more items in another. And as he gives a last prod, he looks about with the furtive air of one who knows that he must now pretend to be blind to deficiencies, yet still fearful that something absolutely indispensable may have been left out.

There are as many stories to be told about the University of Minnesota as there are colleges, schools, institutes and research units within it. Each deserves a book all to itself, and each such study would dramatize, in the careers of vivid crusaders, the faith upon which Minnesota is founded, that "men are ennobled by understanding."

Having written an account the essential purpose of which has been to show by what steps a candlelit schoolroom in a struggling pioneer village managed to evolve into an enormous "thinking device" designed to make important contributions to knowledge, this observer could happily put a fresh sheet in his typewriter and start another account which would be based on any one of a dozen related themes. It would be rewarding, for example, to show how the university has served to transform into professions activities of human society that were once regarded as mere chores or the improvisations of merry vagabonds or the exploits of rugged campaigners with no notion of service to society.

Minnesota's School of Nursing would show, in its history, how the sickroom drudge, quite without prestige as she still is in some societies, has become under the American system of training the discerning, highly disciplined collaborator of the doctor. The University of Minnesota long ago assumed leadership in bringing dignity, along with expertness, to the profession of the nurse. Its five-year program invites and requires a young woman to explore all the possibilities of her work and equips her for a role which she can play with dignity.

The School of Journalism has proved the important point that, though newspapermen may be "born, not made," they must be reborn, by training, in the image of the most highly responsible of public servants. Picturesqueness of temperament, a flair for expression and a liking for adventure are still fine attributes in the occupants of city rooms. But as interpreters of a complex modern world the gentlemen of the press must have more than a chatting acquaintance with history, political science and the psychology of human nature. Minnesota's fine school has undertaken successfully to enrich instruction through the exploration of the resources of all the social sciences. To reveal the basic principles, as well as the subtle arts, of communication is its aim. In 1949 the American Council on Education in Journalism gave its official endorsement to this effort. Not only did it accredit the School of Journalism as a whole but accredited more of its professional sequences than it did those of any other school except one. Minnesota and Missouri were tied.

The School of Business Administration has made the equally important point that to be "in business" is no longer to be in a jungle of ruggedly individualistic enterprise but rather to be in a social situation where a man serves himself best by serving society first. The brilliant men—past and present—of the faculty have built up a distinguished unit which would abundantly have satisfied Folwell's dream of having a "College of Commerce" within the structure of his "University of the Twentieth Century." It did satisfy the exacting and fastidious Vincent when he revisited the university to see his name go up over the building that houses the present-day school.

And there are many others who would have written quite other histories of the University of Minnesota. One such man might well have insisted that the Golden Gophers must be allowed to cast their mighty shadows over any proper study, since the United States would not be what it is without its sporting background. A writer of that faith would look back fondly at the days when Bernie Bierman, the "silver fox" of one sports reporter's admiring recollection, built up a team that lost no game in 1934, none in 1935, and only one in 1936. The Gophers' contributions to the excitement of "Big Ten" affairs have been less dramatic in recent seasons but there would be much to tell of gifted coaches and players in every year.

To another observer it would seem strange not to look behind the imposing façades of fraternity row on University Avenue and into the life of the sorority houses that dot the neighborhood on the edge of the campus. Many men and women have seized in such places on the values of their life careers, and the Greeks have spoken imperishable words into the ears of leaders who have gone out into the towns of Minnesota—and elsewhere—to give color and warmth to their social patterns.

It would not be unreasonable to suggest that there is a certain significance to the fact that Minnesota is the place where a huge indoor arena, named for a football coach ("Doc" Williams), was the only hall large enough to accommodate the thousands of students and citizens who wanted, on a recent occasion, to hear a Nobel prize winner talk about aesthetics. It was the Gideon Seymour lectureship fund, established by Minneapolis newspaper publishers in the name of one of their late editors, that brought T. S. Eliot to

251

"our university." Mr. Eliot was impressed by the size of his audience. He acknowledged the extraordinary aspects of the meeting with a dry wit and rueful modesty that delighted his hearers. "Never," he said, "have I seen so many faces all turned toward me—at least for the moment."

It is, then, a world of many interests, many dramas, many surprises. The pioneers who first imagined it with a vaingloriousness in which they themselves hardly believed would look upon their dream and find it wonderfully amplified, variegated, suffused with shifting lights. They would be pleased, no doubt, with its steady progress—from a dusty corner of a village, to a position of respect in the community, to a commanding authority in the affairs of the state, to a share in the councils of the nation, to a role in the drama of "one world."

An interest that marked this final phase of development is the university's continuing collaboration with the Seoul National University in the work of rehabilitating and modernizing the educational system of South Korea. It was Harold Stassen who, as a creative intelligence of the United States government's service to other peoples, urged this duty on his alma mater.

The proposal was to step up Korea's recovery in the fields of the medical sciences, engineering and agriculture by offering the expert assistance of a more fortunate brother in education. Three men of Minnesota—Dr. Gaylord Anderson, Dean Spilhaus and Dean Macy—went out in 1952 to inspect the university of Seoul and to draft a plan of campaign. Their suggestions were eventually accepted by the Foreign Operations Administration and, in September, 1954, a contract was put into effect.

By its terms the University of Minnesota sent a team to be in residence at Seoul and to supervise the work of building it up both physically and in the intellectual sense. Other special consultants went from Minnesota now and again for brief periods to reorganize certain divisions.

Meanwhile the president of the Korean university and three of his deans visited Minnesota to make arrangements for the reception of members of their faculties who were to be in residence as students. First came senior department heads and, after them, a number of younger teachers. A course in English especially designed for these men and women helped to throw down the language barrier and, because selection had been made carefully among candidates for the adventure in America, most of the visitors were able to take Doctor's or Master's degrees.

The University of Minnesota's team also advised their Korean colleagues on what supplies and equipment were needed to modernize their facilities and acted as procuring agent. The contract has lately been renewed for a longer period of cooperation.

On the friendly territory of the academic world, East and West have met in a rapprochement that can scarcely fail to bear much fruit. The reseeding of the Korean faculty with men of American training has certainly helped to nourish the educational system of a country that was long subjected to the stultifying influence of non-independence.

Correspondingly, a bridge has been thrown from East to West to cover psychological distances. Even when ideological beliefs seem sharply to divide peoples, international cooperation in the academic sphere helps toward mutual understanding. As Dr. Wesley Spink has pointed out in connection with his work as an ambassador of the laboratory:

"When we meet people with whom we disagree politically on the common ground of science, it's at least a first step toward international understanding. After a while we find that there are other things, besides the treatment of brucellosis, on which we agree."

Minnesota lives very much in the great world today. Indeed, its faculty members are called so often into world conferences that a family joke epitomizes a great volume of comment. If a Minnesota man wants to meet a colleague, it is said, the best time and place for an appointment is during the change of planes at Willow Run.

A last sympton of change must be noted—one which indicates clearly that Minnesota will soon have still another story to tell. In March, 1957, the university created a new department of Radio and Television Education. Its old station, KUOM—in existence since 1938—will continue its full program of lectures and concerts. To it has been added the services of KTCA-TV which is now offering, under the auspices of the General Extension Division, television courses which may be taken either simply for enjoyment or for credit.

The triumph of Richard Price is now complete. The man who insisted that education must not be made a matter of the movements of the sun may someday have a successor who will say that it must not be made a matter of the mobility of human beings. The phrase "in residence" may lose its significance, and it is not inconceivable that a Minnesota scholar of the future may take his degree by air without ever leaving his own living room.

Even to those who during the next hundred years will take their degrees in residence the University of Minnesota will look very different from the way it has looked to students in the past. Needing much more space for the reception of its additional thousands, it will escape, sometime in the immediate future, from the tight little island it has occupied so long in the midst of a sea of traffic.

The new land lies not far away from the main campus—just across the Mississippi near a center of urban life called Seven Corners. The popular name itself suggests that when the new buildings, perhaps more skyscrapers, rise they will have the same familiar background of commerce all about.

But if the university never achieves academic seclusion, it may be just as well. Designed to serve a strenuous world of affairs it belongs where it is—in the forefront of the battle.

If the recorder of the events of an academic story must leave his task with an anxious awareness of "the little done, the undone vast," he has the comfort of knowing that his mood is sympathetic to that of the world of learning itself. For it is the thought of the undone vast that alerts and stimulates the mind of the scholar. Undismayed by the dimness of the corridors that lead toward truth, unappalled by the fact that leaps must be taken into the infinity of space to satisfy the Olympian curiosity of modern man, the dedicated investigator now makes ready for a new pursuit of understanding. This time he will be content with nothing less than the ultimate in knowledge not only of his own but of other worlds.

What impresses an observer who stands on the edge of the academic world is the equanimity displayed, in this tense moment, by its best explorers. Such a man is the boldest of adventurers—and the least spectacular. He has an enormous confidence in the ability of the imagination to conquer the untried—and no vanity about his share in the project of doing so. He makes a god of expertness but he almost never mistakes himself as a human manifestation of that godhood. Except for a proper perception of the comfort that art, sport, family environment, food and drink—all the features of a full experience—may offer a wise man, work is in life. But his work is only part of *the* work, which is to discover and make known. You might think to hear the scholar talk that it is a commonplace matter to identfy U 235 as responsible for the slow fission in uranium or to discover cortisone. But if you listen, just a little more closely, you will hear an overtone which confides that these acts by which the mind of man is advanced, ever a small space farther, are parts of the daily worship of deeply reverent men.

In a recent "self-survey" of the university's policies, programs and procedures, one contributing committee offered a variation on President Morrill's principle that education must "open wide the door" on opportunity. "Keep the door open" is their counsel. They mean, keep the door open to students—as many as may deserve to come; but they mean also, keep the door open on the undone vast, on the many-voiced challenge of the modern world.

Minnesota may be listed among the fortunate institutions of our time in that it confronts that challenge with good men, good facilities and, consequently, it may be added, good heart.